EVERYMAN'S LIBRARY
EDITED BY ERNEST RHYS

ESSAYS AND
BELLES LETTRES

PENN'S FRUITS OF SOLITUDE, &
OTHER WRITINGS · WITH AN
INTRODUCTION BY JOSEPH BESSE

THIS IS NO. 724 OF *EVERYMAN'S LIBRARY*. THE PUBLISHERS WILL BE PLEASED TO SEND FREELY TO ALL APPLICANTS A LIST OF THE PUBLISHED AND PROJECTED VOLUMES ARRANGED UNDER THE FOLLOWING SECTIONS:

TRAVEL ❦ SCIENCE ❦ FICTION
THEOLOGY & PHILOSOPHY
HISTORY ❦ CLASSICAL
FOR YOUNG PEOPLE
ESSAYS ❦ ORATORY
POETRY & DRAMA
BIOGRAPHY
REFERENCE
ROMANCE

IN FOUR STYLES OF BINDING: CLOTH, FLAT BACK, COLOURED TOP; LEATHER, ROUND CORNERS, GILT TOP; LIBRARY BINDING IN CLOTH, & QUARTER PIGSKIN

LONDON: J. M. DENT & SONS, LTD.
NEW YORK: E. P. DUTTON & CO.

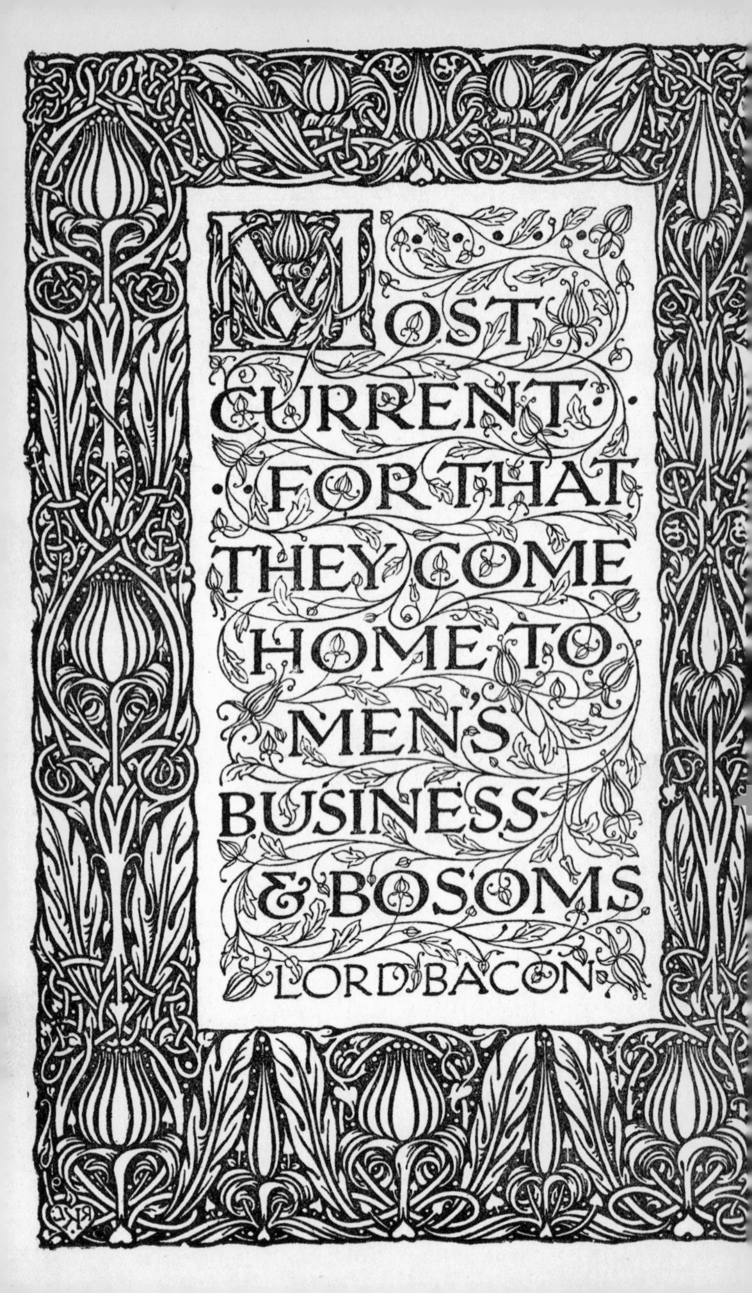
MOST CURRENT FOR THAT THEY COME HOME TO MEN'S BUSINESS & BOSOMS
LORD BACON

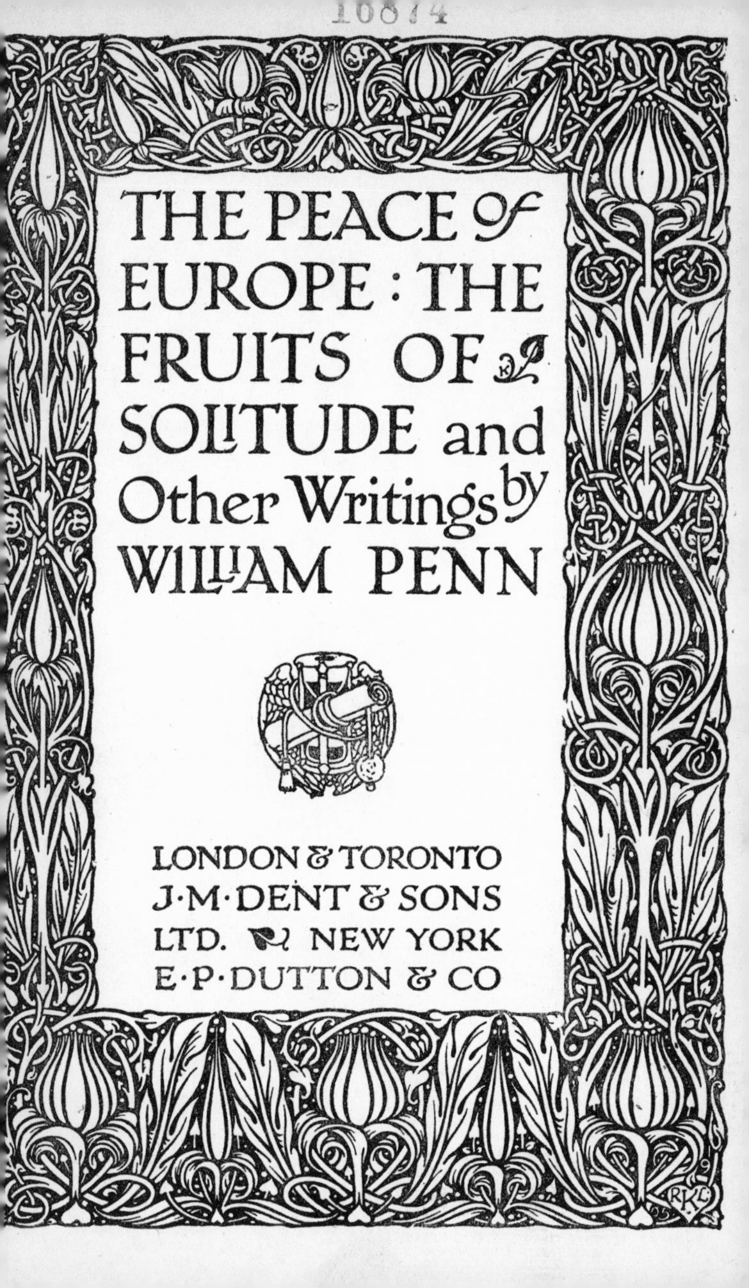

THE PEACE OF EUROPE: THE FRUITS OF SOLITUDE and Other Writings

by

WILLIAM PENN

LONDON & TORONTO
J·M·DENT & SONS
LTD. NEW YORK
E·P·DUTTON & CO

INTRODUCTION

THE AUTHOR'S LIFE

BY JOSEPH BESSE

WILLIAM PENN was born in the parish called St. Katharine's, near the Tower of London, on the 14th day of October, 1644. His father, of the same name, was a man of good estate and reputation, and in the time of the Commonwealth served in some of the highest maritime offices, as those of rear-admiral, vice-admiral, admiral of Ireland, vice-admiral of England, etc., in all which he acquitted himself with honour and fidelity. After the restoration he was knighted by King Charles the Second, and became a peculiar favourite of the then Duke of York. His paternal care and a promising prospect of his son's advancement induced him to give him a liberal education; and the youth, of an excellent genius, made such early improvements in literature that about the fifteenth year of his age he was entered a student at Christ's Church College in Oxford.

Now began his ardent desire after pure and spiritual religion (of which he had before received some taste or relish through the ministry of one Thomas Loe, a Quaker) to show itself; for he, with certain other students of that university, withdrawing from the national way of worship, held private meetings for the exercise of religion, where they both preached and prayed amongst themselves. This gave great offence to the heads of the college, and he, being but sixteen years of age, was fined for nonconformity. Which small stroke of persecution, not at all abating the fervour of his zeal, he was at length, for persevering in the like religious practices, expelled the college.

From thence he returned home, but still took great delight in the company of sober and religious people, which his father, knowing to be a block in the way to preferment, endeavoured both by words and blows to deter him from; but finding those methods ineffectual he was at length so incensed that he turned him out of doors.

Patience surmounted this difficulty, till his father's affection had subdued his anger, who then sent him to France in company with some persons of quality that were making a tour thither. He continued there a considerable time till a quite different conversation had diverted his mind from the serious thoughts of religion; and upon his return his father finding him not only a good proficient in the French tongue, but also perfectly accomplished with a polite and courtly behaviour, joyfully received him, hoping his point was gained; and indeed for some time after his return from France his carriage was such as justly entitled him to the character of a complete young gentleman.

Great, about this time, was his spiritual conflict; his blooming youth, his natural inclination, his lively and active disposition, his acquired accomplishments, his father's favour, the respect of his friends and acquaintance, did strongly press him to embrace the glory and pleasures of this world then as it were courting and caressing him to accept them. Such a combined force might seem almost invincible; but the earnest supplication of his soul being to the Lord for preservation, He was pleased to grant him such a portion of His holy power and spirit as enabled him in due time to overcome all opposition, and with a holy resolution to follow Christ whatsoever reproaches or persecutions might attend him.

About the year 1666, and the twenty-second of his age, his father committed to his care and management a considerable estate in Ireland, which occasioned his residence in that country. Being at Cork he was informed by one of the people called Quakers that Thomas Loe, whom we mentioned before, was to be shortly at a meeting in that city; he went to hear him, who began his declaration with these words, There is a faith that overcomes the world, and there is a faith that is overcome by the world; upon which subject he enlarged with much clearness and energy. By the living and powerful testimony of this man, which had made some impression upon his spirit ten years before, he was now thoroughly and effectually convinced, and afterwards constantly attended the meetings of that people, even through the heat of persecution.

On the third of the 9th month, 1667, being again at a meeting in Cork, he, with many others, were apprehended and carried before the mayor, who observing that his dress discovered not the Quaker, would have set him at liberty upon bond for his good behaviour; which he refusing was with about eighteen others committed to prison. He had during his abode in Ireland contracted an intimate acquaintance with many of the nobility and gentry, and being now a prisoner wrote the following letter to the Earl of Orrery, Lord President of Munster:

"The occasion may seem as strange as my cause is just; but your lordship will no less express your charity in the one than your justice in the other.

"Religion, which is at once my crime and mine innocence, makes me a prisoner to a mayor's malice, but mine own freeman; for being in the assembly of the people called Quakers there came several constables backed with soldiers rudely and arbitrarily requiring every man's appearance before the mayor, and amongst others violently haled me with them. Upon my coming before him he charged me for being present at a tumultuous and riotous assembly, and unless I would give bond for my good behaviour, who challenged the world to accuse me justly with the contrary, he would commit me. I asked for his authority, for I humbly conceive without an act of parliament or an act of state it might be justly termed too much officiousness. His answer was a proclamation in the year 1660, and new instructions to revive that dead and antiquated order. I leave your lordship to be judge if that proclamation relates to this concernment, that only was designed to suppress fifth-monarchy killing spirits; and since the king's lord-lieutenant and yourself, being fully persuaded the intention of these called Quakers by their meetings was really the service of God, have therefore manifested a repeal by a long continuance of freedom, I hope your lordship will not now begin an unusual severity by indulging so much malice in one whose actions savour ill with his nearest neighbours, but that there may be a speedy releasement to all for attending their honest callings with the enjoyment of their families, and not to be longer separated from both.

"And though to differ from a national system imposed by authority renders men heretics, yet I dare believe your lordship is better read in reason and theology than to subscribe a maxim so vulgar and untrue, for imagining most visible constitutions of religious government suited to the nature and genius of a civil empire, it cannot be esteemed heresy but to scare a multitude from such inquiries as may create divisions fatal to a civil policy, and therefore at worst deserves only the name of disturbers.

"But I presume, my lord, the acquaintance you have had with other countries must needs have furnished you with this infallible observation, that diversities of faith and worship contribute not to the disturbance of any place where moral uniformity is barely requisite to preserve the peace. It is not long since you were a good solicitor for the liberty I now crave, and concluded no way so effectual to improve or advantage this country as to dispense with freedom in things relating to conscience; and I suppose were it riotous or tumultuary, as by some vainly imagined, your lordship's inclination as well as duty would entertain a very remote opinion. My humble supplication therefore to you is, that so malicious and injurious a practice to innocent Englishmen may not receive any countenance or encouragement from your lordship; for as it is contrary to the practice elsewhere, and a bad argument to invite English hither, so with submission will it not resemble that clemency and English spirit that hath hitherto made you honourable.

"If in this case I may have used too great a liberty, it is my subject, nor shall I doubt your pardon, since by your authority I expect a favour which never will be used unworthy an honest man."

His request in the letter so far as related to himself was quickly granted, for the earl forthwith ordered his discharge.

His late imprisonment was so far from terrifying that it strengthened him in his resolution of a closer union with that people whose religious innocence was the only crime they suffered for.

And now his more open joining with the Quakers brought himself under that reproachful name; his companions' wonted compliments and caresses were changed into scoffs and derision. He was made a by-word, scorn, and contempt, both to professors and profane; to the latter for being religious, and to the former for having a better than theirs.

His father being informed by letter from a nobleman of his acquaintance what danger his son was in, of being proselyted to Quakerism, remanded him home, and he readily obeyed. Upon his return, although there was no great alteration in his dress, yet his manner of deportment and the solid concern of mind he appeared to be under were manifest indications of the truth of the information his father had received; who thereupon attacked him afresh. And here my pen is diffident of her abilities to describe that most pathetic and moving contest which was betwixt his father and him. His father acted by natural love, principally aiming at his son's temporal honour; he, guided by a divine impulse, having chiefly in view his own eternal welfare. His father grieved to see the well-accomplished son of his hopes, now ripe for worldly promotion, voluntarily turn his back on it; he, no less afflicted, to think that a compliance with his earthly father's pleasure was inconsistent with an obedience to his heavenly One. His father pressing his conformity to the customs and fashions of the times; he modestly craving leave to refrain from what would hurt his conscience. His father earnestly entreating him, and almost on his knees beseeching him to yield to his desire; he, of a loving and tender disposition, in an extreme agony of spirit to behold his father's concern and trouble. His father threatening to disinherit him; he humbly submitting to his father's will therein. His father turning his back on him in anger; he lifting up his heart to God for strength to support him in that time of trial.

And here we may not omit to give our reader a particular and observable instance of his sincerity. His father finding him too fixed to be brought to a general compliance with the customary compliments of the times, seemed inclinable to have borne with him in other respects, provided he would be uncovered in the presence of the king, the duke, and himself. This being proposed he desired time to consider of, which his father supposing to be with an intention of consulting his friends, the Quakers, about it, he assured him that he would see the face of none of them, but retire to his chamber till he should return him an answer. Accordingly he withdrew, and having humbled himself before God, with fasting and supplication, to know His heavenly mind and will, he became so strengthened in his resolution that, returning to his father, he humbly signified that he could not comply with his desire therein.

When all endeavours proved ineffectual to shake his constancy, and his father saw himself utterly disappointed of his hopes, he could no longer endure him in his sight, but turned him out of doors the second time. Thus exposed to the charity of his friends, having no other subsistence (except what his mother privately sent him), he endured the cross with a Christian patience and magnanimity, comforting himself with the promise of Christ, Luke xviii. 29, 30.

After a considerable time, his steady perseverance evincing his integrity, his father's wrath became somewhat mollified, so that he winked at his return to and continuance in his family; and though he did not publicly seem to countenance him, yet when imprisoned for being at meetings he would privately use his interest to get him released.

About the year 1668, being the twenty-fourth of his age, he first came forth in the work of the ministry, rightly called to and qualified for that office, being sent of God to teach others what himself had learnt of Him; commissioned from on high to preach to others that holy self-denial himself had practised; to recommend to all that serenity and peace of conscience himself had felt; walking in the light to call others out of darkness; having drank of the water of life to direct others to the same fountain; having tasted of the heavenly bread, to invite all men to partake of the same banquet; being redeemed by the power of Christ he was sent to call others from under the dominion of Satan into the glorious liberty of the sons of God, that they might receive remission of sins and an inheritance among them that are sanctified through faith in Jesus Christ. One workman thus qualified is able to do his Master's business far more effectually than ten bold intruders who undertake to teach a science themselves never learned.

This year was published the first of his printed works under the title of *Truth Exalted;* and soon after that a second called *The Guide Mistaken*, being a reply to Jonathan Clapham's book, entitled *A Guide to the True Religion.*

About this time two of the auditors of one Thomas Vincent, a presbyter in the Spittle Yard, came over to the Quakers; their pastor, hereat transported with fiery zeal, a thing fertile of ill language, railing to his auditory, accused the Quakers of holding most erroneous and damnable doctrines, and uttered such other invectives against them as his raised choler did suggest. This coming to our author's ears he, together with George Whitehead, demanded of Vincent an opportunity to defend themselves and friends. A conference was agreed to be held at his own meeting-house, at which several points of doctrine were started and debated, but nothing fairly determined: from hence our author took occasion to write a little book entitled *The Sandy Foundation Shaken*, which gave great offence to some then at the helm of the church, who presently took the old method of reforming what they call error by advancing at once their strongest argument, viz., an order for imprisoning him in the Tower of London. There was he under close confinement, and even denied the visits of his friends; but yet his enemies attained not their purpose; for when after some time his servant brought him word that the Bishop of London was resolved he should either publicly recant or die a prisoner he made this reply: All is well: I wish they had told me so before, since the expecting of a release put a stop to some business. Thou mayst tell my father, who I know will ask thee, these words: that my prison shall be my grave before I will budge a jot; for I owe my conscience to no mortal man; I have no need to fear, God will make amends for all. They are mistaken in me; I value not their threats nor resolutions; for they shall know I can weary out their malice and peevishness; and in me shall they all behold a resolution above fear, conscience above cruelty, and a baffle put to all their designs by the spirit of patience, the companion of all the tribulated flock of the blessed Jesus, who is the author and finisher of the faith that overcomes the world, yea, death and hell too. Neither great nor good things were ever attained without loss and hardships. He that would reap and not labour must faint with the wind and perish in disappointments; but a hair of my head shall not fall without the providence of my Father that is over all.

A spirit warmed with the love of God and devoted to His service ever pursues its main purpose: our author, restrained from preaching, applied himself to writing. Several treatises were the fruits of his solitude, particularly that excellent one entitled *No Cross, no Crown*, a book which, tending to promote the general design of religion, was well accepted, and has passed sundry impressions.

He also wrote from the Tower, *A Letter to the Lord Arlington:* and to clear himself from the aspersions cast upon him in relation to the doctrines of the Trinity, the incarnation and satisfaction of Christ, he published a little book called *Innocency with Her Open Face*, by way of apology for the aforesaid *Sandy Foundation Shaken*. In this apology he so successfully vindicated himself that soon after the publication of it he was discharged from his imprisonment, which had been of about seven months' continuance.

On the 15th of the 7th month this year he set out again from London for Ireland, took shipping at Bristol on the 24th of the 8th month, and on the 26th arrived at Cork. In his passage thither we think the following occurrence worth relating. At his former coming from Ireland the conversation and society of a person called a Quaker, who came over in the same vessel, was a strengthening and encouragement to him then newly convinced. This man now happened to return thither again in his company, and observing how effectually the power of truth had wrought upon our author, and the great progress he through a sincere obedience had made in his journey heavenward, and feeling himself not only overtaken, but left far behind, by one that had set out after him, was led to a solid reflection upon his own negligence and unfaithfulness, and expressed with many tears a renewed visitation and deep concern upon his spirit. So forcible is the example of the faithful to the stirring up a holy zeal and emulation in others. Being arrived at Cork he immediately visited his friends imprisoned there, and the next day had a meeting with them, in which they were spiritually refreshed and comforted together. Having tarried there some days he went from thence to Dublin, and on the 5th of the 9th month was at the National Meeting of Friends there, which was held at his lodgings. At this meeting an account of his friends' sufferings being drawn up by way of address he presented the same a few days after to the lord-lieutenant.

During his stay in Ireland, though his business in the care of his father's estate took up a considerable part of his time, yet was he frequently present at and preached in Friends' meetings, especially at Dublin and Cork, in one of which places he usually resided. He also wrote during his residence there several treatises, particularly *A Letter to the Young Convinced,* published in his works. He very frequently visited his friends in prison, and had meetings with them; nor did he let slip any opportunity he had with those in authority to solicit on their behalf, and in the beginning of the 4th month, 1670, through his repeated applications to the chancellor, the Lord Arran, and the lord-lieutenant, an Order of Council was obtained for their release. Having settled his father's concerns to satisfaction, and done his own friends many signal services, he shortly after returned again into England.

In this year 1670 came forth the Conventicle Act, prohibiting dissenters' meetings under severe penalties. The edge of this new weapon was presently turned upon the Quakers, who, not accustomed to flinch in the cause of religion, stood most exposed. Being forcibly kept out of their meeting-house in Grace Church Street, they met as near it in the street as they could, and William Penn there preaching was apprehended, and by warrant from Sir Samuel Starling, then Lord Mayor of London, dated August the 14th, 1670, committed to Newgate, and at the next sessions at the Old Bailey was (together with William Mead) indicted for being present at and preaching to an unlawful, seditious, and riotous assembly. At his trial he made a brave defence, discovering at once both the free spirit of an Englishman and the undaunted magnanimity of a Christian, insomuch that, maugre the most partial frowns and menaces of the bench, the jury acquitted him.

Not long after this trial and his discharge from Newgate his father died, perfectly reconciled to his son, and left him both his paternal blessing and a plentiful estate. His death-bed expressions being very instructive and pathetic deserve a double reading. He was buried in Redcliff Steeple House in the city of Bristol; and over or near his sepulchre is erected a fair monument with the following inscription:

To the just memory of Sir William Penn, knight, and sometimes general, born at Bristol, Anno 1621. Son of Captain Giles Penn, several years consul for the English in the Mediterranean; of the Penns of Pennslodge in the county of Wilts, and those Penns of Penn in the county of Bucks, and by his mother from the Gilberts, in the county of Somerset, originally from Yorkshire, addicted from his youth to maritime affairs: he was made captain at the years of twenty-one, rear-admiral of Ireland at twenty-three, vice-admiral of Ireland at twenty-five, admiral to the Straits at twenty-nine, vice-admiral of England at thirty-one, and general in the first Dutch war at thirty-two. Whence returning Anno 1655, he was a parliament man for the town of Weymouth; 1660, made commissioner of the admiralty and navy, governor of the town and fort of Kingsail, vice-admiral of Munster, and a member of that provincial council, and Anno 1664 was chosen great captain commander under His Royal Highness in that signal and most evidently successful fight against the Dutch fleet.

Thus he took leave of the sea, his old element, but continued still his other employs till 1669, at what time, through bodily infirmities, contracted by the care and fatigue of public affairs, he withdrew, prepared, and made for his end; and with a gentle and even gale in much peace arrived and anchored in his last and best port at Wanstead, in the county of Essex, the 16th of September, 1670, being then but forty-nine and four months old.

To his name and memory his surviving lady hath erected this remembrance.

About this time a public dispute was held at West Wiccomb in Buckinghamshire, between him and one Jeremy Ives, a celebrated Baptist. The subject was the universality of the divine light, which Ives had undertaken to disprove, and came furnished with a stock of syllogisms ready framed for his purpose. It was his place as opponent to speak first, which as soon as he had done, being sensible that his arguments stood in their greatest force while unanswered, he stepped down from his seat, and with an intention of breaking up the assembly departed. Some of his own party followed him, but the generality of the people tarrying, W. Penn had an opportunity of answering, which he did to the great satisfaction of the auditory.

In the ninth month this year being at Oxford, and observing the cruel usage and persecution his innocent friends underwent there from the hands of the junior scholars, too much by the connivance of their superiors, he wrote a letter to the vice-chancellor on that subject.

This winter, having his residence at Penn in Buckinghamshire, he published a book entitled *A Seasonable Caveat against Popery*, wherein he both exposes and confutes many erroneous doctrines of the Church of Rome, and establishes the opposite truths by sound arguments; a work alone sufficient on the one hand to wipe off the calumny cast upon him of being a favourer of the Romish religion, and on the other to show that his principle being for a universal liberty of conscience he would have had it extended even to the Papists themselves, under a security of their not persecuting others.

On the 5th of the 12th month this year he being at a meeting in Wheeler Street, a sergeant with soldiers came and planted themselves at the door where they waited till he stood up and preached, and then the sergeant pulled him down and led him into the street, where a constable and his assistants standing ready to join them they carried him away to the Tower, by order from the lieutenant. A guard was there clapped upon him and a messenger dispatched to the lieutenant then at Whitehall to inform him of the success. After about three hours time, it being evening, he came home, and W. Penn was sent for from the guard by an officer with a file of musketeers. There comely personage rendered well accomplished. He had issue by her several children.

Soon after his marriage, pitching upon a convenient habitation at Rickmersworth in Hertfordshire, he resided there with his family, often visiting the meetings of Friends and returning home again.

In the seventh month this year he took a journey to visit his friends in Kent, Sussex, and Surrey; of which his own memorandums furnish us with an observation of that singular industry which the free ministers of the gospel exercise in the discharge of their office; for in the space of twenty-one days he, with his companion under the like concern, were present at and preached to as many assemblies of people at distant places, viz., Rochester, Canterbury, Dover, Deal, Folkestone, Ashford, and other places in Kent; at Lewis, Horsham, Stenning, etc., in Sussex; and at Charlewood and Rygate in Surrey. Great was their service in these counties: their testimonies effectual to the strengthening of their Friends, silencing of gainsayers, and to a general edification, were received by the people with joy and openness of heart; and themselves in the performance of their duty filled with spiritual consolation.

At this time sundry opposers, some of whom being dissenters themselves, had enough to do in time of persecution by a cautious privacy, which they called Christian prudence, to secure their own heads from the storm the Quakers weathered, began under the sunshine of the king's indulgence to peep out, and by gainsaying the truth to make its defence necessary. So that our author, who never turned his back in the day of battle, had plenty of controversial exercise for his pen the remainder of this year, and the two next ensuing.

The same zeal and affection which made him a constant advocate for his friends at home, led him also to solicit on their behalf with foreign powers and states under whose government they suffered persecution. For there was a decree made this year at Dantzick for banishing the Quakers; and a law of the like nature at Embden, where that people had also undergone other grievous sufferings: whereupon he wrote to the senate of Embden an epistle in Latin, which hath been since translated into English, and is in the collection of his works.

The persecution at home now waxing hot again, and many Quakers being imprisoned for refusing the oath of allegiance, our author publishes their reasons against swearing at all, and confirms the same by numerous authorities in a book entitled *A Treatise of Oaths*.

This year also he published a choice piece entitled *England's Present Interest Discovered*, wherein, to allay the heats of contending parties, he shows the consistency of a general liberty of conscience with the peace of the kingdom, discovering at once the generous charity of a real Christian, and the noble spirit of a true patriot.

Soon after this he presented to the king and both houses of parliament a book called *The Continued Cry of the Oppressed for Justice*, giving an account of the unjust and cruel proceedings against the persons and estates of many of the people called Quakers, with a postscript of the nature, difference, and limits of civil and ecclesiastical authority.

About this time was a controversy between the famous Richard Baxter and our author. They met at a convenient place near Rickmersworth, and in the presence of a numerous auditory held a dispute of six or seven hours' continuance, but no account thereof having ever been published in print (except some hints given by Richard Baxter himself in his life, part 3, p. 174), we know not the particulars.

In the twelfth month this year, one Matthew Hide, a person that had been very troublesome in the Quakers meetings, by opposing their ministers in their public testimony and prayers, was taken sick, and on his death-bed, being under great remorse of conscience for what he had done, he could not be easy till he had sent for some of that people, and particularly G. Whitehead, to whom he expressed great sorrow for the abuses done them; declaring them to be the children of God, and begging mercy of the Lord for his wilful opposition to known truth in gainsaying them; and so died penitent. This gave occasion to our author to publish, as a warning to other opposers, a narrative entitled *Saul Smitten to the Ground*.

In the year 1676 he became one of the proprietors of West Jersey in America, and was instrumental in the first colonising of that province by the English. For King Charles the Second having given the propriety of that country to the Duke of York, he granted the same to Sir George Berkley and the Lord Carteret, the former of whom sold his part to one Edward Billing, a Quaker, whose circumstances in the world afterward declining, he transferred his right to W. Penn, Gawen Lawrey, and Nicholas Lucas, in trust for the payment of his debts; they accordingly allotted out and sold the lands; and many people from England transporting themselves and settling there, in a few years it became a flourishing plantation, and so continues. The chief town of it is Burlington, situate on the great River Delaware. But we return to religious matters.

One John Cheney, near Warrington in Lancashire had written several books against the Quakers, which were replied to by Roger Haydock and William Gibson. In one of those books he made an excursion upon our author about a passage in his answer to Faldo, which occasioned him in his own defence to publish a book called *The Skirmisher Defeated*, etc., the success of which answered its title, for Cheney drew his sword no more.

About this time it pleased God to inspire the hearts of two Protestant ladies of great quality in Germany with a sense of the follies and vanities of the world, and to excite them to an earnest inquiry after the knowledge of himself. The one was the Princess Elizabeth, daughter of Frederick the Fifth, Prince Palatine of the Rhine, and King of Bohemia, granddaughter to King James the First, and sister to Prince Rupert, and the late Princess Sophia, King George's mother. The other, Anna Maria de Hornes, Countess of Hornes, a familiar acquaintance of the said princess. The report of their religious inclination coming to our author's ears, who gladly embraced every opportunity of watering the growing seeds of virtue, he sent them a letter of encouragement and consolation exhorting those noble women to a constancy and perseverance in that holy way which the Lord had directed their feet into.

In the year 1677 he travelled into Holland and Germany, of which an account was written and published by himself.

Soon after his return from Holland he wrote a letter in answer to one he had received from John Pennyman, a person who had once professed himself a Quaker, but was now become an opposer of them, part of which letter contained advice well adapted to the case of such a backslider.

The people called Quakers being now harassed with severe prosecutions in the exchequer, on penalties of £20 per month or two thirds of their estates, by laws made against Papists, but unjustly turned upon them, William Penn soliciting the parliament for redress of those grievances presented petitions, viz.:—(1) To the Commons of England assembled in Parliament. The Request of the People called Quakers; and (2) The Request of some called Quakers presented to the House of Lords on the Behalf of their Suffering Friends.

Being thereupon admitted to a hearing before a committee on the 22nd of the month called March, 1678, he made two speeches.

The committee thereupon agreed to insert in a bill then depending a proviso or clause for relief in the case complained of; and the same did pass the House of Commons: but before it had gone through the House of Lords it was quashed by a sudden prorogation of the parliament.

This year some sneaking adversary, who showed more wisdom in concealing his name than in publishing his work, put forth a libel called *The Quakers' Opinions;* to which our author replied in a brief answer to a false and foolish libel.

The generality of people being now in a hurry and consternation of mind upon the discovery of the Popish plot, and apprehensions of a French invasion, he, lest the minds of any of his friends the Quakers should be drawn from their wonted dependence upon God to partake of the popular uneasiness, wrote an epistle to them directed *To the Children of Light in this Generation.*

And in the next year the nation still continuing under fears of wicked designs on foot for subverting the Protestant religion, and introducing Popery, he published a book entitled *An Address to Protestants*, wherein he sets forth the reigning evils of the times, and endeavours to excite men to repentance and amendment of life as the best means to cure their fears and prevent the impending dangers.

The rising hopes of Papists and the just fears of Protestants kept the nation still in a ferment, and writs being issued for summoning a new parliament, party struggles for power ran high, on which occasion our author dedicated to the freeholders and electors a sheet called *England's great Interest in the Choice of this New Parliament*, and soon after the parliament sitting he presented to them a book entitled *One Project for the Good of England*.

In this year 1680 died that excellent Princess, Elizabeth, of the Rhine, before mentioned, to whose real worth our author's religious gratitude dedicated a memorial by transmitting to posterity her exemplary character in the second edition of his *No Cross, no Crown*, printed Anno 1682.

On the eighth of the eighth month this year also departed this life his dear friend and father-in-law, Isaac Pennington, to whose virtues he published a testimony and prefixed it to his works that year printed in folio.

There being about this time some difference in judgment among his friends the Quakers about establishing church discipline, a point not easily fixed, so as neither to subject the conscience to an ecclesiastical authority, nor yet to give an unlimited liberty of running into anarchy and confusion, he published a little book called *A Brief Examination of Liberty Spiritual*.

A fresh persecution being now raised in the city of Bristol where Sir John Knight, sheriff, John Helliar, attorney at law, and other their accomplices put the penal laws in a rigorous execution, many of the people called Quakers there were fined and imprisoned. To whom W. P. wrote an epistle for their Christian consolation and encouragement, directed *To the Friends of God in the City of Bristol*.

Having hitherto attended our author through a continued series of his labours and travails in the service of the gospel and work of the ministry in these parts of the world, we shall now accompany him to his province of Pennsylvania.

King Charles the Second (in consideration of the services of Sir W. Penn, and sundry debts due to him from the crown at the time of his decease) by letters patent bearing date the 4th of March, 1680-1, granted to W. P. and his heirs that province lying on the west side of the River Delaware in N. America, formerly belonging to the Dutch, and then called the New Netherlands. The name was now changed by the king in honour of W. P., whom, and his heirs, he made absolute proprietors and governors of it. Upon this he presently publishes an *Account of the Province of Pennsylvania*, with the king's patent and other papers relating thereto, describing the country and its produce, and proposing an easy purchase of lands, and good terms of settlement, for such as might incline to transport themselves. Many single persons, and some families out of England and Wales, went over; and with singular industry and application, having cleared their purchased lands, settled and soon improved plantations to good advantage, and began to build the city of Philadelphia, in a commodious situation on the aforesaid navigable River Delaware. And to secure the new planters from the native Indians (who in some other provinces, being injuriously dealt with, had made reprisals to the loss of many lives) the governor gave orders to treat them with all candour and humanity; and appointed commissioners to confer with them about land, and to confirm a league of peace; by whom he also sent them the following letter.

LONDON, *the 18th of the 8th month*, 1681.

MY FRIENDS,—There is a great God and power that hath made the world and all things therein, to whom you and I and all people owe their being and well-being; and to whom you and I must one day give an account for all that we do in the world. This great God hath written His law in our hearts, by which we are taught and commanded to love and help and do good to one another, and not to do harm and mischief one unto another. Now this great God hath been pleased to make me concerned in your part of the world, and the king of the country where I live hath given me a great province therein, but I desire to enjoy it with your love and consent, that we may always live together as neighbours and friends; else what would the great God do to us? who hath made us not to devour and destroy one another, but to live soberly and kindly together in the world. Now I would have you well observe that I am very sensible of the unkindness and injustice that hath been too much exercised towards you by the people of these parts of the world, who have sought themselves and to make great advantages by you rather than to be examples of justice and goodness unto you, which I hear hath been matter of trouble to you, and caused great grudgings and animosities, sometimes to the shedding of blood, which hath made the great God angry. But I am not such a man, as is well known in my own country. I have great love and regard towards you, and I desire to win and gain your love and friendship by a kind, just, and peaceable life, and the people I send are of the same mind, and shall in all things behave themselves accordingly, and if in anything any shall offend you or your people you shall have a full and speedy satisfaction for the same by an equal number of just men on both sides, that by no means you may have just occasion of being offended against them. I shall shortly come to you myself, at what time we may more largely and freely confer and discourse of these matters, in the meantime I have sent my commissioners to treat with you about land and a firm league of peace. Let me desire you to be kind to them and the people, and receive these presents and tokens which I have sent you as a testimony of my good will to you and my resolution to live justly, peaceably, and friendly with you.—I am your loving friend,

W. PENN.

His friendly and pacific manner of treating the Indians begat in them an extraordinary love and regard to him and his people, so that they have maintained a perfect amity with the English of Pennsylvania ever since. And it is observable that upon renewing the treaty with the present governor, Sir William Keith, bart., in 1722, they mention the name of William Penn with much gratitude and affection, calling him a good man, and as their highest compliment to Sir William use this expression, we esteem and love you as if you were William Penn himself. So universally doth a principle of peace, justice, and morality operate on the hearts even of those we call heathens.

He also drew up the Fundamental Constitutions of Pennsylvania in twenty-four articles consented to and subscribed by the first adventurers and freeholders of that province as the ground and rule of all future government. The first of which articles, showing that his principle was to give as well as take liberty of conscience in matters of religion, we shall transcribe.

"In reverence to God, the Father of light and spirits, the author as well as object of all divine knowledge, faith, and worship, I do for me and mine declare and establish for the first fundamental of the government of this country that every person that doth or shall reside therein shall have and enjoy the free profession of his or her faith and exercise of worship toward God, in such way and manner as every such person shall in conscience believe is most acceptable to God. And so long as every such person useth not this Christian liberty to licentiousness or the destruction of others, that is to say, to speak loosely and profanely or contemptuously of God, Christ, the Holy Scripture, or religion, or commit any moral evil or injury against others in their conversation, he or she shall be protected in the enjoyment of the aforesaid Christian liberty by the civil magistrate."

In the next year, 1682, he published *The Frame of Government of Pennsylvania,* containing twenty-four articles somewhat varying from the aforesaid constitutions, together with certain other laws to the number of forty, agreed on in England by the governor and diverse freemen of the said province. Of which laws one was:

"That all persons living in this province, who confess and acknowledge the one Almighty and Eternal God to be the creator, upholder, and ruler of the world, and that hold themselves obliged in conscience to live peaceably and justly in civil society, shall in no wise be molested or prejudiced for their religious persuasion or practice in matters of faith and worship; nor shall they be compelled at any time to frequent or maintain any religious worship, place, or ministry whatsoever."

In the sixth month, 1682, himself, accompanied with diverse of his friends, took shipping for his province of Pennsylvania, and on the 30th of the same month he wrote from the Downs *A Farewell to England,* being an epistle containing a salutation to all faithful friends.

After a prosperous voyage of six weeks they came within sight of the American coast, from whence the air at twelve leagues distance smelt as sweet as a new-blown garden.

Sailing up the river the inhabitants, as well Dutch and Swedes as English, met him with demonstrations of joy and satisfaction. He landed at Newcastle, a place mostly inhabited by the Dutch, and the next day he summoned the people to the Court House, where possession of the country was legally given him; he then made a speech setting forth the purpose of his coming, and the ends of government, giving them assurances of a free enjoyment of liberty of conscience in things spiritual, and of civil freedom in temporal, and recommending to them to live in sobriety and peace one with another. After which he renewed the magistrates' commissions, and then departed to Upland or Chester, where he called an assembly, to whom he made the like declaration and received their thankful acknowledgments. Here also the Swedes deputed one Captain Lucey Cook in their names to congratulate him upon his safe arrival, and to assure him of their fidelity, love, and obedience.

By this time some progress had been made in building at Philadelphia, and several pretty houses were run up on the side of the River Delaware. The governor himself had a fair mansion house erected at Penn's Bury, near the fall of the said river, at which he sometimes resided. The country was unexceptionable, the air exceeding clear, sweet, and healthy; and provisions, both meat and drink, good and plentiful.

In the tenth month following, a general assembly of the freeholders was held at Chester aforesaid, at which Newcastle was annexed to Pennsylvania; the foreigners there inhabiting were naturalised, and the laws before agreed on in England, with some amendments and alterations, were confirmed and ratified; and the whole proceedings of the assembly carried on with love and unanimity.

After the adjournment of that assembly he went to Maryland, and was there kindly received by the Lord Baltimore and the chiefs of that colony. They held a treaty about settling the bounds of their provinces; but the season of the year not admitting the conclusion of that business after two days' conference he took his leave, and the Lord Baltimore accompanied him back some miles to the house of one William Richardson; from thence he went two miles farther to a meeting of his friends, at the house of

Thomas Hooker, and afterward forwarded his journey to Choptank, on the eastern shore, where was to be an appointed meeting of colonels, magistrates, and people of several ranks and qualities. Thus he proceeded to settle his government and province, and to establish a good correspondence with his neighbours. Nor was the advancement of himself or his family in worldly wealth and grandeur his aim in the administration of government; but in the greatest honour of his public station he still retained the meekness and humility of a private Christian.

In the sixth month, 1683, having been about a year in Pennsylvania, he wrote a letter to the Free Society of Traders of that province residing at London, wherein he describes the country, relates the customs and manners of the Indians, the condition of the first planters, and the present state and settlement of that province, with an account of the new laid out city of Philadelphia; which the reader may find no small pleasure in perusing.

And being no less solicitous for the spiritual good than for the temporal advantages of his people, he wrote in the year 1684 *An Epistle to the People of God called Quakers in the Province of Pennsylvania*, etc.

After about two years' residence there, having settled all things in a thriving and prosperous condition, he returned to England where he arrived safe the 12th of the 6th month, 1684.

On the 6th of the 12th month following King Charles the Second died and was succeeded by his brother the Duke of York, by the name of King James the Second, who being a professed Papist, his accession to the crown filled the people's hearts with just apprehensions and fears lest he should take into the wonted measures of those of his persuasion, and establish his own religion by the destruction of others; and had W. P. at that time fomented the general uneasiness by encouraging multitudes then upon the wing, he might, as himself said, have put many thousands of people into his province, as well as pounds into his pocket. But he who had been intimate with that king when Duke of York, and for whom, excepting their difference in matters of religion, the Duke had always shown a personal respect and esteem, was induced by the repeated protestations he had heard him make to believe that he was really principled for granting liberty of conscience; and accordingly embraced the present opportunity of soliciting afresh for the relief of his innocent and suffering Friends, who at that time filled the jails; and that he might be the nearer on all occasions for the service of them and his country, he took lodgings in 1685 near Kensington.

And now his acquaintance and frequency at court subjected him to the undeserved censure of such as least knew him as being a Papist or Jesuit; and about this time two copies of verses were printed with the initial letters of his name subscribed, condoling the late king's death and congratulating the accession of the present. These verses, though savouring both of Popery and flattery, were, as perhaps the publisher's malice intended, presently imputed to him: whereupon to undeceive the world and clear himself he published a paper called *Fiction Found Out.*

But yet the mistaken notions entertained by the common people of his being a Papist, or at least holding a correspondence with Jesuits at Rome, began to enter the minds of some of better judgment; and among others his acquaintance, Dr. Tillotson (afterwards Archbishop of Canterbury), having let in a suspicion of him, dropped some expressions which were improved to his disadvantage. W. P. being informed of this wrote a letter to the doctor on that subject, which was followed by several others that passed between them, until at last the doctor declared himself fully satisfied that his suspicion was groundless.

In this year he published *A Farther Account of the Province of Pennsylvania ;* and about this time the Duke of Buckingham having written a book in favour of liberty of conscience, for which he was always a known advocate, a nameless author put forth an answer reflecting not only on the Duke himself, but also on W. P., saying the Pennsylvanian had entered him (*i.e.*, the Duke) with his Quakeristical doctrine. W. P. gave that answerer a reply entitled *A Defence of the Duke of Buckingham's Book of Religion and Worship*, etc., a small piece, in the conclusion of which he refers to another excellent and larger discourse soon after published by himself, entitled *A Persuasive to Moderation to Dissenting Christians, in Prudence and Conscience, humbly submitted to the King and his Great Council,* in which he confutes the several pleas for persecution, and confirms his own arguments for a toleration by the testimonies of authors and the examples of flourishing kingdoms and states, and shows the dismal effects and consequences of the contrary. A treatise well worthy the reader's serious perusal.

How far this book and other solicitations of its author did influence the king and council we determine not, but shortly after, viz., on the 14th of the month called March, 1685-6, came forth the king's proclamation for a general pardon; and instructions being given to the judges of assize in their several circuits to extend the benefit of it to the Quakers, about thirteen hundred of that people, most of whom had been diverse years imprisoned, were set at liberty. Joyful, no doubt, to their distressed families, as well as beneficial to the country, was the restoring so many industrious people to their own homes and lawful employments; and, whatever private views some in authority may be supposed to have had in granting that general amnesty, it was certainly the duty of the afflicted to receive the present favour with a becoming gratitude.

On the 4th of the month called April, 1687, came forth the king's declaration for liberty of conscience, suspending the execution of all penal laws in matters ecclesiastical; by which (though probably done in favour of the Papists) Dissenters received a general ease, and enjoyed their meetings peaceably. The people called Quakers having smarted by those laws more than others could not be less sensible of the present relief, wherefore at their next annual assembly held at London, in the third month this year, they drew up an address of thanks to the king, deputing W. P. and others to present the same.

Some have objected against the Quakers and other Dissenters for addressing King James upon the aforesaid declaration of indulgence, as though they had thereby countenanced the king's dispensing with the laws in general; let such observe their imputation, as to our author and his friends the Quakers, sufficiently guarded against in that part of their address where they say, We hope the good effects thereof for the peace, trade, and prosperity of the kingdom will produce such a concurrence from the parliament as may secure it to our posterity. It is plain, therefore, they gratefully accepted of the suspension of the penal laws by the king's prerogative (as who in their case would not?), a thing in itself just and reasonable, in hopes of having the same afterwards confirmed by the legislative authority; there being at that time much talk of an approaching parliament. And that their expectation centred not in the king's dispensing power is evident by our author's continuing his endeavours to show the necessity of abolishing the penal laws, for soon after this he wrote a large tract called *Good Advice to the Church of England, Roman Catholics, and Protestant Dissenters*, in which he shows the disannulling of those laws to be their general interest.

He wrote also presently after this a book entitled *The Great and Popular Objection against the Repeal of the Penal Laws, Briefly Stated and Considered.*

On the 27th of April, 1688, King James renewed his declaration for liberty of conscience, with an order of council for the reading of it in churches, against which seven bishops petitioning were committed to the Tower.

On the 5th of November this year, William Prince of Orange landed at Torbay in Devonshire, to the great joy of the English nation. Many of King James's officers and army soon joined the prince, and the king perceiving the hearts of the people alienated from him, withdrew himself and went over to France; and by a convention called shortly after the said Prince of Orange and the Princess Mary his spouse, King James's daughter, were declared king and queen of England, etc., and were proclaimed on the 13th of the month called February, 1688-9. Upon this turn of the times our author's late friendship at court made him suspected of disaffection to the present government, so that on the 10th of December, 1688, walking in Whitehall, he was sent for by the lords of the council then sitting; and though nothing appeared against him, and himself assured them that he had done nothing but what he could answer before God and all the princes in the world, that he loved his country and the Protestant religion above his life, and never acted against either, that all he ever aimed at in his public endeavours was no other than what the prince himself had declared for; that King James was always his friend, and his father's friend, and in gratitude he was the king's and did ever, as much as in him lay, influence him to his true interest. Notwithstanding they obliged him to give sureties for his appearance the first day of the next term; which he did, and then was continued on the same security to Easter term following, on the last day of which nothing having been laid to his charge he was cleared in open court.

In the year 1690 he was again brought before the lords of the council upon an accusation of holding correspondence with the late King James, and they requiring sureties for his appearance he appealed to King William himself, who, after a conference of near two hours, inclined to acquit him; but to please some of the council he was held upon bail for a while, and in Trinity term the same year again discharged.

He was yet attacked a third time, and his name inserted in a proclamation dated July the 18th this year, wherein he with divers lords and others, to the number of eighteen, were charged with adhering to the kingdom's enemies; but proof failing respecting him, he was again cleared by order of the King's Bench Court at Westminster, on the last day of Michaelmas term, 1690.

Being now again at liberty he purposed to go over a second time to Pennsylvania and published proposals in print for another settlement there. He had so far prepared for his transportation that an order for a convoy was granted him by the Secretary of State, when his voyage was prevented by a fresh accusation against him, backed with the oath of one William Fuller, a wretch, afterward by parliament declared a cheat and impostor; and a warrant was thereupon granted for his apprehension, which he narrowly escaped at his return from G. Fox's burial on the 16th of the month called January, 1690.

He had hitherto defended himself before the king and council, but now thought it rather advisable to retire for a time than hazard the sacrificing his innocence to the oaths of a profligate villain; and accordingly he appeared but little in public for two or three years. During this recess he applied himself to writing; and first lest his own friends, the Quakers, should entertain any sinister thought of him he sent an epistle to their yearly meeting in London.

His excellent preface to Robert Barclay's works, and another to those of John Burnyeat, both printed this year, were farther fruits of his retirement, as were also: 1. A small treatise entitled *Just Measures in an Epistle of Peace and Love*. 2. *A Key opening the Way to every Common Understanding*. 3. *An Essay toward the Present Peace of Europe*. A work so adapted to the unsettled condition of the times, and so well received, that it was reprinted the same year. 4. *Reflections and Maxims Relating to the Conduct of Human Life*.

Having thus improved the times of his retirement to his own comfort and the common good, it pleased God to dissipate that cloud and open his way again to a public service; for in the latter end of the year 1693, through the mediation of his friends, the Lord Ranelagh, Lord Somers, Duke of Buckingham, and Sir John Trenchard, or some of them, he was admitted to appear before the king and council, where he so pleaded his innocency that he was acquitted.

In the twelfth month, 1693, departed this life his beloved wife, Gulielma Maria, with whom he had lived in all the endearments of that nearest relation about twenty-one years. The loss of her was a very great exercise, such, himself said, as all his other troubles were nothing in comparison of. Her character, dying expressions, and pious end were related by himself in an account he published.

In the ninth, tenth, and eleventh months this year he travelled in the work of the ministry in the counties of Gloucester, Somerset, Devon, and Dorset, having meetings almost daily in the most considerable towns, and other places in those counties, at which the people flocked in abundantly; and his testimony to the truth, answering to that of God in their consciences, was assented to by many.

About the latter end of the summer this year he again went down into the west of England, and was present in the eighth month at a dispute held at Melksham in Wiltshire, between one John Plympton, a Baptist, and John Clark, a Quaker. The Baptist had dared the Quakers to a conference on five heads, viz., 1. The Universality of Grace. 2. Baptism. 3. The Supper. 4. Perfection. 5. The

Resurrection. John Clark notably answered his objections; but Plympton continuing to cavil against the plainest scripture proofs, even when the auditors were satisfied, would not be silent. The evening approaching, and William Penn finding himself under a concern to bear his testimony to the truth in that assembly, terminated the dispute by an open and free declaration, which the auditory received with singular attention; and he concluded the meeting with prayer.

On the fifteenth of the ninth month a meeting was appointed at Wells, and a large room at an inn with a balcony next the street was taken for that purpose; and the bishop duly certified of the same. The room was quickly filled, and there was also a great concourse of people in the street; so that for the conveniency of his double auditory, W. P. placed himself in the balcony, and thence preached to the people; but in the midst of his declaration came officers from the mayor with a warrant.

The officers rudely officious, though desired to tarry till he had done, forced him away instantly before the magistrates; who upon examination finding the house was certified, and that by disturbing a lawful for an unlawful assembly they had overshot themselves, excused the matter as well as they could, and presently dismissed him; having done just enough to manifest the keenness of their stomachs for the old work of devouring, in that they could not refrain from whetting their teeth again after the Act of Toleration had blunted them.

About this time the people called Quakers soliciting the parliament in the case of oaths, W. P. presented to the House of Commons, before whom a bill for their ease was then depending, "a few words to crave their perusal upon occasion of the Bill to excuse the people called Quakers from swearing."

On the 5th of the first month, 1695-6, he consummated his second marriage at Bristol, with Hannah the daughter of Thomas Callowhill, and granddaughter of Dennis Hollister, an eminent man of that city; she was a sober and religious young woman; with whom he had a comfortable cohabitation during the rest of his life, and had issue by her four sons and one daughter.

In the second month, 1696, his eldest son by his former wife, named Springett, died at Worminghurst, in Sussex, of a consumption, in the twenty-first year of his age: a most hopeful and promising young man; whose character being published (together with that of his mother) in the account before mentioned, we recommend to our reader's perusal.

At this time George Keith, having been disowned by the Quakers for his contentious and disorderly spirit, kept up a meeting with some adherents at Turner's Hall, London, where under the name of religion he fostered strife and debate; sending out peremptory challenges and summons to the Quakers to dispute with him; and mustering up against them quotations out of their books, such as himself formerly could candidly interpret, and had successfully vindicated against other opposers. To put a check to his confidence by employing him to beat down the batteries himself had raised, W. P. sets before him his own vindications of the Quakers from those very lies, when told by others, which himself had now licked up afresh. This book our author entitled *More Work for George Keith*. It has a suitable preface, wherein he aptly describes the man and his self-contradictious methods of procedure.

There being about this time a Bill depending in the House of Lords against blasphemy, he presented to that House a caution requisite in the consideration of that Bill, wherein he advises that the word blasphemy be so explained as that no ambiguous interpretation might minister occasion to malicious or envious persons to prosecute under that name whatsoever they should be pleased to call so. After which the House thought fit to drop the Bill.

In the second month, 1698, he set out together with John Everot and Thomas Story from Bristol, where he then dwelt, for Ireland. Some time after his arrival there John Plympton, the tenacious Baptist disputant mentioned before, being at Dublin, published a paper entitled *A Quaker No Christian*, to which W. P. replied under the title of *The Quaker a Christian*. After this he travelled to other parts of that nation in the work of the ministry to the edification of the churches.

The next winter residing at Bristol he, together with

Benjamin Coole, wrote a book entitled *The Truth of God as held by the People called Quakers farther cleared from Mistakes*, etc., a choice piece, which was reprinted next year.

In 1699, the sixth month, himself with his wife and family took shipping for his province of Pennsylvania, and on the third of the seventh month following, from on board the ship lying in Cowes Road near the Isle of Wight, he took his farewell of his friends in an epistle directed *To the People of God called Quakers, wherever scattered or gathered in England, Ireland, Scotland, Holland, Germany, or in any other Parts of Europe*.

On the 9th of the same month they set sail, and were near three months out at sea, Providence by the tediousness of their voyage protracting the time of their arrival until the danger of a contagious distemper then reigning in that country was over. Upon their coming thither they were received with the universal joy of the inhabitants.

Being now determined to settle in his province he applied himself to the offices of government, always preferring the good of the country and its inhabitants to his own private interest; rather remitting than rigorously exacting his lawful revenues: so that under the influence of his paternal administration the province was in an easy and flourishing condition: when some persons here in England, taking advantage of his absence, were endeavouring to undermine both his and other proprietary governments, under the specious pretence of advancing the prerogative of the crown; and a Bill for that purpose was brought into the House of Lords. His friends, the proprietors and adventurers here, presently represented the hardship of their case to the parliament, soliciting time for his return to answer for himself; and accordingly giving him a speedy account how matters stood, they pressed his coming over forthwith; with which he seeing it necessary to comply, summoned an assembly to meet at Philadelphia, to whom, on the 15th of September, 1701, he made the governor's speech.

The next month he took shipping for England, and safely arrived at Portsmouth, about the middle of December; and the same month came up to London. After his return the

Bill, which through his friends' solicitations had been postponed the last sessions of parliament, was wholly dropped, and no farther progress made in that affair.

About two months after this, viz., on the eighth of the month called March, 1701-2, King William died; and the Princess Ann of Denmark ascended the throne, who began her reign with moderation and clemency, and declared for maintaining the Act of Toleration. Our author being in the queen's favour was often at court, and for his conveniency took lodgings at Kensington; where he wrote *More Fruits of Solitude, being a Second Part of Reflections and Maxims relating to the Conduct of Human Life.* After which he removed to Knightsbridge over against Hyde Park Corner, where he resided for some years.

About this time a Bill to prevent occasional conformity was brought into the House of Commons, on which occasion he wrote a sheet entitled *Considerations upon the Bill against Occasional Conformity.*

In this year he again visited the meetings of his friends in the western parts of England, where he had good service, and his testimony was effectual to the information of many.

In the year 1706, he removed with his family to a convenient habitation about a mile from Brentford, and eight from London, where he dwelt some years; and frequently attended the meeting at Brentford, which his friends, as well for the accommodation of his family, as the general service of their persuasion, then first appointed to be held there once a month.

In the year 1707, he was unhappily involved in a suit of law with the executors of a person who had been formerly his steward, against whose demands he thought both conscience and justice required his endeavours to defend himself. But his cause (though many thought him aggrieved) was attended with such circumstances as that the Court of Chancery did not think it proper to relieve him, wherefore he was obliged to dwell in the Old Bailey within the rules of the Fleet, some part both of this and the next ensuing year, until such time as the matter in dispute was accommodated.

Now although the infirmities of old age began to visit

him, and to lessen his abilities of continuing his service in the work of the ministry with his wonted alacrity, yet he travelled as his strength and health would admit into the west of England, as also the counties of Berks, Buckingham, Surrey, and other places.

In the year 1710, the air near London not being agreeable to his declining constitution, he took a handsome seat at Rushcomb, near Tywford in Buckinghamshire, where he had his residence during the remainder of his life.

In the year 1712 he was seized at distant times with three several fits, supposed to be apoplectic, by the last of which, though beyond all probability or expectation he survived it, his understanding and memory were so impaired as to render him incapable of public action for the future. Nevertheless we shall continue our annals to the close of his days from the accounts an intimate friend hath left of his condition at the visits he yearly made him.

In the third month, 1713, the aforesaid friend, being at his house some days, found him to appearance pretty well in health and cheerful of disposition, but defective in memory, so that though he could relate many past transactions yet could he not readily recollect the names of absent persons: nor could he deliver his words so readily as heretofore; yet many sensible and savoury expressions came from him, rendering his company even yet acceptable, and manifesting the religious settlement and stability of his mind.

At a second visit made him in the spring, 1714, he was very little altered from what he had been the last year. The friend accompanied him in his chariot to Reading meeting, where he spake several sensible sentences; but was not able to say much. At parting he took leave of his friends with much tenderness and affection.

In the year 1715 his memory became yet more deficient, but his love to and his sense of religious enjoyment apparently continued, for he still often went in his chariot to the meeting at Reading, and there sometimes uttered short, but very sound and savoury expressions. One morning, while the friend was at his house, being about to go to the meeting, he expressed his desires to the Lord that they might receive some good from him. This year he went to

Bath, but the waters there proved of no benefit to his long continued distemper.

In the year 1716, the said friend and another went to visit him, at whose coming he seemed glad, and though he could not then remember their names, yet by his answers it appeared he knew their persons. He was now much weaker than last year, but still expressed himself sensibly at times, and particularly took his leave of them at their going away in these words, My love is with you; the Lord preserve you, and remember me in the everlasting covenant.

In the 5th month, 1717, being the last visit the said friend made him, he found his understanding so much weakened as that he scarce knew his old acquaintance, and his bodily strength so much decayed that he could not well walk without leading, nor scarce express himself intelligibly.

After a continued and gradual declension for about six years, his body drew near to its dissolution; and on the thirtieth day of the fifth month, 1718, in the seventy-fourth year of his age, his soul, prepared for a more glorious habitation, forsook the decayed tabernacle, which was committed to the earth on the fifth of the sixth month following at Jordans in Buckinghamshire, where his former wife and several of his family had been before interred.

As he had led in this life a course of patient continuance in well-doing, and through faith in our Lord Jesus Christ had been enabled to overcome the world, the flesh, and the devil, the grand enemies of man's salvation; he is, we doubt not, admitted to that everlasting inheritance which God hath prepared for his people, and made partaker of the promise of Christ, Rev. iii. 21, To him that overcometh will I grant to sit with Me in My throne, even as I also overcame, and am set down with my Father in His throne.

BIBLIOGRAPHY

Some elegiacs in the "Epicedia" published on the occasion of the death of Henry, Duke of Gloucester, 1660; The Guide Mistaken, 1668; Truth Exalted; in a short, but sure, testimony against all those Religions, Faiths, and Worships that have been formed and followed in the darkness of apostacy, 1668; The Sandy Foundation Shaken, 1668, edited by J. Barker, 1845?; No Cross, no Crown; or, several sober reasons against hat-honour, titular respects, you to a single person, with the apparel and recreations of the times being inconsistent with Scripture, reason and the practice . . . of holymen, 1669; Innocency with her Open Face, 1669; The People's Ancient and Just Liberties asserted in the trial of William Penn and William Mead, at the session held at the Old Baily against the most arbitrary proceedings of that Court, 1670 (a new edition of Pt. I. with appendix by W. Penn, edited by B. Flower, 1810); Truth Rescued from Imposture, or, a brief reply to a meer rapsodie of lies, folly, and slander, but a pretended answer to the tryal of William Penn and William Mead, 1670; A Seasonable Caveat against Popery, or a pamphlet entitled, An Explanation of the Roman Catholic Belief, briefly examined, 1670 (with notes by R. Macbeth, 1852); The Great Case of Liberty of Conscience once more debated and defended by the authority of reason, Scripture and antiquity: which may serve the place of a general reply to such late discourses as have opposed a toleration, 1670; A Letter of Love to the Young convinced of that blessed everlasting way of truth and righteousness, now testified unto by the people of England, Ireland and Scotland, but particularly those of London, 1670; The Spirit of Truth Vindicated, against that of error and envy unseasonably manifested, in a . . . libel entitled "The Spirit of the Quakers' Tryal," 1672; Quakerism, a New Nickname for Old Christianity, being an answer to a book entitled "Quakerism No Christianity," 1672; Plain Dealing with a Traducing Anabaptist, or three letters writ upon occasion of some slanderous reflections, given and promoted against William Penn by one J. Morse, 1672; The New Witnesses proved Old Heretics, or Information to the Ignorant, 1672; A Winding-Sheet for Controversie Ended (an answer to "Controversie Ended," by H. Hedworth, attacking William Penn and George Fox), 1672; The Proposed Comprehension soberly considered, 1672?; The Invalidity of J. Faldo's Vindication of his Book called "Quakerism no Christianity," 1673; Reason against Railing, and Truth against Fiction in answer to "A Dialogue between a Christian and a Quaker," by T. Hicks, 1673; Wisdom Justified of her Children, from the ignorance and calumny of H. Hallywell in his book "An Account of Familism as it is revived and propagated by the Quakers," 1673; The Spirit of Alexander the Copper-Smith justly rebuk'd, or an answer to a late pamphlet entitled "The Spirit of the Hat, or the Government of the Quakers," 1673; Judas and the Jews combined against Christ and his followers, being a rejoynder to the late nameless reply called "Tyranny and Hypocrisie detected" made against a book entitled "The Spirit of Alexander the Coppersmith rebuked, etc.," which was an answer to a pamphlet called "The Spirit of the Hat," 1673; The Christian Quaker, and his divine testimony vindicated by Scripture, reason, and authorities against the injurious attempts . . . to render him odiously inconsistent with Christianity and Civil Society, in two parts. Part I. by William Penn, Part II. by G. Whitehead, 1673; The Counterfeit Christian detected; and the Real Quaker justified . . . against the language of T. Hicks . . . in his 3rd dialogue called "The Quaker Condemned," etc. 1674; A Just Rebuke to one and twenty learned Divines, being an answer to an abusive epistle against the Quakers, subscribed by T. Manton, J. Jacomb, etc., 1674; Naked Truth needs no Shift, or an answer to a libellous Sheet entituled "The Quaker's last Shift found out," 1674; A Discourse of the General Rule of Faith and Life and Judge of Controversie, 1674; Urim and Thummim; or The Apostolical doctrines of light and perfection maintained, 1674; Return to J. Faldo's Reply, called "A Curb for William Penn's Confidence, 1674; (with Richard Richardson) A Treatise of Oaths, containing several . . . reasons why the . . . Quakers refuse to swear, 1675; Saul Smitten to the Ground, 1675 (appendix only by Penn); The Continued Cry of the Oppressed for Justice, 1675; England's Present Interest discover'd with honour to the Prince, and safety to the People. In answer to this one question: what is most fit at this juncture of affairs to be done for composing, at least quieting of differences, 1675; An Epistle to the Princess Elizabeth of the Rhine and Countess of Hornes, 1676; The Skirmisher defeated and Truth Defended, being an answer to a pamphlet (by I. C.) entitled "A Skirmish made upon Quakerism," 1676; A Brief Answer to a false and foolish libell called "The Quakers' Opinions," 1678; To the Children of Light in this Generation, 1678; An Address to Protestants upon the present conjuncture, 1679; England's Great Interest in the Choice of this new Parliament, 1680; The Case of William Penn, Esq., as to the Proprietary Government of Pensilvania, which together with Carolina, etc., is intended to be taken away by a Bill in Parliament, 1680; The Great Question to be considered by the King and this approaching Parliament, 1680?; A Brief Examination and State of Liberty Spiritual, both with respect to persons in their private capacity and in their Church Society and Communion, 1681; A Brief Account of the Province of Pensilvania lately granted under the Great Seal of England to William Penn, 1681; A Brief Account of the Province of Pennsylvania lately granted by the King under the great seal of England to William Penn, and his heirs and assigns, 1681 (a different work from the preceding); The Protestant's Remonstrance against Pope and Presbyter, 1681; The Frame of the Government of the Province of Pennsilvania, together with certain laws agreed upon in England, 1682; An Epistle containing a salutation to all faithful friends . . . in a solemn farewell to them all in the land of my nativity, 1682 (another edition, William Penn's Last Farewell to England: being an epistle containing a salutation to all faithful friends, a reproof to the unfaithful, 1682); A Letter from William Penn, Proprietary and Governor of Pennsilvania, containing a general description of the said province, to which is added an account of the city of Philadelphia, 1683; Annimadversions on the Apology of the Clamorous Squire against the Duke of Buckingham's Seconds, as men of no conscience, 1685; Fiction Found Out. To my esteemed Friends, call'd Quakers, on the occasion of two copies of verses (on Charles II. and James II.) in disavowal of the said verses, 1685; A Further Account of the Province of Pennsilvania, and its improvements, 1685; The Speech of William Penn to his Majesty upon his delivering the Quakers' Address, 1687; Good Advice to the Church of England, Roman Catholick and Protestant Dissenter, in which it is endeavoured to make appear, that it is their duty, principle and interest, to abolish the Penal Laws and Tests, 1687; A Persuasive to moderation to Church Dissenters, 1687; The Great and Popular Objection against the Repeal of the Penal Laws and Tests, 1688; Mr. Penn's Advice in the Choice of Parliament-Men in his England's Great Interest in the choice of this New Parliament, etc., 1688; Some Proposals for a Second Settlement in the Province of Pennsylvania, 1690; A Key opening the way to every common understanding to discern the difference between the religion professed by the people called Quakers and the perversions, misrepresentations, and calumnies of their several Adversaries, 1692; (A Reply to a pretended Answer by a nameless author, to this Key, 1695); The New Athenians no noble Bereans (the 2nd part of Athenians no noble Bereans) 1692; Some Fruits of Solitude, in reflections and maxims relating to the conduct of human life, 1693—the 10th edition (Fruits of a Father's Love), 1790—with Introduction by Edmund Gosse, 1900—edited by C. R. Ashbee, 1901—with Introduction by John Clifford, 1905—edited by J. V. Cheney, 1906; Essay towards the Present and Future Peace of Europe, 1693; An Account of William Penn's Travels in Holland and Germany, anno 1677, by way of a journal, containing also divers letters writ to several great persons, 1694—2nd edition corrected 1694—3rd edition corrected by the Author's own copy with some answers not printed in the first to which is added 2 Epistles formerly printed in Dutch, 1714—4th edition, 1835; A Brief Account of the Rise and Progress of the people called Quakers, 1694 (first appeared as a preface to George Fox's Journal); Tender Counsel and Advice, by way of an epistle to all those who are sensible of their day of visitation, 2nd edition, 1695; A Call to Christendom, 2nd edition, 1695; Primitive Christianity revived, 1696; An Account of the blessed end of Gulielma Maria Penn and of Springet Penn, the beloved wife and eldest son of William Penn, 1696; A Defence of a paper, entituled Gospel Truths, against the Exceptions of the Bishop of Cork's testimony, 1698; An Epistle of Farewell to the people of God called Quakers wherever scattered or gathered in England, Ireland, Scotland, etc., 1699; A Just Censure of Francis Bigg's Address to the Parliament against the Quakers, 1699; The Benefit of Plantations or Colonies, 1700?; Primitive Christianity revived in the faith and practice of the people called Quakers, 1702; More Fruits of Solitude, 1703. Posthumous: Fruits of a Father's Love. Being the Advice of William Penn to his children, 1726; A Call to Repentance (extracted from "An Address to Protestants," published in 1679), 1745; Christian Discipline or certain good and wholesome orders for the well-governing of my family in a right Christian Conversation . . . 1751; Sermon preached April 13, 1694, 1775; Sermon preached on the occasion of the death of Mrs. Rebecca Travers, June 19, 1688, 1775; A Letter from William Penn to his Wife and Children, 1797; Letters to various People, 1826, etc.; An Epistle to the Churches of Jesus throughout the world, 1835; A Summons or Call to Christendom, 1835; A Sermon (on John iii. 16) preached August 12, 1694, Salvation from Sin by Christ alone, 1836; Immediate Revelation considered and explained: being an extract from the preface to the works of R. Barclay, 1854;

A Tender Visitation in the Love of God, 1855; On our National History and Education (a reprint of his preface to Whitelock's "Memorials"), 2nd edition, 1870.

COLLECTED EDITIONS OF WORKS.—An edition with life by Joseph Besse, 2 vols., 1726; Select works to which is prefixed a journal of his Life, 1771—3rd edition, 5 vols., 1782—4th edition, 3 vols., 1825.

WORKS WITH PREFACES, APPENDIXES, ETC., BY PENN.—Journal of the life, etc., of J. Banks, 1712; Barclay's works, 1692; The Harmony of the Old and New Testaments, appendix on the Jews by Penn, 1694; Truth Exalted in the writings of J. Burnyeat, 1691; The Works of J. Coale, 1671; Fox's Journal, 1694; E. Hide's "Saul smitten to the ground," 1675; C. Marshall's Journal, 1840; C. Marshall's "Sion's Travellers Comforted," 1704; I. Pennington's works, 1681; D. Phillips' "Vindiciæ Veritatis," 1703; J. Whitehead's Written Gospel-Labours, 1704; J. Whitehead's Life and Writings, 1852; B. Whitelocke's "Memorials of English Affairs," 1709; B. Whitelock's "Quench not the Spirit," 1711.

LIFE.—Those lives prefixed to the collective works, also those of Clarkson, 1849; Hepworth Dixon, new edition, 1856; R. J. Burdette, 1882; Stoughton, new edition, 1883; S. M. Janney, 1852; Mrs. Colquhoun Grant's "Quaker and Courtier. The Life and Work of William Penn," 1907.

CONTENTS

An Essay towards the Present and Future Peace of Europe 1
Some Fruits of Solitude 23
The Advice of William Penn to His Children . 93
A Tender Visitation 129
A Summons or Call to Christendom . . . 145
A Brief Account of the Rise and Progress of the People called Quakers 167
Primitive Christianity revived 229
A Description of Pennsylvania 277

AN ESSAY TOWARDS THE PRESENT AND FUTURE PEACE OF EUROPE

WILLIAM PENN

AN ESSAY TOWARDS THE PRESENT AND FUTURE PEACE OF EUROPE

By the Establishment of an European Diet, Parliament, or Estates

Beati Pacifici. Cedant arma togæ

To the Reader,—I have undertaken a subject that I am very sensible requires one of more sufficiency than I am master of to treat it as, in truth, it deserves and the groaning state of Europe calls for; but since bunglers may stumble upon the game as well as masters, though it belongs to the skilful to hunt and catch it, I hope this essay will not be charged upon me for a fault if it appear to be neither chimerical nor injurious, and may provoke abler pens to improve and perform the design with better judgment and success. I will say no more in excuse of myself for this undertaking but that it is the fruit of my solicitous thoughts for the peace of Europe, and they must want charity as much as the world needs quiet to be offended with me for so pacific a proposal. Let them censure my management, so they prosecute the advantage of the design; for until the millenary doctrine be accomplished, there is nothing appears to me so beneficial an expedient to the peace and happiness of this quarter of the world.

I. Of Peace and its Advantages

He must not be a man but a statue of brass or stone whose bowels do not melt when he beholds the bloody tragedies of this war, in Hungary, Germany, Flanders, Ireland, and at sea, the mortality of sickly and languishing camps and navies, and the mighty prey the devouring winds and waves have made upon ships and men since '88. And as this with reason ought to affect human nature, and deeply kindred, so there is something very moving that becomes prudent men to consider, and that is the vast charge that has accompanied that blood, and which makes no mean part of these tragedies; especially if they deliberate upon the uncertainty of the war, that they know not how or when it will end, and that the expense cannot be less, and the hazard is as great as before. So that in the contraries of peace we see the beauties and benefits of it; which under it, such is the unhappiness of mankind, we are too apt to nauseate, as the full stomach loathes the honeycomb; and like that unfortunate gentleman, that having a fine and a good woman to his wife, and searching his pleasure in forbidden and less agreeable company, said, when reproached with his neglect of better enjoyments, that he could love his wife of all women if she were not his wife, though that increased his obligation to prefer her. It is a great mark of the corruption of our natures, and what ought to humble us extremely, and excite the exercise of our reason to a nobler and juster sense, that we cannot see the use and pleasure of our comforts but by the want of them. As if we could not taste the benefit of health but by the help of sickness; nor understand the satisfaction of fulness without the instruction of want; nor, finally, know the comfort of peace but by the smart and penance of the vices of war: and without dispute that is not the least reason that God is pleased to chastise us so frequently with it. What can we desire better than peace but the grace to use it? Peace preserves our possessions; we are in no danger of invasions: our trade is free and safe, and we rise and lie down without anxiety. The rich bring out their hoards, and employ the poor manufacturers; buildings and divers projections for profit and pleasure go on: it excites industry, which brings wealth, as that gives the means of charity and hospitality, not the lowest ornaments of a kingdom or commonwealth. But war, like the frost of '83, seizes all these comforts at once, and stops the civil channel of society. The rich draw in their stock, the poor turn soldiers, or thieves, or starve: no industry, no building, no manufactory, little hospitality or charity; but what the peace gave, the war devours. I need say no more upon this head, when the advantages of peace, and mischiefs of war, are so many and sensible to every capacity under all governments, as either of them prevails. I shall proceed to the next point. What is the best means of Peace? which will conduce much to open my way to what I have to propose.

II. Of the Means of Peace, which is Justice rather than War

As justice is a preserver, so it is a better procurer of peace than war. Though *Pax quæritur bello* be a usual saying, *Peace is the end of war*, and as such it was taken up by O. C. for his motto; yet the use generally made of that expression shows us that, properly and truly speaking, men seek their wills by war rather than peace, and that as they will violate it to obtain them, so they will hardly be brought to think of peace unless their appetites be some way gratified. If we look over the stories of all times, we shall find the aggressors generally moved by ambition; the pride of conquest and greatness of dominion more than right. But as those leviathans appear rarely in the world, so I shall anon endeavour to make it evident they had never been able to devour the peace of the world, and ingross whole countries as they have done, if the proposal I have to make for the benefit of our present age had been then in practice. The advantage that justice has upon war is seen by the success of embassies, that so often prevent war by hearing the pleas and memorials of justice in the hands and mouths of the wronged party. Perhaps it may be in a good degree owing to reputation or poverty, or some particular interest or conveniency of princes and states, as much as justice; but it is certain that, as war cannot in any sense be justified, but upon wrongs received and right, upon complaint refused; so the generality of wars have their rise from some such pretension. This is better seen and understood at home; for that which prevents a civil war in a nation is that which may prevent it abroad, viz., justice; and we see where that is notably obstructed, war is kindled between the magistrates and people in particular kingdoms and states; which, however it may be unlawful on the side of the people, we see never fails to follow, and ought to give the same caution to princes as if it were the right of the people to do it: Though I must needs say the remedy is almost ever worse than the disease: the aggressors seldom getting what they seek, or performing, if they prevail, what they promised: and the blood and poverty that usually attend the enterprise weigh more on earth, as well as in heaven, than what they lost or suffered, or what they get by endeavouring to mend their condition, comes to: which disappointment seems to be the voice of heaven and judgment of God against those violent attempts. But to return, I say, justice is the means of peace, betwixt the government and the people, and one man and company and another. It prevents strife, and at last ends it: for besides shame or fear, to contend longer, he or they being under government, are constrained to bound their desires and resentment with the satisfaction the law gives. Thus peace is maintained by justice, which is a fruit of government, as government is from society, and society from consent.

III. Government, its Rise and End under all Models

Government is an expedient against confusion; a restraint upon all disorder; just weights and an even balance: that one may not injure another, nor himself, by intemperance.

This was at first without controversy patrimonial, and upon the death of the father or head of the family the eldest son or male of kin succeeded. But time breaking in upon this way of governing, as the world multiplied, it fell under other claims and forms; and is as hard to trace to its original as are the copies we have of the first writings of sacred or civil matters. It is certain the most natural and human is that of consent, for that binds freely (as I may say), when men hold their liberty by true obedience to rules of their own making. No man is judge in his own cause, which ends the confusion and blood of so many judges and executioners. For out of society every man is his own king, does what he lists at his own peril: but when he comes to incorporate himself, he submits that royalty to the conveniency of the whole, from whom he receives the returns of protection. So that he is not now his own judge nor avenger, neither is his antagonist, but the law, in indifferent hands between both. And if he be servant to others that before was free, he is also served of others that formerly owed him no obligation. Thus while we are not our own, every body is ours, and we get more than we lose, the safety of the society being the safety of the particulars that constitute it. So that while we seem to submit to, and hold all we have from society, it is by society that we keep what we have.

Government then is the prevention or cure of disorder, and the means of justice, as that is of peace: for this cause they have sessions, terms, assizes, and parliaments, to overrule men's passions and resentments, that they may not be judges in their own cause, nor punishers of their own wrongs, which, as it is very incident to men in their corrupt state, so, for that reason, they would observe no measure; nor on the other hand would any be easily reduced to their duty. Not that men know not what is right, their excesses, and wherein they are to blame, by no means; nothing is plainer to them: but so depraved is human nature that, without compulsion some way or other, too many would not readily be brought to do what they know is right and fit, or avoid what they are satisfied they should not do. Which brings me near to the point I have undertaken, and for the better understanding of which I have thus briefly treated of peace, justice, and government, as a necessary introduction, because the ways and methods by which peace is preserved in particular governments will help those readers most concerned in my proposal to conceive with what ease as well as advantage the peace of Europe might be procured and kept; which is the end designed by me, with all submission to those interested in this little treatise.

IV. Of a General Peace, or the Peace of Europe, and the Means of it

In my first section, I showed the desirableness of peace; in my next, the truest means of it; to wit, justice not war. And in my last, that this justice was the fruit of government, as government itself was the result of society which first came from a reasonable design in men of peace. Now if the sovereign princes of Europe, who represent that society, or independent state of men that was previous to the obligations of society, would, for the same reason that engaged men first into society, viz., love of peace and order, agree to meet by their stated deputies in a general diet, estates, or parliament, and there establish rules of justice for sovereign princes to observe one to another; and thus to meet yearly, or once in two or three years at farthest, or as they shall see cause, and to be styled, the Sovereign or Imperial Diet, Parliament, or State of Europe; before which sovereign assembly should be brought all differences depending between one sovereign and another that cannot be made up by private embassies before the sessions begin; and that if any of the sovereignties that constitute these imperial states shall refuse to submit their claim or pretensions to them, or to abide and perform the judgment thereof, and seek their remedy by arms, or delay their compliance beyond the time prefixed in their resolutions, all the other sovereignties, united as one strength, shall compel the submission and performance of the sentence, with damages to the suffering party, and charges to the sovereignties that obliged their submission. To be sure, Europe would quietly obtain the so much desired and needed peace to her harassed inhabitants; no sovereignty in Europe having the power and therefore cannot show the will to dispute the conclusion; and, consequently, peace would be procured and continued in Europe.

V. Of the Causes of Difference, and Motives to violate Peace

There appears to me but three things upon which peace is broken, viz., to keep, to recover, or to add. First, to keep what is one's right from the invasion of an enemy; in which I am purely defensive. Secondly, to recover, when I think myself strong enough, that which by violence I or my ancestors have lost by the arms of a stronger power; in which I am offensive. Or, lastly, to increase my dominion by the acquisition of my neighbour's countries, as I find them weak and myself strong. To gratify which passion there will never want some accident or other for a pretence: and knowing my own strength, I will be my own judge and carver. This last will find no room in the imperial states: they are an unpassable limit to that ambition. But the other two may come as soon as they please and find the justice of the sovereign court. And considering how few there are of those sons of prey, and how early they show themselves, it may be not once in an age or two, this expedition being established, the balance cannot well be broken.

VI. Of Titles, upon which those Differences may arise

But I easily foresee a question that may be answered in our way, and that is this: What is right? Or else we can never know what is wrong: It is very fit that this should be established. But that is fitter for the sovereign states to resolve than me. And yet that I may lead a way to the matter, I say that title is either by a long and undoubted succession, as the crowns of Spain, France, and England; or by election, as the crown of Poland and the Empire; or by marriage, as the family of the Stewarts came by England; the elector of Brandenburg to the Duchy of Cleve: and we, in ancient time, to divers places abroad; or by purchase, as hath been frequently done in Italy and Germany; or by conquest, as the Turk in Christendom, the Spaniards in Flanders, formerly mostly in the French hands, and the French in Burgundy, Normandy, Lorraine, French-County, etc. This last title is, morally speaking, only questionable. It has indeed obtained a place among the rolls of titles, but it was engrossed and recorded by the point of the sword and in bloody characters. What cannot be controlled or resisted must be submitted to; but all the world knows the date of the length of such empires, and that they expire with the power of the possessor to defend them. And yet there is a little allowed to conquest too, when it has the sanction of articles of peace to confirm it: though that hath not always extinguished the fire, but it lies, like embers and ashes, ready to kindle so soon as there is fit matter prepared for it. Nevertheless, when conquest has been confirmed by a treaty, and conclusion of peace, I must confess it is an adopted title; and if not so genuine and natural, yet being engrafted, it is fed by that which is the security of better titles, consent. There is but one thing more to be mentioned in this section, and that is from what time titles shall take their beginning, or how far back we may look to confirm or dispute them. It would be very bold and inexcusable in me to determine so tender a point, but be it more or less time, as to the last general peace at Nimeguen, or to the commencing of this war, or to the time of the beginning of the treaty of peace, I must submit it to the great pretenders and masters in that affair. But something everybody must be willing to give or quit, that he may keep the rest, and by this establishment be forever freed of the necessity of losing more.

VII. Of the Composition of these Imperial States

The composition and proportion of this Sovereign Part, or Imperial State, does, at the first look, seem to carry with it no small difficulty what votes to allow for the inequality of the princes and states. But with submission to better judgments, I cannot think it invincible; for if it be possible to have an estimate of the yearly value of the several sovereign countries, whose delegates are to make up this august assembly, the determination of the number of persons or votes in the states for every sovereignty will not be impracticable. Now that England, France, Spain, the Empire, etc., may be pretty exactly estimated is so plain a case, by considering the revenue of lands, the exports and entries at the custom houses, the books of rates, and surveys that are in all governments, to proportion taxes for the support of them, that the least inclination to the peace of Europe will not stand or halt at this objection. I will, with pardon on all sides, give an instance far from exact; nor do I pretend to it, or offer it for an estimate; for I do it at random: only this, as wide as it is from the just proportion, will give some aim to my judicious reader, what I would be at: Remembering I design not by any computation an estimate from the revenue of the prince, but the value of the territory, the whole being concerned as well as the prince. And a juster measure it is to go by, since one prince may have more revenue than another, who has much a richer country: though in the instance I am now about to make, the caution is not so necessary, because, as I said before, I pretend to no manner of exactness, but go wholly by guess, being but for example's sake. I suppose the Empire of Germany to send twelve; France, ten; Spain, ten; Italy, which comes to France, eight; England, six; Portugal, three; Sweedland, four; Denmark, three; Poland, four; Venice, three; the seven provinces, four; the thirteen cantons and little neighbouring sovereignties, two; dukedoms of Holstein and Courland, one; and if the Turks and Muscovites are taken in, as seems but fit and just, they will make ten apiece more. The whole makes ninety. A great presence when they represent the fourth, and now the best and wealthiest part of the known world; where religion and learning, civility and arts have their seat and empire. But it is not absolutely necessary there should be always so many persons to represent the larger sovereignties; for the votes may be given by one man of any sovereignty as well as by ten or twelve: though the fuller the assembly of states is, the more solemn, effectual, and free the debates will be, and the resolutions must needs come with greater authority. The place of their first session should be central, as much as is possible, afterwards as they agree.

VIII. Of the Regulations of the Imperial States in Session

To avoid quarrel for precedency, the room may be round, and have divers doors to come in and go out at, to prevent exceptions. If the whole number be cast in tens, each choosing one, they may preside by turns, to whom all speeches should be addressed, and who should collect the sense of the debates, and state the question for a vote, which, in my opinion, should be by the ballot after the prudent and commendable method of the Venetians: which, in a great degree, prevents the ill effects of corruption; because if any of the delegates of that high and mighty Estates could be so vile, false, and dishonourable as to be influenced by money, they have the advantage of taking their money that will give it them and of voting undiscovered to the interest of their principles and their own inclinations; as they that do understand the balloting box do very well know. A shrewd stratagem and an experimental remedy against corruption, at least corrupting: for who will give their money where they may so easily be cozened, and where it is two to one they will be so; for they that will take money in such cases will not stick to lie heartily to them that give it, rather than wrong their country, when they know their lie cannot be detected.

It seems to me that nothing in this Imperial Parliament should pass but by three quarters of the whole, at least seven above the balance. I am sure it helps to prevent treachery, because if money could ever be a temptation in such a court, it would cost a great deal of money to weigh down the wrong scale. All complaints should be delivered in writing in the nature of memorials and journals kept by a proper person, in a trunk or chest, which should have as many differing locks as there are tens in the states. And if there were a clerk for each ten, and a pew or table for those clerks in the assembly; and at the end of every session one out of each ten were appointed to examine and compare the journals of those clerks, and then lock them up as I have before expressed, it would be clear and satisfactory. And each sovereignty if they please, as is but very fit, may have an exemplification, or copy of the said memorials, and the journals of proceedings upon them. The liberty and rules of speech, to be sure, they cannot fail in, who will be wisest and noblest of each sovereignty, for its own honour and safety. If any difference can arise between those that come from the same sovereignty that then one of the major number do give the balls of that sovereignty. I should think it extremely necessary that every sovereignty should be present under great penalties, and that none leave the session without leave, till all be finished; and that neutralities in debates should by no means be endured: for any such latitude will quickly open a way to unfair proceedings, and be followed by a train, both of seen and unseen inconveniences. I will say little of the language in which the session of the Sovereign Estates should be held, but to be sure it must be in Latin or French; the first would be very well for civilians, but the last most easy for men of quality.

IX. Of the Objections that may be advanced against the Design

I will first give an answer to the objections that may be offered against my proposal: and in my next and last section I shall endeavour to show some of the manifold conveniences that would follow this European league or confederacy.

The first of them is this, that the strongest and richest sovereignty will never agree to it, and if it should, there would be danger of corruption more than of force one time or other. I answer to the first part, he is not stronger than all the rest, and for that reason you should promote this and compel him into it; especially before he be so, for then it will be too late to deal with such a one. To the last part of the objection, I say the way is as open now as then; and it may be the number fewer, and as easily come at. However, if men of sense and honour and substance are chosen, they will either scorn the baseness, or have wherewith to pay for the knavery: at least they may be watched so that one may be a check upon the other, and all prudently limited by the sovereignty they represent. In all great points, especially before a final resolve, they may be obliged to transmit to their principals the merits of such important cases depending, and receive their last instructions: which may be done in four and twenty days at the most, as the place of their session may be appointed.

The second is that it will endanger an effeminacy by such a disuse of the trade of soldiery; that if there should be any need for it, upon any occasion, we should be at a loss as they were in Holland in '72.

There can be no danger of effeminacy, because each sovereignty may introduce as temperate or severe a discipline in the education of youth as they please, by low living and due labour. Instruct them in mechanical knowledge and in natural philosophy by operation, which is the honour of the German nobility. This would make them men: neither women nor lions: for soldiers are the other extreme to effeminacy. But the knowledge of nature, and the useful as well as agreeable operations of art, give men an understanding of themselves, of the world they are born into, how to be useful and serviceable, both to themselves and others:

and how to save and help, not injure or destroy. The knowledge of government in general; the particular constitutions of Europe; and above all of his own country, are very recommending accomplishments. This fits him for the parliament and council at home, and the courts of princes and services in the imperial states abroad. At least, he is a good commonwealth's man, and can be useful to the public or retire as there may be occasion.

To the other part of the objection, of being at a loss for soldiery as they were in Holland in '72. The proposal answers for it itself. One has war no more than the other; and will be as much to seek upon occasion. Nor is it to be thought that any one will keep up such an army after such an empire is on foot, which may hazard the safety of the rest. However, if it be seen requisite, the question may be asked, by order of the sovereign states, why such a one either raises or keeps up a formidable body of troops, and he obliged forthwith to reform or reduce them; lest any one, by keeping up a great body of troops, should surprise a neighbour. But a small force in every other sovereignty, as it is capable or accustomed to maintain, will certainly prevent that danger, and vanquish any such fear.

The third objection is, that there will be great want of employment for younger brothers of families; and that the poor must either turn soldiers or thieves. I have answered that in my return to the second objection. We shall have the more merchants and husbandmen, or ingenious naturalists, if the government be but anything solicitous of the education of their youth: which, next to the present and immediate happiness of any country, ought of all things to be the care and skill of the government. For such as the youth of any country is bred, such is the next generation, and the government in good or bad hands.

I am come now to the last objection, that sovereign princes and states will hereby become not sovereign: a thing they will never endure. But this also, under correction, is a mistake, for they remain as sovereign at home as ever they were. Neither their power over their people, nor the usual revenue they pay them, is diminished: it may be the war establishment may be reduced, which will indeed of course follow, or be better employed to the advantage of the public.

So that the sovereignties are as they were, for none of them have now any sovereignty over one another: And if this be called a lessening of their power, it must be only because the great fish can no longer eat up the little ones, and that each sovereignty is equally defended from injuries, and disabled from committing them: *Cedant Arma Togæ* is a glorious sentence; the voice of the dove; the olive branch of peace. A blessing so great, that when it pleases God to chastise us severely for our sins, it is with the rod of war that for the most part He whips us: and experience tells us none leaves deeper marks behind it.

X. Of the Real Benefits that flow from this Proposal about Peace

I am come to my last section, in which I shall enumerate some of those many *real benefits* that flow from this proposal for the present and future peace of Europe.

Let it not, I pray, be the least that it prevents the spilling of so much human and Christian blood. For a thing so offensive to God, and terrible and afflicting to men, as that has ever been, must recommend our expedient beyond all objections. For what can a man give in exchange for his life as well as soul? And though the chiefest in government are seldom personally exposed, yet it is a duty incumbent upon them to be tender of the lives of their people; since without all doubt, they are accountable to God for the blood that is spilt in their service. So that besides the loss of so many lives, of importance to any government, both for labour and propagation, the cries of so many widows, parents, and fatherless are prevented, that cannot be very pleasant in the ears of any government, and is the natural consequence of war in all government.

There is another *manifest benefit* which redounds to Christendom by this peaceable expedient, the reputation of Christianity will in some degree be recovered in the sight of infidels; which, by the many bloody and unjust wars of Christians, not only with them, but one with another, hath been greatly impaired. For, to the scandal of that holy profession, Christians, that glory in their Saviour's name, have long devoted the credit and dignity of it to their worldly passions, as often as they have been excited by the impulses of ambition or revenge. They have not always been in the right: nor has right been the reason of war: and not only Christians against Christians, but the same sort of Christians have imbrued their hands in one another's blood; invoking and interesting all they could the good and merciful God to prosper their arms to their brethren's destruction: yet their Saviour has told them that He came to save, and not to destroy the lives of men: to give and plant peace among men: and if in any sense He may be said to send war, it is the holy war indeed; for it is to send against the devil, and not the persons of men. Of all His titles this seems the most glorious as well as comfortable for us, that He is the prince of peace. It is His nature, His office, His work, and the end and excellent blessings of His coming, who is both the maker and preserver of our peace with God. And it is very remarkable, that in all the New Testament He is but once called lion, but frequently the Lamb of God; to denote to us His gentle,meek, and harmless nature, and that those who desire to be the disciples of His cross and kingdom, for they are inseparable, must be like Him, as St. Paul, St. Peter, and St. John tell us. Nor is it said the lamb shall lie down with the lion, but the lion shall lie down with the lamb. That is war shall yield to peace, and the soldier turn hermit. To be sure, Christians should not be apt to strive, not swift to anger against anybody, and less with one another, and least of all for the uncertain and fading enjoyments of this lower world: and no quality is exempted from this doctrine. Here is a wide field for the reverend clergy of Europe to act their part in, who have so much the possession of princes and people too. May they recommend and labour this pacific means I offer, which will end blood, if not strife; and then reason, upon free debate, will be judge, and not the sword. So that both right and peace, which are the desire and fruit of wise governments, and the choice blessings of any country, seem to succeed the establishment of this proposal.

The *third benefit* is that it saves money, both to the prince and people; and thereby prevents those grudgings and misunderstandings between them that are wont to follow the devouring expenses of war; and enables both to perform public acts for learning, charity, manufactures, etc. The virtues of government and ornaments of countries. Nor is this all the advantage that follows to sovereignties, upon this head of money and good husbandry, to whose service and happiness this short discourse is dedicated; for it saves the great expense that frequent and splendid embassies require, and all their appendages of spies and intelligence, which in the most prudent governments have devoured mighty sums of money; and that not without some immoral practices also: such as corrupting of servants to betray their masters, by revealing their secrets; not to be defended by Christian or old Roman virtues. But here where there is nothing to fear there is little to know, and therefore the purchase is either cheap, or may be wholly spared. I might mention pensions to the widows and orphans of such as die in wars, and of those that have been disabled in them; which rise high in the revenue of some countries.

Our *fourth advantage* is that the towns, cities, and countries that might be laid waste by the rage of war are thereby preserved. A blessing that would be very well understood in Flanders and Hungary, and indeed upon all the borders of sovereignties, which are almost ever the stages of spoil and misery; of which the stories of England and Scotland do sufficiently inform us without looking over the water.

The *fifth benefit* of this peace is the ease and security of travel and traffic: a happiness never understood since the Roman Empire has been broken into so many sovereignties. But we may easily conceive the comfort and advantage of travelling through the governments of Europe by a pass from any of the sovereignties of it, which this league and state of peace will naturally make authentic. They that have travelled Germany, where is so great a number of sovereignties, know the want and value of this privilege, by the many stops and examinations they meet with by the way: but especially such as have made the great tour of Europe. This leads to the benefit of a universal monarchy, without the inconveniences that attend it: for when the whole was one empire, though these advantages were enjoyed, yet the several provinces, that now make the kingdoms and states of Europe, were under some hardship from the great sums of money remitted to the imperial seat, and the ambition and avarice of their several proconsuls and governors, and the great taxes they paid to the numerous legions of soldiers, that they maintained for their own subjection, who were not wont to entertain that concern for them (being uncertainly there, and having their fortunes to make) which their respective and proper sovereigns have always shown for them. So that to be ruled by native princes or states, with the advantage of that peace and security that can only render a universal monarchy desirable, is peculiar to our proposal, and for that reason it is to be preferred.

Another advantage is the great security it will be to Christians against the inroads of the Turk, in their most prosperous fortune. For it had been impossible for the Porte to have prevailed so often, and so far from Christendom, but by the carelessness, or wilful connivence, if not aid, of some Christian princes. And for the same reason, why no Christian monarch will adventure to oppose or break such a union, the Grand Seignior will find himself obliged to concur, for the security of what he holds in Europe: where with all his strength he would feel it an over-match for him. The prayers, tears, treason, blood, and devastation that war has cost in Christendom, for these two last ages especially, must add to the credit of our proposal, and the blessing of the peace thereby humbly recommended.

The *seventh advantage* of a European Imperial Diet, Parliament, or Estates is that it will beget and increase personal friendship between princes and states, which tends to the rooting up of wars, and planting peace in a deep and fruitful soil. For princes have the curiosity of seeing the courts and cities of other countries, as well as private men, if they could as securely and familiarly gratify their inclinations. It were a great motive to the tranquillity of the world that they could freely converse face to face, and personally and reciprocally give and receive marks of civility and kindness. A hospitality that leaves these impressions behind it will hardly let ordinary matters prevail to mistake or quarrel one another. Their emulation would be in the instances of goodness, laws, customs, learning, arts, buildings; and in particular those that relate to charity, the true glory of some governments, where beggars are as much a rarity as in other places it would be to see none.

Nor is this all the benefit that would come by this freedom

and interview of princes. For natural affection would hereby be preserved, which we see little better than lost, from the time their children, or sisters, are married into other courts. For the present state of insincerity of princes forbid them the enjoyment of that natural comfort which is possessed by private families: insomuch that from the time a daughter or sister is married to another crown, nature is submitted to interest, and that, for the most part, grounded not upon solid or commendable foundations, but ambition or unjust avarice. I say this freedom that is the effect of our pacific proposal restores nature to her just right and dignity in the families of princes, and them to the comfort she brings, wherever she is preserved in her proper station. Here daughters may personally entreat their parents, and sisters, their brothers, for a good understanding between them and their husbands, where nature not crushed by absence and sinister interests, but acting by the sight and lively entreaties of such near relations, is almost sure to prevail. They cannot easily resist the most affectionate addresses of such powerful solicitors as their children and grandchildren, and their sisters, nephews, and nieces; and so backward from children to parents, and sisters to brothers, to keep up and preserve their own families, by a good understanding between their husbands and them.

To conclude this section, there is yet *another manifest privilege* that follows this intercourse and good understanding, which methinks should be very moving with princes, viz., that hereby they may choose wives for themselves such as they love, and not by proxy merely to gratify interest; an ignoble motive; and that rarely begets or continues that kindness which ought to be between men and their wives. A satisfaction very few princes ever knew, and to which all other pleasures ought to resign. Which has often obliged me to think that the advantage of private men upon princes, by family comforts, is a sufficient balance against their greater power and glory: the one being more in imagination than real; and often unlawful; but the other natural, solid, and commendable. Besides, it is certain, parents loving well before they are married, which very rarely happens to princes, has kind and generous influences upon their offspring: which with their example makes them better husbands and wives in their turn. This in great measure prevents unlawful love, and the mischiefs of those intrigues that are wont to follow them. What hatred, feuds, wars, and desolations have in divers ages flown from unkindness between princes and their wives? What unnatural divisions among their children, and ruin to their families, if not loss of their countries by it? Behold an expedient to prevent it, a natural and efficacious one. Happy to princes and happy to their people also. For nature being renewed and strengthened by these mutual pledges and endearments I have mentioned will leave those soft and kind impressions behind in the minds of princes that court and country will very easily discern and feel the good effects of: especially if they have the wisdom to show that they interest themselves in the prosperity of the children and relations of their princes. For it does not only incline them to be good, but engage those relations to become powerful suitors to their princes for them if any misunderstanding should unhappily arise between them and their sovereigns. Thus ends this section. It now rests to conclude the discourse in which, if I have not pleased my reader or answered his expectation, it is some comfort to me I meant well, and have cost him but little money and time; and brevity is an excuse, if not a virtue, where the subject is not agreeable, or is but ill prosecuted.

The Conclusion

I will conclude this my proposal of a European Sovereign, or Imperial Diet, Parliament, or Estates with that which I have touched upon before, and which falls under the notice of every one concerned, by coming home to their particular and respective experience within their own sovereignties. That by the same rules of justice and prudence by which parents and masters govern their families, and magistrates their cities, and estates their republics, and princes and kings their principalities and kingdoms, Europe may obtain and preserve peace among her sovereignties. For wars are the duels of princes; and as government in kingdoms and states prevents men being judges and executioners for themselves, over-rules private passions as to injuries or revenge, and subjects the great as well as the small to the rule of justice that power might not vanquish or oppress right nor one neighbour act an independency and sovereignty upon another, while they have resigned that original claim to the benefit and comfort of society; so this being soberly weighed in the whole and parts of it, it will not be hard to conceive or frame, nor yet to execute, the design I have here proposed.

And for the better understanding and perfecting of the idea I here present to the sovereign princes and estates of Europe for the safety and tranquillity of it, I must recommend to their perusals Sir William Temple's account of the United Provinces; which is an instance and answer upon practice to all the objections that can be advanced against the practicability of my proposal: nay, it is an experiment that not only comes to our case, but exceeds the difficulties that can render its accomplishment disputable. For there we shall find three degrees of sovereignties to make up every sovereignty in the general states. I will reckon them backwards. First, the states general themselves; then the immediate sovereignties that constitute them, which are those of the provinces, answerable to the sovereignties of Europe, that by their deputies are to compose the European diet, parliament, or estates in our proposal; and then there are the several cities of each province that are so many independent or distinct sovereignties, which compose those of the provinces as those of the provinces do compose the states general at the Hague.

But I confess I have the passion to wish heartily that the honour of proposing and effecting so great and good a design might be owing to England, of all the countries in Europe, as something of the nature of our expedient was, in design and preparation, to the wisdom, justice, and valour of Henry the Fourth of France, whose superior qualities raising his character above those of his ancestors or contemporaries deservedly gave him the style of Henry the Great. For he was upon obliging the princes and estates of Europe to a political balance when the Spanish faction for that reason contrived and accomplished his murder by the hands of Ravilliac. I will not then fear to be censured for proposing an expedient for the present and future peace of Europe when it was not only the design but glory of one of the greatest princes that ever reigned in it; and is found practicable in the constitution of one of the wisest and powerfullest states of it. So that to conclude, I have very little to answer for in all this affair; because if it succeed I have so little to deserve. For this great king's example tells us it is fit to be done; and Sir William Temple's history shows us by a surpassing instance that it may be done; and Europe, by her incomparable miseries, makes it now necessary to be done: that my share is only thinking of it at this juncture, and putting it into the common light for the peace and prosperity of Europe.

SOME FRUITS OF SOLITUDE

IN

REFLECTIONS AND MAXIMS RELATING TO THE CONDUCT OF HUMAN LIFE

SOME FRUITS OF SOLITUDE

In Reflections and Maxims Relating to the Conduct of Human Life

PART I

THE PREFACE

Reader,—This Enchiridion I present thee with is the Fruit of Solitude, a school few care to learn in, though none instructs us better. Some parts of it are the result of serious reflection: others the flashing of lucid intervals: written for private satisfaction, and now published for a help to human conduct.

The author blesseth God for his retirement, and kisses that gentle hand which led him into it. For though it should prove barren to the world, it can never do so to him.

He has now had some time he could call his own, a property he was never so much master of before, in which he has taken a view of himself and the world and observed wherein he hath hit and missed the mark; what might have been done, what mended, and what avoided in his human conduct; together with the omissions and excesses of others, as well societies and governments, as private families and persons. And he verily thinks were he to live over his life again, he could not only with God's grace serve him, but his neighbour and himself, better than he hath done, and have seven years of his time to spare. And yet perhaps he hath not been the worst or the idlest man in the world; nor is he the oldest. And this is the rather said that it might quicken thee, reader, to lose none of the time that is yet thine.

There is nothing of which we are apt to be so lavish as of time, and about which we ought to be more solicitous; since without it we can do nothing in this world. Time is what we want most, but what, alas! we use worst; and for which God will certainly most strictly reckon with us when time shall be no more.

It is of that moment to us in reference to both worlds that I can hardly wish any man better than that he would seriously consider what he does with his time; how and to what ends he employs it; and what returns he makes to God, his neighbour, and himself for it. Will he never have a ledger for this? This, the greatest wisdom and work of life.

To come but once into the world, and trifle away our true enjoyment of it, and of ourselves in it, is lamentable indeed. This one reflection would yield a thinking person great instruction. And since nothing below man can so think, man, in being thoughtless, must needs fall below himself. And that, to be sure, such do as are unconcerned in the use of their most precious time.

This is but too evident, if we will allow ourselves to consider that there's hardly anything we take by the right end or improve to its just advantage.

We understand little of the works of God, either in nature or grace. We pursue false knowledge and mistake education extremely. We are violent in our affections, confused and immethodical in our whole life; making that a burthen which was given for a blessing; and so of little comfort to ourselves or others. Misapprehending the true notion of happiness, and so missing of the right use of life and way of happy living.

And until we are persuaded to stop and step a little aside, out of the noisy crowd and encumbering hurry of the world, and calmly take a prospect of things, it will be impossible we should be able to make a right judgment of ourselves, or know our own misery. But after we have made the just reckonings which retirement will help us to, we shall begin to think the world in great measure mad, and that we have been in a sort of bedlam all this while.

Reader, whether young or old, think it not too soon or too late to turn over the leaves of thy past life. And be sure to fold down where any passage of it may affect thee and bestow thy remainder of time to correct those faults in thy future conduct, be it in relation to this or the next life. What thou wouldst do, if what thou hast done were to do again, be sure to do as long as thou livest, upon the like occasions.

Our resolutions seem to be vigorous, as often as we reflect upon our past errors. But, alas! they are apt to flat again upon fresh temptations to the same things.

The author does not pretend to deliver thee an exact piece, his business not being ostentation but charity. It is miscellaneous in the matter of it, and by no means artificial in the composure. But it contains hints that may serve thee for texts to preach to thyself upon, and which comprehend much of the course of human life, since, whether thou art parent or child, prince or subject, master or servant, single or married, public or private, mean or honourable, rich or poor, prosperous or improsperous, in peace or controversy, in business or solitude, whatever be thy inclination or aversion, practice or duty, thou wilt find something not unsuitably said for thy direction and advantage. Accept and improve what deserves thy notice; the rest excuse and place to account of good will to thee and the whole creation of God.

REFLECTIONS AND MAXIMS

1. *Ignorance.*—It is admirable to consider how many millions of people come into and go out of the world, ignorant of themselves and of the world they have lived in.

2. If one went to see Windsor Castle or Hampton Court it would be strange not to observe and remember the situation, the building, the gardens, fountains, etc., that make up the beauty and pleasure of such a seat. And yet few people know themselves; no, not their own bodies, the houses of their minds, the most curious structure of the world, a living walking tabernacle; nor the world of which it was made, and out of which it is fed; which would be so much our benefit as well as our pleasure to know. We cannot doubt of this when we are told that the invisible things of God are brought to light by the things that are seen, and consequently we read our duty in them, as often as we look upon them, to Him that is the great and wise author of them if we look as we should do.

3. The world is certainly a great and stately volume of natural things, and may be not improperly styled the hieroglyphics of a better. But, alas! how very few leaves of it do we seriously turn over! This ought to be the subject of the education of our youth, who at twenty, when they should be fit for business, know little or nothing of it.

4. *Education.*—We are in pain to make them scholars, but not men! To talk, rather than to know; which is true canting.

5. The first thing obvious to children is what is sensible; and that we make no part of their rudiments.

6. We press their memory too soon, and puzzle, strain, and load them with words and rules; to know grammar and rhetoric, and a strange tongue or two, that it is ten to one may never be useful to them; leaving their natural genius to mechanical and physical or natural knowledge uncultivated and neglected; which would be of exceeding use and pleasure to them through the whole course of their life.

7. To be sure languages are not to be despised or neglected. But things are still to be preferred.

8. Children had rather be making of tools and instruments of play; shaping, drawing, framing, and building, etc., than getting some rules of propriety of speech by heart. And those also would follow with more judgment and less trouble and time.

9. It were happy if we studied nature more in natural things; and acted according to nature; whose rules are few, plain, and most reasonable.

10. Let us begin where she begins, go her pace, and close always where she ends, and we cannot miss of being good naturalists.

11. The creation would not be longer a riddle to us. The heavens, earth, and waters, with their respective, various, and numerous inhabitants; their productions, natures, seasons, sympathies, and antipathies; their use, benefit, and pleasure would be better understood by us; and an eternal wisdom, power, majesty, and goodness very conspicuous to us, through those sensible and passing forms, the world wearing the mark of its maker, whose stamp is everywhere visible, and the characters very legible to the children of wisdom.

12. And it would go a great way to caution and direct people in their use of the world that they were better studied and knowing in the creation of it.

13. For how could men find the confidence to abuse it while they should see the Great Creator look them in the face in all and every part thereof?

14. Therefore ignorance makes them insensible, and that insensibility hardly misusing this noble creation that has the stamp and voice of a deity everywhere and in everything to the observing.

15. It is a pity therefore that books have not been composed for youth by some curious and careful naturalists, and also mechanics, in the Latin tongue, to be used in schools that they might learn things with words, things obvious and familiar to them, and which would make the tongue easier to be attained by them.

16. Many able gardeners and husbandmen are yet ignorant of the reason of their calling; as most artificers are of the reason of their own rules that govern their excellent workmanship. But a naturalist and mechanic of this sort is master of the reason of both, and might be of the practice too, if his industry kept pace with his speculation; which were very commendable; and without which he cannot be said to be a complete naturalist or mechanic.

17. Finally, if man be the index or epitome of the world, as philosophers tell us, we have only to read ourselves well to be learned in it. But because there is nothing we less regard than the characters of the power that made us, which are so clearly written upon us and the world He has given us, and can best tell us what we are and should be, we are even strangers to our own genius. The glass in which we should see that true instructing and agreeable variety which is to be observed in nature to the admiration of that wisdom and adoration of that power which made us all.

18. *Pride.*—And yet we are very apt to be full of ourselves, instead of Him that made what we so much value; and but for whom we can have no reason to value ourselves. For we have nothing that we can call our own; no, not ourselves. For we are all but tenants, and at will too, of the great lord of ourselves, and the rest of this great farm, the world that we live upon.

19. But methinks we cannot answer it to ourselves as well as our Maker, that we should live and die ignorant of ourselves, and thereby of Him, and the obligations we are under to Him for ourselves.

20. If the worth of a gift sets the obligation and directs the return of the party that receives it: he that is ignorant of it will be at a loss to value it and the Giver for it.

21. Here is man in his ignorance of himself. He knows not how to estimate his Creator, because he knows not how to value his creation. If we consider his make and lovely compositure; the several stories of his lovely structure; his divers members, their order, function, and dependency; the instruments of food, the vessels of digestion, the several transmutations it passes, and how nourishment is carried and diffused throughout the whole body, by most innate and imperceptible passages; how the animal spirit is thereby refreshed, and with an unspeakable dexterity and motion sets all parts at work to feed themselves; and last of all, how the rational soul is seated in the animal, as its proper house, as is the animal in the body—I say, if this rare fabric alone were but considered by us, with all the rest by which it is fed and comforted, surely man would have a more reverent sense of the power, wisdom, and goodness of God, and of that duty he owes to Him for it. But if he would be acquainted with his own soul, its noble faculties, its union with the body, its nature and end, and the providences by which the whole frame of humanity is preserved, he would admire and adore his good and great God. But man is become a strange contradiction to himself; but it is of himself, not being by constitution, but corruption such.

22. He would have others obey him, even his own kind; but he will not obey God that is so much above him, and who made him.

23. He will lose none of his authority: no, not bate an ace of it. He is humourous to his wife, he beats his children, is angry with his servants, strict with his neighbours, revenges all affronts to extremity; but, alas! forgets all the while that he is the man; and is more in arrear to God that is so very patient with him than they are to him with whom he is so strict and impatient.

24. He is curious to wash, dress, and perfume his body,

but careless of his soul. The one shall have many hours, the other not so many minutes. This shall have three or four new suits in a year, but that must wear its old clothes still.

25. If he be to receive or see a great man, how nice and anxious is he that all things be in order? And with what respect and address does he approach and make his court? But to God how dry and formal and constrained is his devotion?

26. In his prayers he says, Thy Will be done: but means his own. At least acts so.

27. It is too frequent to begin with God and end with the world. But He is the good man's beginning and end; his Alpha and Omega.

28. *Luxury.*—Such is now become our delicacy, that we will not eat ordinary meat, nor drink small, palled liquor; we must have the best and the best cooked for our bodies, while our souls feed on empty or corrupted things.

29. In short, man is spending all upon a bare house, and hath little or no furniture within to recommend it; which is preferring the cabinet before the jewel, a lease of seven years before an inheritance. So absurd a thing is man, after all his proud pretences to wit and understanding.

30. *Inconsideration.*—The want of due consideration is the cause of all the unhappiness man brings upon himself. For his second thoughts rarely agree with his first, which pass not without a considerable retrenchment or correction. And yet that sensible warning is too frequently not precaution enough for his future conduct.

31. Well may we say our infelicity is of ourselves; since there is nothing we do that we should not do, but we know it, and yet do it.

32. *Disappointments and Resignation.*—For disappointments that come not by our own folly, they are the trials or correction of heaven. And it is our own fault if they prove not our advantage.

33. To repine at them does not mend the matter: it is only to grumble at our Creator. But to see the hand of God in them, with a humble submission to His will, is the way to turn our water into wine, and engage the greatest love and mercy on our side.

34. We must needs disorder ourselves if we only look at

our losses. But if we consider how little we deserve what is left our passion will cool and our murmurs will turn into thankfulness.

35. If our hairs fall not to the ground, less do we or our substance without God's Providence.

36. Nor can we fall below the arms of God, how low soever it be we fall.

37. For though our Saviour's passion is over, His compassion is not. That never fails His humble, sincere disciples. In Him they find more than all that they love in the world.

38. *Murmuring.*—Is it reasonable to take it ill that anybody desires of us that which is their own? All we have is the Almighty's. And shall not God have His own when He calls for it?

39. Discontentedness is not only in such a case ingratitude, but injustice. For we are both unthankful for the time we had it, and not honest enough to restore it, if we could keep it.

40. But it is hard for us to look on things in such a glass and at such a distance from this low world; and yet it is our duty, and would be our wisdom and our glory to do so.

41. *Censoriousness.*—We are apt to be very pert at censuring others, where we will not endure advice ourselves. And nothing shows our weakness more than to be so sharp-sighted at spying other men's faults, and so purblind about our own.

42. When the actions of a neighbour are upon the stage, we can have all our wits about us, are so quick and critical we can split a hair and find out every failure and infirmity. But are without feeling or have but very little sense of our own.

43. Much of this comes from ill nature, as well as from an inordinate value of ourselves. For we love rambling better than home, and blaming the unhappy rather than covering and relieving them.

44. In such occasions some show their malice and are witty upon misfortunes; others their justice, they can reflect apace; but few or none their charity; especially if it be about money matters.

45. You shall see an old miser come forth with a set gravity, and so much severity against the distressed to excuse his purse, that he will, ere he has done, put it out of all question that riches is righteousness with him. This, says

he, is the fruit of your prodigality (as if, poor man, covetousness were no fault) or of your projects or grasping after a great trade. While he himself would have done the same thing but that he had not the courage to venture so much ready money out of his own trusty hands, though it had been to have brought him back the Indies in return. But the proverb is just, vice should not correct sin.

46. They have a right to censure that have a heart to help. The rest is cruelty, not justice.

47. *Bounds of Charity.*—Lend not beyond thy ability, nor refuse to lend out of thy ability; especially when it will help others more than it can hurt thee.

48. If thy debtor be honest and capable, thou hast thy money again, if not with increase with praise. If he prove insolvent, don't ruin him to get that which it will not ruin thee to lose. For thou art but a steward, and another is thy owner, master, and judge.

49. The more merciful acts thou dost, the more mercy thou wilt receive; and if with a charitable employment of thy temporal riches thou gainest eternal treasure, thy purchase is infinite. Thou wilt have found the art of multiplying indeed.

50. *Frugality or Bounty.*—Frugality is good if liberality be joined with it. The first is leaving off superfluous expenses; the last bestowing them to the benefit of others that need. The first without the last begins covetousness; the last without the first begins prodigality. Both together make an excellent temper. Happy the place where that is found.

51. Were it universal we should be cured of two extremes, want and excess. And the one would supply the other and so bring both nearer to a mean, the just degree of earthly happiness.

52. It is a reproach to religion and government to suffer so much poverty and excess.

53. Were the superfluities of a nation valued and made a perpetual tax or benevolence, there would be more almshouses than poor; schools than scholars; and enough to spare for government besides.

54. Hospitality is good if the poorer sort are the subjects of our bounty; else too near a superfluity.

55. *Discipline.*—If thou wouldst be happy and easy in thy family, above all things observe discipline.

56. Every one in it should know their duty; and there should be a time and place for everything; and whatever else is done or omitted, be sure to begin and end with God.

57. *Industry.*—Love labour. For if thou dost not want it for food, thou mayst for physic. It is wholesome for thy body and good for thy mind. It prevents the fruits of idleness, which many times comes of nothing to do, and leads too many to do what is worse than nothing.

58. A garden, an elaboratory, a workhouse, improvements, and breeding are pleasant and profitable diversions to the idle and ingenious. For here they miss ill company, and converse with nature and art; whose variety are equally grateful and instructing; and preserve a good constitution of body and mind.

59. *Temperance.*—To this a spare diet contributes much. Eat therefore to live, and do not live to eat. That's like a man, but this below a beast.

60. Have wholesome but not costly food, and be rather cleanly than dainty in ordering it.

61. The receipts of cookery are swelled to a volume, but a good stomach excels them all; to which nothing contributes more than industry and temperance.

62. It is a cruel folly to offer up to ostentation so many lives of creatures as make up the state of our treats; as it is a prodigal one to spend more in sauce than in meat.

63. The proverb says that enough is as good as a feast. But it is certainly better if superfluity be a fault which never fails to be at festivals.

64. If thou rise with an appetite thou art sure never to sit down without one.

65. Rarely drink but when thou art dry; nor then between meals, if it can be avoided.

66. The smaller the drink the clearer the head and the cooler the blood; which are great benefits in temper and business.

67. Strong liquors are good at some times, and in small proportions; being better for physic than food, for cordials than common use.

68. The most common things are the most useful; which

shows both the wisdom and goodness of the great Lord of the family of the world.

69. What therefore he has made rare, don't thou use too commonly, lest thou shouldst invert the use and order of things; become wanton and voluptuous; and thy blessings prove a curse.

70. Let nothing be lost, said our Saviour. But that is lost that is misused.

71. Neither urge another to that thou wouldst be unwilling to do thyself; nor do thyself what looks to thee unseemly and intemperate in another.

72. All excess is ill; but drunkenness is of the worst sort. It spoils health, dismounts the mind, and unmans men. It reveals secrets, is quarrelsome, lascivious, impudent, dangerous, and mad. In fine, he that's drunk is not a man; because he is so long void of reason, that distinguishes a man from a beast.

73. *Apparel.*—Excess in apparel is another costly folly. The very trimming of the vain world would clothe all the naked one.

74. Choose thy clothes by thine own eyes, not another's. The more plain and simple they are, the better. Neither unshapely nor fantastical; and for use and decency, and not for pride.

75. If thou art clean and warm, it is sufficient; for more doth but rob the poor and please the wanton.

76. It is said of the true church, the King's daughter is all glorious within. Let our care therefore be of our minds more than of our bodies if we would be of her communion.

77. We are told with truth that meekness and modesty are the rich and charming attire of the soul. And the plainer the dress the more distinctly and with greater lustre their beauty shines.

78. It is a great pity such beauties are so rare, and those of Jezebel's forehead are so common. Whose dresses are incentives to lust; but bars, instead of motives, to love or virtue.

79. *Right Marriage.*—Never marry but for love; but see that thou lovest what is lovely.

80. If love be not thy chiefest motive, thou wilt soon grow

weary of a married state, and stray from thy promise to search out thy pleasures in forbidden places.

81. Let not enjoyment lessen, but augment affection; it being the basest of passions to like when we have not what we slight when we possess.

82. It is the difference between lust and love that this is fixed, that volatile. Love grows, lust wastes by enjoyment. And the reason is that one springs from a union of souls, and the other springs from a union of sense.

83. They have divers originals, and so are of different families. That inward and deep, this superficial; this transient, and that permanent.

84. They that marry for money cannot have the true satisfaction of marriage, the requisite means being wanting.

85. Men are generally more careful of the breed of their horses and dogs than of their children.

86. Those must be of the best sort for shape, strength, courage, and good conditions. But as for these, their own posterity, money shall answer all things. With such it makes the crooked straight, sets squint-eyes right, cures madness, covers folly, changes ill conditions, mends the skin, gives a sweet breath, repairs honours, makes young, works wonders.

87. O how sordid is man grown! man, the noblest creature of the world, as a God on earth and the image of Him that made it; thus to mistake earth for heaven, and worship gold for God!

88. *Avarice.*—Covetousness is the greatest of monsters, as well as the root of all evil. I have once seen the man that died to save charges. What! give ten shillings to a doctor and have an apothecary's bill besides, that may come to I know not what! No, not he. Valuing life less than twenty shillings. But indeed such a man could not well set too low a price upon himself; who, though he lived up to the chin in bags, had rather die than find in his heart to open one of them to help to save his life.

89. Such a man is *felo de se*, and deserves not Christian burial.

90. He is a common nuisance, a weir cross the stream that stops the current. An obstruction to be removed by a purge of the law. The only gratification he gives his neighbours is to let them see that he himself is as little the

better for what he has as they are. For he always looks like Lent; a sort of lay-minim. In some sense he may be compared to Pharaoh's lean kine, for all that he has does him no good. He commonly wears his clothes till they leave him, or that nobody else can wear them. He affects to be thought poor to escape robbery and taxes. And by looking as if he wanted an alms, excuses himself from giving any. He ever goes late to markets to cover buying the worst, but does it because that is cheapest. He lives of the offal. His life were an insupportable punishment to any temper but his own. And no greater torment to him on earth than to live as other men do. But the misery of his pleasure is that he is never satisfied with getting, and always in fear of losing what he cannot use.

91. How vilely has he lost himself that becomes a slave to his servant; and exalts him to the dignity of his Maker. Gold is the god, the wife, the friend of the money-monger of the world.

92. But in marriage do thou be wise; prefer the person before money, virtue before beauty, the mind before the body. Then thou hast a wife, a friend, a companion, a second self; one that bears an equal share with thee in all thy toils and troubles.

93. Choose one that measures her satisfaction, safety, and danger by thine; and of whom thou art sure as of thy secretest thoughts. A friend as well as a wife, which indeed a wife implies. For she is but half a wife that is not, or is not capable of being such a friend.

94. Sexes make no difference; since in souls there is none. And they are the subjects of friendship.

95. He that minds a body and not a soul has not the better part of that relation; and will consequently want the noblest comfort of a married life.

96. The satisfaction of our senses is low, short, and transient, But the mind gives a more raised and extended pleasure, and is capable of a happiness founded upon reason; not bounded and limited by the circumstances that bodies are confined to.

97. Here it is we ought to search out our pleasure, where the field is large and full of variety, and of an enduring nature; sickness, poverty, or disgrace being not able

to shake it because it is not under the moving influences of worldly contingencies.

98. The satisfaction of those that do so is in well-doing and in the assurance they have of a future reward. That they are best loved of those that love most, and that they enjoy and value the liberty of their minds above that of their bodies; having the whole creation for their prospect; the most noble and wonderful works and providences of God, the histories of the ancients, and in them the actions and examples of the virtuous; and lastly, themselves, their affairs and family to exercise their minds and friendship upon.

99. Nothing can be more entire and without reserve; nothing more zealous, affectionate, and sincere; nothing more contented and constant than such a couple; nor no greater temporal felicity than to be one of them.

100. Between a man and his wife nothing ought to rule but love. Authority is for children and servants; yet not without sweetness.

101. As love ought to bring them together, so it is the best way to keep them well together.

102. Wherefore use her not as a servant whom thou wouldst perhaps have served seven years to have obtained.

103. A husband and wife that love and value one another show their children and servants that they should do so too. Others visibly lose their authority in their families by their contempt of one another; and teach their children to be unnatural by their own examples.

104. It is a general fault not to be more careful to preserve nature in children; who at least in the second descent hardly have the feeling of their relation; which must be an unpleasant reflection to affectionate parents.

105. Frequent visits, presents, intimate correspondence, and intermarriages within allowed bounds are means of keeping up the concern and affection that nature requires from relations.

106. *Friendship.*—Friendship is the next pleasure we may hope for. And where we find it not at home, or have no home to find it in, we may seek it abroad. It is a union of spirits, a marriage of hearts, and the bond thereof virtue.

107. There can be no friendship where there is no freedom.

Friendship loves a free air, and will not be penned up in straight and narrow enclosures. It will speak freely and act so too; and take nothing ill where no ill is meant; nay, where it is it will easily forgive and forget too upon small acknowledgments.

108. Friends are true twins in soul; they sympathise in everything, and have the same love and aversion.

109. One is not happy without the other, nor can either of them be miserable alone. As if they could change bodies, they take their turns in pain as well as in pleasure; relieving one another in their most adverse conditions.

110. What one enjoys the other cannot want. Like the Primitive Christians, they have all things in common, and no property but in one another.

111. *Qualities of a Friend.*—A true friend unbosoms freely, advises justly, assists readily, adventures boldly, takes all patiently, defends courageously, and continues a friend unchangeably.

112. These being the qualities of a friend, we are to find them before we choose one.

113. The covetous, the angry, the proud, the jealous, the talkative cannot but make ill friends as well as false.

114. In short, choose a friend as thou dost a wife, till death separate you.

115. Yet be not a friend beyond the altar. But let virtue bound thy friendship. Else it is not friendship, but an evil confederacy.

116. If my brother or kinsman will be my friend, I ought to prefer him before a stranger, or I show little duty or nature to my parents.

117. And as we ought to prefer our kindred in point of affection, so too in point of charity, if equally needing and deserving.

118. *Caution and Conduct.*—Be not easily acquainted, lest finding reason to cool thou makest an enemy instead of a good neighbour.

119. Be reserved, but not sour, grave but not formal, bold but not rash, humble but not servile, patient not insensible, constant not obstinate, cheerful not light, rather sweet than familiar, familiar than intimate, and intimate with very few, and upon very good grounds.

120. Return the civilities thou receivest, and be ever grateful for favours.

121. *Reparation.*—If thou hast done an injury to another, rather own it than defend it. One way thou gainest forgiveness, the other thou doublest the wrong and reckoning.

122. Some oppose honour to submission: but it can be no honour to maintain what it is dishonourable to do.

123. To confess a fault, that is none, out of fear is indeed mean: but not to be afraid of standing in one is brutish.

124. We should make more haste to right our neighbour than we do to wrong him, and instead of being vindictive we should leave him to judge of his own satisfaction.

125. True honour will pay treble damages, rather than justify one wrong by another.

126. In such controversies it is but too common for some to say both are to blame to excuse their own unconcernedness, which is a base neutrality. Others will cry, they are both alike; thereby involving the injured with the guilty, to mince the matter for the faulty, or cover their own injustice to the wronged party.

127. Fear and gain are great perverters of mankind, and where either prevail the judgment is violated.

128. *Rules of Conversation.*—Avoid company where it is not profitable or necessary; and in those occasions speak little and last.

129. Silence is wisdom where speaking is folly, and always safe.

130. Some are so foolish as to interrupt and anticipate those that speak instead of hearing and thinking before they answer; which is uncivil as well as silly.

131. If thou thinkest twice before thou speakest once thou wilt speak twice the better for it.

132. Better say nothing than not to the purpose. And to speak pertinently, consider both what is fit and when it is fit to speak.

133. In all debates let truth be thy aim, not victory or an unjust interest: and endeavour to gain rather than to expose thy antagonist.

134. Give no advantage in argument, nor loose any that is offered. This is a benefit which arises from temper.

135. Don't use thyself to dispute against thine own judgment to show wit, lest it prepare thee to be too indifferent about what is right: nor against another man to vex him or for mere trial of skill; since to inform or to be informed ought to be the end of all conferences.

136. Men are too apt to be concerned for their credit more than for the cause.

137. *Eloquence.*—There is a truth and beauty in rhetoric, but it oftener serves ill turns than good ones.

138. Elegancy is a good mien and address given to matter, be it by proper or figurative speech. Where the words are apt and allusions very natural, certainly it has a moving grace. But it is too artificial for simplicity and oftentimes for truth. The danger is lest it delude the weak, who in such cases may mistake the handmaid for the mistress, if not error for truth.

139. It is certain truth is least indebted to it because she has least need of it and least uses it.

140. But it is a reprovable delicacy in them that despise truth in plain clothes.

141. Such luxuriants have but false appetites; like those gluttons that by sauces force them where they have no stomach, and sacrifice to their palate not their health. Which cannot be without great vanity, nor that without some sin.

142. *Temper.*—Nothing does reason more right than the coolness of those that offer it. For truth often suffers more by the heat of its defenders than from the arguments of its opposers.

143. Zeal ever follows an appearance of truth, and the assured are too apt to be warm; but it is their weak side in argument; zeal being better shown against sin than persons or their mistakes.

144. *Truth.*—Where thou art obliged to speak, be sure to speak the truth. For equivocation is half way to lying; as lying, the whole way to hell.

145. *Justice.*—Believe nothing against another but upon good authority. Nor report what may hurt another, unless it be a greater hurt to others to conceal it.

146. *Secrecy.*—It is wise not to seek a secret, and honest not to reveal one.

147. Only trust thyself and another shall not betray thee.

148. Openness has the mischief though not the malice of treachery.

149. *Complacency.*—Never assent merely to please others. For that is beside flattery oftentimes untrue; and discovers a mind liable to be servile and base: nor contradict to vex others, for that shows an ill temper, and provokes but profits nobody.

150. *Shifts.*—Do not accuse others to excuse thyself; for that is neither generous nor just. But let sincerity and ingenuity be thy refuge rather than craft and falsehood. For cunning borders very near upon knavery.

151. Wisdom never uses nor wants it. Cunning to wife is as an ape to a man.

152. *Interest.*—Interest has the security though not the virtue of a principle. As the world goes it is the surer side. For men daily leave both relations and religion to follow it.

153. It is an odd sight but very evident that families and nations of cross religions and humours unite against those of their own, where they find an interest to do it.

154. We are tied down by our senses to this world; and where that is in question it can be none with worldly men, whether they should not forsake all other considerations for it.

155. *Inquiry.*—Have a care of vulgar errors. Dislike as well as allow reasonably.

156. Inquiry is human; blind obedience, brutal. Truth never loses by the one but often suffers by the other.

157. The usefullest truths are plainest. And while we keep to them our differences cannot rise high.

158. There may be a wantonness in search as well as a stupidity in trusting. It is great wisdom equally to avoid the extremes.

159. *Right Timing.*—Do nothing improperly. Some are witty, kind, cold, angry, easy, stiff, jealous, careless, cautious, confident, close, open, but all in the wrong place.

160. It is ill mistaking where the matter is of importance.

161. It is not enough that a thing be right, if it be not fit to be done. If not prudent, though just, it is not advisable. He that loses by getting had better lose than get.

162. *Knowledge.*—Knowledge is the treasure, but judgment the treasurer of a wise man.

163. He that has more knowledge than judgment is made for another man's use more than his own.

164. It cannot be a good constitution where the appetite is great and the digestion weak.

165. There are some men like dictionaries; to be looked into upon occasion, but have no connection and are little entertaining.

166. Less knowledge than judgment will always have the advantage upon the injudicious knowing man.

167. A wise man makes what he learns his own, the other shows he is but a copy or a collection at most.

168. *Wit.*—Wit is a happy and striking way of expressing a thought.

169. It is not often, though it be lively and mantling, that it carries a great body with it.

170. Wit therefore is fitter for diversion than business, being more grateful to fancy than judgment.

171. Less judgment than wit is more sail than ballast.

172. Yet it must be confessed that wit gives an edge to sense, and recommends it extremely.

173. Where judgment has wit to express it, there's the best orator.

174. *Obedience to Parents.*—If thou wouldst be obeyed, being a father; being a son, be obedient.

175. He that begets thee owes thee; and has a natural right over thee.

176. Next to God thy parents; next them the magistrate.

177. Remember that thou art not more indebted to thy parents for thy nature than for their love and care.

178. Rebellion therefore in children was made death by God's law, and the next sin to idolatry in the people; which is renouncing of God, the great parent of all.

179. Obedience to parents is not only our duty, but our interest. If we received our life from them we prolong it by obeying them. For obedience is the first commandment with promise.

180. The obligation is as indissoluble as the relation.

181. If we must not disobey God to obey them, at least we must let them see that there is nothing else in our refusal. For some unjust commands cannot excuse the general

neglect of our duty. They will be our parents and we must be their children still. And if we cannot act for them against God neither can we act against them for ourselves or anything else.

182. *Bearing.*—A man in business must put up many affronts if he loves his own quiet.

183. We must not pretend to see all that we see if we would be easy.

184. It were endless to dispute upon everything that is disputable.

185. A vindictive temper is not only uneasy to others, but to them that have it.

186. *Promising.*—Rarely promise. But if lawful constantly perform.

187. Hasty resolutions are of the nature of vows; and to be equally avoided.

188. I will never do this, says one, yet does it. I am resolved to do that, says another, but flags upon second thoughts. Or does it, though awkwardly, for his word's sake. As if it were worse to break his word than to do amiss in keeping it.

189. Wear none of thine own chains; but keep free whilst thou art free.

190. It is an effect of passion that wisdom corrects to lay thyself under resolutions that cannot be well made and worse performed.

191. *Fidelity.*—Avoid all thou canst being entrusted. But do thy utmost to discharge the truth thou undertakest. For carelessness is injurious if not unjust.

192. The glory of a servant is fidelity; which cannot be without diligence as well as truth.

193. Fidelity has enfranchised slaves and adopted servants to be sons.

194. Reward a good servant well: and rather quit than disquiet thyself with an ill one.

195. *Master.*—Mix kindness with authority; and rule more by discretion than rigour.

196. If thy servant be faulty, strive rather to convince him of his error than discover thy passion: and when he is sensible, forgive him.

197. Remember he is thy fellow creature, and that God's

goodness, not thy merit, has made the difference betwixt thee and him.

198. Let not thy children domineer over thy servants: nor suffer them to slight thy children.

199. Suppress tales in the general: but where a matter requires notice encourage the complaint and right the aggrieved.

200. If a child, he ought to entreat and not to command; and if a servant, to comply where he does not obey.

201. Though there should be but one master and mistress in a family, yet servants should know that children have the reversion.

202. *Servants.*—Indulge not unseemly things in thy master's children, nor refuse them what is fitting. For one is the highest unfaithfulness and the other indiscretion as well as disrespect.

203. Do thine own work honestly and cheerfully, and when that is done help thy fellow; that so another time he may help thee.

204. If thou wilt be a good servant thou must be true and thou canst not be true if thou defraudest thy master.

205. A master may be defrauded many ways by a servant, as in time, care, pains, money, trust.

206. But a true servant is the contrary. He is diligent, careful, trusty. He tells no tales, reveals no secrets, refuses no pains. Not to be tempted by gain, nor awed by fear to unfaithfulness.

207. Such a servant serves God in serving his master; and has double wages for his work, to wit, here and hereafter.

208. *Jealous.*—Be not fancifully jealous: for that is foolish; as to be reasonably so is wise.

209. He that superfines upon other men's actions cozens himself as well as injures them.

210. To be very subtle and scrupulous in business is as hurtful as being over-confident and secure.

211. In difficult cases such a temper is timorous; and in dispatch irresolute.

212. Experience is a safe guide. And a practical head is a great happiness in business.

213. *Posterity.*—We are too careless of posterity, not considering that as they are so the next generation will be.

214. If we would amend the world we should mend ourselves and teach our children to be not what we are but what they should be.

215. We are too apt to awaken and tune up their passions by the example of our own; and to teach them to be pleased not with what is best but with what pleases best.

216. It is our duty, and ought to be our care, to ward against that passion in them which is more especially our own weakness and affliction. For we are in great measure accountable for them as well as for ourselves.

217. We are in this also true turners of the world upside down. For money is first and virtue last and least in our care.

218. It is not how we leave our children, but what we leave them.

219. To be sure virtue is but a supplement and not a principal in their portion and character: and therefore we see so little wisdom or goodness among the rich in proportion to their wealth.

220. *A Country Life.*—The country life is to be preferred, for there we see the works of God; but in cities little else but the works of men. And the one makes a better subject for our contemplation than the other.

221. As puppets are to men and babies to children, so is man's workmanship to God's. We are the picture, he the reality.

222. God's works declare his power, wisdom, and goodness; but man's works, for the most part, his pride, folly, and excess. The one is for use, the other chiefly for ostentation and lust.

223. The country is both the philosopher's garden and library, in which he reads and contemplates the power, wisdom, and goodness of God.

224. It is his food as well as study; and gives him life as well as learning.

225. A sweet and natural retreat from noise and talk; and allows opportunity for reflection, and gives the best subjects for it.

226. In short, it is an original, and the knowledge and improvement of it man's oldest business and trade, and the best he can be of.

227. *Art and Project.*—Art is good where it is beneficial. Socrates wisely bounded his knowledge and instruction by practice.

228. Have a care therefore of projects. And yet despise nothing rashly or in the lump.

229. Ingenuity as well as religion sometimes suffers between two thieves: pretenders and despisers.

230. Though injudicious and dishonest projectors often discredit art, yet the most useful and extraordinary inventions have not at first escaped the scorn of ignorance; as their authors rarely have cracking of their heads or breaking of their backs.

231. Undertake no experiment in speculation that appears not true in art; nor then at thine own cost if costly or hazardous in making.

232. As many hands make light work, so several purses make cheap experiments.

233. *Industry.*—Industry is certainly very commendable and supplies the want of parts.

234. Patience and diligence like faith remove mountains.

235. Never give out while there is hope; but hope not beyond reason, for that shows more desire than judgment.

236. It is a profitable wisdom to know when we have done enough. Much time and pains are spared in not flattering ourselves against probabilities.

237. *Temporal Happiness.*—Do good with what thou hast, or it will do thee no good.

238. Seek not to be rich but happy. The one lies in bags, the other in content; which wealth can never give.

239. We are apt to call things by wrong names. We will have prosperity to be happiness, and adversity to be misery; though that is the school of wisdom, and oftentimes the way to eternal happiness.

240. If thou wouldst be happy bring thy mind to thy condition, and have an indifferency for more than what is sufficient.

241. Have but little to do, and do it thyself. And do to others as thou wouldst have them do to thee. So thou canst not fail of temporal felicity.

242. The generality are the worse for their plenty. The voluptuous consumes it, the miser hides it. It is the good

man that uses it, and to good purposes. But such are hardly found among the prosperous.

243. Be rather bountiful than expensive.

244. Neither make nor go to feasts, but let the laborious poor bless thee at home in their solitary cottages.

245. Never voluntarily want what thou hast in possession; nor so spend it as to involve thyself in want unavoidable.

246. Be not tempted to presume by success: for many that have got largely have lost all by coveting to get more.

247. To hazard much to get much has more of avarice than wisdom.

248. It is great prudence both to bound and use prosperity.

249. Too few know when they have enough; and fewer know how to employ it.

250. It is equally advisable not to part lightly with what is hardly gotten, and not to shut up closely what flows in freely.

251. Act not the shark upon thy neighbour; nor take advantage of the ignorance, prodigality, or necessity of anyone: for that is next door to fraud, and at best makes but an unblessed gain.

252. It is oftentimes the judgment of God upon greedy rich men that he suffers them to push on their desires of wealth to the excess of overreaching, grinding, or oppression which poisons all they have gotten; so that it commonly runs away as fast and by as bad ways as it was heaped up together.

253. *Respect.*—Never esteem any man or thyself the more for money; nor think the meaner of thyself or another for want of it. Virtue being the just reason of respecting, and the want of it, of slighting any one.

254. A man like a watch is to be valued for his goings.

255. He that prefers him upon other accounts bows to an idol.

256. Unless virtue guide us, our choice must be wrong.

257. An able bad man is an ill instrument, and to be shunned as the plague.

258. Be not deceived with the first appearances of things, but give thyself time to be in the right.

259. Show is not substance: realities govern wise men.

260. Have a care therefore where there is more sail than ballast.

261. *Hazard.*—In all business it is best to put nothing to hazard. But where it is unavoidable be not rash, but firm and resigned.

262. We should not be troubled for what we cannot help. But if it was our fault let it be so no more. Amendment is repentance if not reparation.

263. As a desperate game needs an able gamester, so consideration often would prevent what the best skill in the world cannot recover.

264. Where the probability of advantage exceeds not that of loss, wisdom never adventures.

265. To shoot well flying is well; but to choose it has more of vanity than judgment.

266. To be dexterous in danger is a virtue; but to court danger to show it is weakness.

267. *Detraction.*—Have a care of that base evil detraction. It is the fruit of envy as that is of pride, the immediate offspring of the devil; who of an angel, a Lucifer, a son of the morning, made himself a serpent, a devil, a Beelzebub, and all that is obnoxious to the Eternal Goodness.

268. Virtue is not secure against envy. Men will lessen what they will not imitate.

269. Dislike what deserves it, but never hate; for that is of the nature of malice; which is almost ever to persons not things, and is one of the blackest qualities sin begets in the soul.

270. *Moderation.*—It were a happy day if men could bound and qualify their resentments with charity to the offender. For then our anger would be without sin, and better convict and edify the guilty; which alone can make it lawful.

271. Not to be provoked is best. But if moved never correct till the fume is spent. For every stroke our fury strikes is sure to hit ourselves at last.

272. If we did but observe the allowances our reason makes upon reflection when our passion is over, we could not want a rule how to behave ourselves again on the like occasions.

273. We are more prone to complain than redress, and to censure than excuse.

274. It is next to unpardonable that we can so often blame what we will not once mend. It shows we know, but will not do our Master's will.

275. They that censure should practise: or else let them have the first stone and the last too.

276. *Trick.*—Nothing needs a trick but a trick; sincerity loathes one.

277. We must take care to do right things rightly. For a just sentence may be unjustly executed.

278. Circumstances give great light to true judgment if well weighed.

279. *Passion.*—Passion is a sort of fever in the mind, which ever leaves us weaker than it found us.

280. But being intermitting to be sure it is curable with care.

281. It more than anything deprives us of the use of our judgment; for it raises a dust very hard to see through.

282. Like wine whose lees fly up being jogged it is too muddy to drink.

283. It may not unfitly be termed the mob of the man that commits a riot upon his reason.

284. I have oftentimes thought that a passionate man is like a weak spring that cannot stand long locked.

285. And it is as true that those things are unfit for use that cannot bear small knocks without breaking.

286. He that will not hear can't judge, and he that cannot bear contradiction may with all his wits miss the mark.

287. Objection and debate sift out truth, which needs temper as well as judgment.

288. But above all observe it in resentments; for there passion is most extravagant.

289. Never chide for anger but instruction.

290. He that corrects out of passion raises revenge sooner than repentance.

291. It has more of wantonness than wisdom, and resembles those that eat to please their palate rather than their appetite.

292. It is the difference between a wise and a weak man; this judges by the lump, that by parts and their connection.

293. The Greeks use to say all cases are governed by their

circumstances. The same thing may be well and ill as they change or vary the matter.

294. A man's strength is shown by his bearing. *Bonum agere, et male pati, regis est.*

295. *Personal Caution.*—Reflect without malice, but never without need.

296. Despise nobody nor no condition; lest it come to be thine own.

297. Never rail nor taunt. The one is rude, the other scornful, and both evil.

298. Be not provoked by injuries to commit them.

299. Upbraid only ingratitude.

300. Haste makes work which caution prevents.

301. Tempt no man; lest thou fall for it.

302. Have a care of presuming upon after games. For if that miss all is gone.

303. Opportunities should never be lost, because they can hardly be regained.

304. It is well to cure, but better to prevent a distemper. The first shows more skill, but the last more wisdom.

305. Never make a trial of skill in difficult or hazardous cases.

306. Refuse not to be informed: for that shows pride or stupidity.

307. Humility and knowledge in poor clothes excel pride and ignorance in costly attire.

308. Neither despise nor oppose what thou dost not understand.

309. *Balance.*—We must not be concerned above the value of the thing that engages us; nor raised above reason in maintaining what we think reasonable.

310. It is too common an error to invert the order of things by making an end of that which is a means and a means of that which is an end.

311. Religion and government escape not this mischief. The first is too often made a means instead of an end; the other an end instead of a means.

312. Thus men seek wealth rather than subsistence; and the end of clothes is the least reason of their use. Nor is the satisfying of our appetite our end in eating so much as the pleasing of our palate. The like may also be said of building,

furniture, etc., where the man rules not the beast, and appetite submits not to reason.

313. It is great wisdom to proportion our esteem to the nature of the thing. For as that way things will not be undervalued, so neither will they engage us above their intrinsic worth.

314. If we suffer little things to have great hold upon us we shall be as much transported for them as if they deserved it.

315. It is an old proverb, *Maxima bella ex levissimis causis*, the greatest feuds have had the smallest beginnings.

316. No matter what the subject of the dispute be, but what place we give it in our minds. For that governs our concern and refinement.

317. It is one of the fatalest errors of our lives when we spoil a good cause by an ill management. And it is not impossible but we may mean well in an ill business; but that will not defend it.

318. If we are but sure the end is right we are too apt to gallop over all bounds to compass it; not considering that lawful ends may be very unlawfully attained.

319. Let us be careful to take just ways to compass just things; that they may last in their benefits to us.

320. There is a troublesome humour some men have, that if they may not lead they will not follow; but had rather a thing were never done than not done their own way, though otherwise very desirable.

321. This comes of an over fulness of ourselves, and shows we are more concerned for praise than the success of what we think a good thing.

322. *Popularity*.—Affect not to be seen and men will less see thy weakness.

323. They that show more than they are raise an expectation they cannot answer; and so lose their credit as soon as they are found out.

324. Avoid popularity. It has many snares and no real benefit to thyself, and uncertainty to others.

325. *Privacy*.—Remember the proverb, *Benè qui latuit, benè vixit*, they are happy that live retiredly.

326. If this be true princes and their grandees of all men are the unhappiest. For they live least alone. And they

that must be enjoyed by everybody can never enjoy themselves as they should.

327. It is the advantage little men have upon them; they can be private and have leisure for family comforts, which are the greatest worldly contents men can enjoy.

328. But they that place pleasure in greatness seek it there. And we see rule is as much the ambition of some natures as privacy is the choice of others.

329. *Government.*—Government has many shapes, but it is sovereignty though not freedom in all of them.

330. *Rex et tyrannus* are very differing characters. One rules his people by laws to which they consent; the other by his absolute will and power. That is called freedom, this tyranny.

331. The first is endangered by the ambition of the populace which shakes the constitution: the other by an ill administration which hazards the tyrant and his family.

332. It is great wisdom in princes of both sorts not to strain points too high with their people. For whether the people have a right to oppose them or not they are ever sure to attempt it when things are carried too far; though the remedy oftentimes proves worse than the disease.

333. Happy that king who is great by justice, and that people who are free by obedience.

334. Where the ruler is just he may be strict; else it is two to one it turns upon him. And though he should prevail he can be no gainer where his people are the losers.

335. Princes must not have passions in government, nor resent beyond interest and religion.

336. Where example keeps pace with authority power hardly fails to be obeyed and magistrates to be honoured.

337. Let the people think they govern and they will be governed.

338. This cannot fail if those they trust are trusted.

339. That prince that is just to them in great things and humours them oftentimes in small ones is sure to have and keep them from all the world.

340. For the people is the politic wife of the prince that may be better managed by wisdom than ruled by force.

341. But where the magistrate is partial and serves ill turns he loses his authority with the people and gives the

populace opportunity to gratify their ambition: and so lays a stumbling-block for his people to fall.

342. It is true that where a subject is more popular than the prince the prince is in danger. But it is as true that it is his own fault. For nobody has the like means, interest, or reason to be popular as he.

343. It is an unaccountable thing that some princes incline rather to be feared than loved, when they see that fear does not oftener secure a prince against the dissatisfaction of his people than love makes a subject too many for such a prince.

344. Certainly service upon inclination is like to go farther than obedience upon compulsion.

345. The Romans had a just sense of this when they placed optimus before maximus to their most illustrious captains and Cæsars.

346. Besides, experience tells us that goodness raises a nobler passion in the soul, and gives a better sense of duty than severity.

347. What did Pharaoh get by increasing the Israelites' task? Ruin to himself in the end.

348. Kings chiefly in this should imitate God. Their mercy should be above all their works.

349. The difference between the prince and the peasant is in this world. But a temper ought to be observed by him that has the advantage here because of the judgment of the next.

350. The end of everything should direct the means. Now that of government being the good of the whole, nothing less should be the aim of the prince.

351. As often as rulers endeavour to attain just ends by just mediums they are sure of a quiet and easy government; and as sure of convulsions where the nature of things are violated and their order overruled.

352. It is certain princes ought to have great allowances made them for faults in government, since they see by other people's eyes and hear by their ears. But ministers of state, their immediate confidents and instruments, have much to answer for if to gratify private passions they misguide the prince to do public injury.

353. Ministers of state should undertake their posts at their peril. If princes overrule them, let them show the law

and humbly resign. If fear, gain, or flattery prevail let them answer it to the law.

354. The prince cannot be preserved but where the minister is punishable. For people as well as princes will not endure *imperium in imperio*.

355. If ministers are weak or ill men, and so spoil their places, it is the prince's fault that choose them. But if their places spoil them it is their own fault to be made worse by them.

356. It is but just that those that reign by their princes should suffer for their princes. For it is a safe and necessary maxim not to shift heads in government while the hands are in being that should answer for them.

357. And yet it were intolerable to be a minister of state if everybody may be accuser and judge.

358. Let therefore the false accuser no more escape an exemplary punishment than the guilty minister.

359. For it profanes government to have the credit of the leading men in it subject to vulgar censure; which is often ill-grounded.

360. The safety of a prince therefore consists in a well chosen council: and that only can be said to be so where the persons that compose it are qualified for the business that comes before them.

361. Who would send to a tailor to make a lock, or to a smith to make a suit of clothes?

362. Let there be merchants for trade, seamen for the admiralty, travellers for foreign affairs, some of the leading men of the country for home business, and common and civil lawyers to advise of legality and right: who should always keep to the strict rules of law.

363. Three things contribute much to ruin government: looseness, oppression, and envy.

364. Where the reins of government are too slack, there the manners of the people are corrupted. And that destroys industry, begets effeminacy, and provokes heaven against it.

365. Oppression makes a poor country and a desperate people, who always wait an opportunity to change.

366. He that ruleth over men must be just, ruling in the fear of God, said an old and wise king.

367. Envy disturbs and distracts government, clogs the

wheels, and perplexes the administration. And nothing contributes more to this disorder than a partial distribution of rewards and punishments in the sovereign.

368. As it is not reasonable that men should be compelled to serve, so those that have employments should not be endured to leave them humourously.

369. Where the state intends a man no affront, he should not affront the state.

370. *A Private Life.*—A private life is to be preferred; the honour and gain of public posts bearing no proportion with the comfort of it. The one is free and quiet, the other servile and noisy.

371. It was a great answer of the Shunamite woman, "I dwell among my own people."

372. They that live of their own neither need nor often list to wear the livery of the public.

373. Their subsistence is not during pleasure, nor have they patrons to please or present.

374. If they are not advanced, neither can they be disgraced. And as they know not the smiles of majesty so they feel not the frowns of greatness or the effects of envy.

375. If they want the pleasures of a court they also escape the temptations of it.

376. Private men, in fine, are so much their own that, paying common dues, they are sovereigns of all the rest.

377. *A Public Life.*—Yet the public must and will be served; and they that do it well deserve public marks of honour and profit.

378. To do so men must have public minds as well as salaries; or they will serve private ends at the public cost.

379. Governments can never be well administered but where those entrusted make conscience of well discharging their places.

380. *Qualifications.*—Five things are requisite to a good officer: ability, clean hands, dispatch, patience, and impartiality.

381. *Capacity.*—He that understands not his employment, whatever else he knows must be unfit for it; and the public suffers by his inexpertness.

382. They that are able should be just too; or the government may be the worse for their capacity.

383. *Clean Hands.*—Covetousness in such men prompts them to prostitute the public for gain.

384. The taking of a bribe or gratuity should be punished with as severe penalties as the defrauding of the state.

385. Let men have sufficient salaries and exceed them at their peril.

386. It is a dishonour to government that its officers should live of benevolence; as it ought to be infamous for officers to dishonour the public by being twice paid for the same business.

387. But to be paid and not to do business is rank oppression.

388. *Dispatch.*—Dispatch is a great and good quality in an officer, where duty not gain excites it. But of this too many make their private market and overplus to their wages. Thus the salary is for doing, and the bribe for dispatching the business. As if business could be done before it were dispatched. Or they were to be paid a part, one by the government, the other by the party.

389. Dispatch is as much the duty of an officer as doing, and very much the honour of the government he serves.

390. Delays have been more injurious than direct injustice.

391. They too often starve those they dare not deny.

392. The very winner is made a loser because he pays twice for his own; like those that purchase estates mortgaged before to the full value.

393. Our law says well to delay justice is injustice.

394. Not to have a right and not to come at it differs little.

395. Refusal or dispatch is the duty and wisdom of a good officer.

396. *Patience.*—Patience is a virtue everywhere; but it shines with greatest lustre in the men of government.

397. Some are so proud or testy they won't hear what they should redress.

398. Others so weak they sink or burst under the weight of their office though they can lightly run away with the salary of it.

399. Business can never be well done that is not well understood: which cannot be without patience.

400. It is cruelty indeed not to give the unhappy a hearing whom we ought to help. But it is the top of oppression to

browbeat the humble and modest miserable when they seek relief.

401. Some it is true are unreasonable in their desires and hopes. But then we should inform not rail at and reject them.

402. It is therefore as great an instance of wisdom as a man in business can give to be patient under the impertinences and contradictions that attend it.

403. Method goes far to prevent trouble in business. For it makes the task easy, hinders confusion, saves abundance of time, and instructs those that have business depending what to do and what to hope.

404. *Impartiality.*—Impartiality, though it be the last, is not the least part of the character of a good magistrate.

405. It is noted as a fault in Holy Writ even to regard the poor: how much more the rich in judgment.

406. If our compassions must not sway us, less should our fears, profits, or prejudices.

407. Justice is justly represented blind, because she sees no difference in the parties concerned.

408. She has but one scale and weight for rich and poor, great and small.

409. Her sentence is not guided by the person but the cause.

410. The impartial judge in judgment knows nothing but the law; the prince no more than the peasant, his kindred than a stranger; nay, his enemy is sure to be upon equal terms with his friend, when he is upon the bench.

411. Impartiality is the life of justice, as that is of government.

412. Nor is it only a benefit to the state, for private families cannot subsist comfortably without it.

413. Parents that are partial are ill obeyed by their children; and partial masters not better served by their servants.

414. Partiality is always indirect, if not dishonest. For it shows a bias where reason would have none; if not an injury which justice everywhere forbids.

415. As it makes favourites without reason, so it uses no reason in judging of actions: confirming the proverb, the crow thinks her own bird the fairest.

416. What some see to be no fault in one, they will have criminal in another.

417. Nay, how ugly do our failings look to us in the persons of others; which yet we see not in ourselves.

418. And but too common it is for some people not to know their own maxims and principles in the mouths of other men, when they give occasion to use them.

419. Partiality corrupts our judgment of persons and things, of ourselves and others.

420. It contributes more than anything to factions in government and feuds in families.

421. It is a prodigal passion that seldom returns till it is hunger bit, and disappointments bring it within bounds.

422. And yet we may be indifferent to a fault.

423. *Indifferency.*—Indifference is good in judgment, but bad in relation, and stark naught in religion.

424. And even in judgment our indifferency must be to the persons not causes, for one to be sure is right.

425. *Neutrality.*—Neutrality is something else than indifferency; and yet of kin to it too.

426. A judge ought to be indifferent, and yet he cannot be said to be neutral.

427. The one being to be even in judgment and the other not to meddle at all.

428. And where it is lawful to be sure it is best to be neutral.

429. He that espouses parties can hardly divorce himself from their fate; and more fall with their party than rise with it.

430. A wise neuter joins with neither; but uses both as his honest interest leads him.

431. A neuter only has room to be a peacemaker. For being of neither side he has the means of mediating a reconciliation of both.

432. *A Party.*—And yet where right or religion gives a call, a neuter must be a coward or a hypocrite.

433. In such cases we should never be backward nor yet mistaken.

434. When our right or religion is in question then is the fittest time to assert it.

435. Nor must we always be neutral where our neighbour

is concerned. For though meddling is a fault, helping is a duty.

436. We have a call to do good as often as we have the power and occasion.

437. If heathens could say we are not born for ourselves, surely Christians should practice it.

438. They are taught so by His example as well as doctrine from whom they have borrowed their name.

439. *Ostentation.*—Do what good thou canst unknown; and be not vain of what ought rather to be felt than seen.

440. The humble in the parable of the day of judgment forgot their good works. Lord, when did we so and so?

441. He that does good for good's sake seeks neither praise nor reward; though sure of both at last.

442. *Complete Virtue.*—Content not thyself that thou art virtuous in the general. For one link being wanting the chain is defective.

443. Perhaps thou art rather innocent than virtuous, and owest more to thy constitution than thy religion.

444. Innocent is not to be guilty; but virtuous is to overcome our evil inclinations.

445. If thou hast not conquered thyself in that which is thy own particular weakness, thou hast no title to virtue though thou art free of other men's.

446. For a covetous man to inveigh against prodigality, an atheist against idolatry, a tyrant against rebellion, or a liar against forgery, and a drunkard against intemperance, is for the pot to call the kettle black.

447. Such reproof would have but little success; because it would carry but little authority with it.

448. If thou wouldst conquer thy weakness, thou must never gratify it.

449. No man is compelled to evil; his consent only makes it his.

450. It is no sin to be tempted, but to be overcome.

451. What man in his right mind would conspire his own hurt? Men are beside themselves when they transgress their convictions.

452. If thou wouldst not sin, don't desire, and if thou wouldst not lust, don't embrace the temptation. No, not look at it nor think of it.

453. Thou wouldst take much pains to save thy body. Take some, prithee, to save thy soul.

454. *Religion.*—Religion is the fear of God, and its demonstration good works; and faith is the root of both. For without faith we cannot please God, nor can we fear what we do not believe.

455. The devils also believe and know abundance. But in this is the difference, their faith works not by love, nor their knowledge by obedience; and therefore they are never the better for them. And if ours be such we shall be of their church not of Christ's. For as the head is so must the body be.

456. He was holy, humble, harmless, meek, merciful, etc., when among us; to teach us what we should be when He was gone. And yet He is among us still, and in us too, a living and perpetual preacher of the same grace by His spirit in our consciences.

457. A minister of the gospel ought to be one of Christ's making, if he would pass for one of Christ's ministers.

458. And if he be one of His making, he knows and does as well as believes.

459. That minister whose life is not the model of his doctrine is a babbler rather than a preacher, a quack rather than a physician of value.

460. Of old time they were made ministers by the Holy Ghost. And the more that is an ingredient now the fitter they are for that work.

461. Running streams are not so apt to corrupt; nor itinerant as settled preachers. But they are not to run before they are sent.

462. As they freely receive from Christ so they give.

463. They will not make that a trade which they know ought not in conscience to be one.

464. Yet there is no fear of their living that design not to live by it.

465. The humble and true teacher meets with more than he expects.

466. He accounts content with godliness great gain, and therefore seeks not to make a gain of godliness.

467. As the ministers of Christ are made by him and are like him, so they beget people into the same likeness.

468. To be like Christ then is to be a Christian. And regeneration is the only way to the kingdom of God, which we pray for.

469. Let us to-day therefore hear His voice, and not harden our hearts; who speaks to us many ways: in the Scriptures, in our hearts, by his servants and providences. And the sum of all is holiness and charity.

470. St. James gives a short draught of the matter, but very full and reaching, pure religion and undefiled before God and the Father is this, to visit the fatherless and the widows in their affliction, and to keep ourselves, unspotted from the world. Which is comprised in these two words, charity and piety.

471. They that truly make these their aim will find them their attainment; and with them the peace that follows so excellent a condition.

472. Amuse not thyself therefore with the numerous opinions of the world, nor value thyself upon verbal orthodoxy, philosophy, or thy skill in tongues or knowledge of the fathers (too much the business and vanity of the world). But in this rejoice that thou knowest God that is the Lord who exerciseth loving kindness, and judgment, and righteousness in the earth.

473. Public worship is very commendable if well performed. We owe it to God and good example. But we must know that God is not tied to time or place who is everywhere at the same time. And this we shall know as far as we are capable, if whereever we are our desires are to be with Him.

474. Serving God people generally confine to the acts of public and private worship. And those the more zealous do often repeat in hopes of acceptance.

475. But if we consider that God is an infinite spirit, and as such everywhere; and that our Saviour has taught us that he will be worshipped in spirit and in truth; we shall see the shortness of such a notion.

476. For serving God concerns the frame of our spirits in the whole course of our lives; in every occasion we have in which we may show our love to His law.

477. For as men in battle are continually in the way of shot, so we in this world are ever within the reach of tempta-

tion. And herein do we serve God if we avoid what we are forbid, as well as do what he commands.

478. God is better served in resisting a temptation to evil than in many formal prayers.

479. This is but twice or thrice a day, but that every hour and moment of the day. So much more is our continual watch than our evening and morning devotion.

480. Wouldst thou then serve God? Do not that alone which thou wouldst not that another should see thee do.

481. Don't take God's name in vain, or disobey thy parents, or wrong thy neighbour, or commit adultery, even in thine heart.

482. Neither be vain, lascivious, proud, drunken, revengeful, or angry: nor lie, detract, backbite, overreach, oppress, deceive, or betray. But watch vigorously against all temptations to these things, as knowing that God is present, the overseer of all thy ways and most inward thoughts, and the avenger of His own law upon the disobedient, and thou wilt acceptably serve God.

483. Is it not reason if we expect the acknowledgments of those to whom we are bountiful, that we should reverently pay ours to God, our most magnificent and constant benefactor?

484. The world represents a rare and sumptuous palace, mankind the great family in it, and God the mighty Lord and Master of it.

485. We are all sensible what a stately seat it is; the heavens adorned with so many glorious luminaries; and the earth with groves, plains, valleys, hills, fountains, ponds, lakes, and rivers; and variety of fruits, and creatures for food, pleasure, and profit. In short, how noble a house he keeps, and the plenty and variety and excellency of his table; his orders, seasons, and suitableness of every time and thing. But we must be as sensible, or at least ought to be, what careless and idle servants we are, and how short and disproportionable our behaviour is to His bounty and goodness: how long He bears, and often he reprieves and forgives us. Who, notwithstanding our breach of promises and repeated neglects, has not yet been provoked to break up house and send us to shift for ourselves. Should not this great goodness raise a due sense in us of our undutifulness, and a resolution

to alter our course and mend our manners; that we may be for the future more worthy communicants at our Master's good and great table? Especially since it is not more certain that we deserve His displeasure than that we shall feel it, if we continue to be unprofitable servants.

486. But though God has replenished this world with abundance of good things for man's life and comfort, yet they are all but imperfect goods. He only is the perfect good to whom they point. But, alas! men cannot see Him for them; though they should always see Him in them.

487. I have often wondered at the unaccountableness of man in this among other things; that though he loves changes so well he should care so little to hear or think of his last, great, and best change too, if he pleases.

488. Being as to our bodies composed of changeable elements, we with the world are made up of and subsist by revolution. But our souls being of another and nobler nature we should seek our rest in a more enduring habitation.

489. The truest end of life is to know the life that never ends.

490. He that makes this his care will find it his crown at last.

491. Life else were a misery rather than a pleasure, a judgment not a blessing.

492. For to know, regret, and resent; to desire, hope, and fear more than a beast, and not live beyond him, is to make a man less than a beast.

493. It is the amends of a short and troublesome life, that doing well, and suffering ill, entitles man to one longer and better.

494. This ever raises the good man's hope, and gives him tastes beyond the other world.

495. As it is his aim, so none else can hit the mark.

496. Many make it their speculation, but it is the good man's practice.

497. His work keeps pace with his life, and so leaves nothing to be done when he dies.

498. And he that lives to live ever, never fears dying.

499. Nor can the means be terrible to him that heartily believes the end.

500. For though death be a dark passage, it leads to

immortality, and that is recompense enough for suffering of it.

501. And yet faith lights us even through the grave, being the evidence of things not seen.

502. And this is the comfort of the good, that the grave cannot hold them, and that they live as soon as they die.

503. For death is no more than a turning of us over from time to eternity.

504. Nor can there be a revolution without it; for it supposes the dissolution of one form in order to the succession of another.

505. Death then being the way and condition of life, we cannot love to live, if we cannot bear to die.

506. Let us then not cozen ourselves with the shells and husks of things; nor prefer form to power, nor shadows to substance; pictures of bread will not satisfy hunger, nor those of devotion please God.

507. This world is a form; our bodies are forms; and no visible acts of devotion can be without forms. But yet the less form in religion the better, since God is a spirit. For the more mental our worship the more adequate to the nature of God; the more silent, the more suitable to the language of a spirit.

508. Words are for others not for ourselves: nor for God who hears not as bodies do; but as spirits should.

509. If we would know this dialect we must learn of the divine principle in us. As we hear the dictates of that so God hears us.

510. There we may see Him too in all His attributes; though but in little yet as much as we can apprehend or bear. For as He is in Himself, He is incomprehensible, and dwelleth in that light which no eye can approach. But in His image we may behold His glory; enough to exalt our apprehensions of God, and to instruct us in that worship which pleaseth Him.

511. Men may tire themselves in a labyrinth of search, and talk of God: but if we would know Him indeed it must be from the impressions we receive of Him; and the softer our hearts are the deeper and livelier those will be upon us.

512. If He has made us sensible of His justice by His reproof; of his patience, by His forbearance; of His mercy,

by His forgiveness; of His holiness, by the sanctification of our hearts through His spirit; we have a grounded knowledge of God. This is experience, that speculation; this enjoyment, that report. In short, this is undeniable evidence with the realities of religion, and will stand all winds and weathers.

513. As our faith so our devotion should be lively. Cold meat won't serve at those repasts.

514. It is a coal from God's altar must kindle our fire. And without fire, true fire, no acceptable sacrifice.

515. Open thou my lips and then, said the Royal Prophet, my mouth shall praise God. But not until then.

516. The preparation of the heart, as well as answer of the tongue, is of the Lord. And to have it our prayers must be powerful and our worship grateful.

517. Let us choose, therefore, to commune where there is the warmest sense of religion; where devotion exceeds formality, and practice most corresponds with profession, and where there is at least as much charity as zeal. For where this society is to be found, there shall we find the Church of God.

518. As good so ill men are all of a church; and everybody knows who must be head of it.

519. The humble, meek, merciful, just, pious, and devout souls are everywhere of one religion; and when death has taken off the mask, they will know one another, though the diverse liveries they wear here make them strangers.

520. Great allowances are to be made for education and personal weaknesses. But it is a rule with me that man is truly religious that loves the persuasion he is of for the piety rather than ceremony of it.

521. They that have one end,can hardly disagree when they meet. At least their concern in the greater moderates their value and difference about the lesser things.

522. It is a sad reflection that many men hardly have any religion at all; and most men have none of their own. For that which is the religion of their education and not of their judgment is the religion of another, and not theirs.

523. To have religion upon authority and not upon conviction is like a finger watch, to be set forwards or backwards as he pleases that has it in keeping.

524. It is a preposterous thing that men can venture their souls where they will not venture their money; for they will take their religion upon trust, but not trust a synod about the goodness of half-a-crown.

525. They will follow their own judgment when their money is concerned, whatever they do for their souls.

526. But to be sure that religion cannot be right that a man is the worse for having.

527. No religion is better than an unnatural one.

528. Grace perfects but never sours or spoils nature.

529. To be unnatural in defence of grace is a contradiction.

530. Hardly anything looks worse than to defend religion by ways that show it has no credit with us.

531. A devout man is one thing, a stickler is quite another.

532. When our minds exceed their just bounds we must needs discredit what we would recommend.

533. To be furious in religion is to be irreligiously religious.

534. If he that is without bowels is not a man, how then can he be a Christian?

535. It were better to be of no church than to be bitter for any.

536. Bitterness comes very near to enmity, and that is Beelzebub, because the perfection of wickedness.

537. A good end cannot sanctify evil means; nor must we ever do evil that good may come of it.

538. Some folk think they may scold, rail, hate, rob, and kill too, so it be but for God's sake.

539. But nothing in us unlike Him can please Him.

540. It is as great presumption to send our passions upon God's errands as it is to palliate them with God's name.

541. Zeal dropped in charity is good; without it good for nothing. For it devours all it comes near.

542. They must first judge themselves that presume to censure others. And such will not be apt to overshoot the mark.

543. We are too ready to retaliate rather than forgive, or gain by love and information.

544. And yet we could hurt no man that we believe loves us.

545. Let us then try what love will do. For if men do once see we love them, we should soon find they would not harm us.

546. Force may subdue, but love gains: and he that forgives first wins the laurel.

547. If I am even with my enemy, the debt is paid; but if I forgive it I oblige him for ever.

548. Love is the hardest lesson in Christianity; but for that reason it should be most our care to learn it. *Difficilia quæ pulchra.*

549. It is a severe rebuke upon us that God makes us so many allowances, and we make so few to our neighbour. As if charity had nothing to do with religion; or love with faith, that ought to work by it.

550. I find all sorts of people agree, whatsoever were their animosities, when humbled by the approaches of death. Then they forgive, then they pray for, and love one another. Which shows us that it is not our reason but our passion that makes and holds up the feuds that reign among men in their health and fulness. They, therefore, that live nearest to that which they should die must certainly live best.

551. Did we believe a final reckoning and judgment, or did we think enough of what we do believe, we would allow more love in religion than we do; since religion itself is nothing else but love to God and man.

552. He that lives in love lives in God, says the beloved disciple. And to be sure a man can live nowhere better.

553. It is most reasonable men should value that benefit which is most durable. Now tongues shall cease, and prophecy fail, and faith shall be consummated in sight, and hope in enjoyment; but love remains.

554. Love is indeed heaven upon earth; since heaven above would not be heaven without it. For where there is not love there is fear. But perfect love casts out fear. And yet we naturally fear most to offend what we most love.

555. What we love we will hear, what we love we will trust, and what we love we will serve, ay, and suffer for too. If you love me (says our Blessed Redeemer) keep my commandments. Why? Why then He will love us; then we shall be His friends; then He will send us the comforter; then whatever we ask we shall receive; and then where He is we

shall be also, and that for ever. Behold the fruits of love; the power, virtue, benefit, and beauty of love!

556. Love is above all; and when it prevails in us all we shall all be lovely, and in love with God and one with another.

Amen.

PART II

THE INTRODUCTION TO THE READER

THE title of this treatise shows there was a former of the same nature; and the author hopes he runs no hazard in recommending both to his reader's perusal. He is well aware of the low reckoning the labours of indifferent authors are under at a time when hardly anything passes for current that is not calculated to flatter the sharpness of contending parties. He is also sensible that books grow a very drug where they cannot raise and support their credit by their own usefulness; and how far this will be able to do it he knows not; yet he thinks himself tolerably safe in making it public in three respects.

First, that the purchase is small, and the time but little that is requisite to read it.

Next, though some men should not find it relished high enough for their finer wits or warmer palates, it may not perhaps be useless to those of lower flights, and who are less engaged in public heats.

Lastly, the author honestly aims at as general a benefit as the thing will bear; to youth especially, whether he hits the mark or not. And that without the least ostentation or any private regards.

Let not envy misinterpret his intention, and he will be accountable for all other faults.

Vale.

REFLECTIONS AND MAXIMS

1. *The Right Moralist.*—A right moralist is a great and good man, but for that reason he is rarely to be found.

2. There are a sort of people that are fond of the character who, in my opinion, have but little title to it.

3. They think it enough not to defraud a man of his pay, or betray his friend; but never consider that the law forbids the one at his peril, and that virtue is seldom the reason of the other.

4. But certainly he that covets can no more be a moral man than he that steals; since he does so in his mind. Nor can he be one that robs his neighbour of his credit, or that craftily undermines him of his trade or office.

5. If a man pays his tailor but debauches his wife, is he a current moralist?

6. But what shall we say of the man that rebels against his father, is an ill husband, or an abusive neighbour; one that is lavish of his time, of his health, and of his estate in which his family is so nearly concerned? Must he go for a right moralist because he pays his rent well?

7. I would ask some of those men of morals whether he that robs God and himself too, though he should not defraud his neighbour, be the moral man?

8 Do I owe myself nothing? And do I not owe all to God? And if paying what we owe makes the moral man, is it not fit we should begin to render our dues where we owe our very beginning; ay, our all?

9 The complete moralist begins with God; he gives Him his due, his heart, his love, his service; the Bountiful Giver of his well-being as well as being.

10. He that lives without a sense of this dependency and obligation cannot be a moral man, because he does not know his returns of love and obedience: as becomes an honest and a sensible creature. Which very term implies he is not his own; and it cannot be very honest to misemploy another's goods.

11. But how can there be no debt but to a fellow creature? Or will our exactness in paying those dribbling ones, while we

neglect our weightier obligations, cancel the bonds we lie under, and render us right and thorough moralists?

12. As judgments are paid before bonds and bonds before bills or book debts, so the moralist considers his obligations according to their several dignities.

In the first place, Him to whom he owes himself. Next, himself in his health and livelihood. Lastly, his other obligations, whether rational or pecuniary; doing to others to the extent of his ability as he would have them do unto him.

13. In short, the moral man is he that loves God above all, and his neighbour as himself, which fulfils both tables at once.

14. *The World's Able Man.*—It is by some thought the character of an able man to be dark and not understood. But I am sure that is not fair play.

15. If he be so by silence it is better; but if by disguises it is insincere and hateful.

16. Secrecy is one thing, false lights are another.

17. The honest man that is rather free than open is ever to be preferred; especially when sense is at helm.

18. The glorying of the other humour is in a vice. For it is not human to be cold, dark, and unconversable. I was going to say, they are like pickpockets in a crowd, where a man must ever have his hand on his purse; or as spies in a garrison that if not prevented betray it.

19. They are the reverse of human nature, and yet this is the present world's wise man and politician. Excellent qualities for Lapland, where they say witches though not many conjurors dwell.

20. Like highwaymen that rarely rob without vizards, or in the same wigs and clothes, but have a dress for every enterprise.

21. At best, he may be a cunning man, which is a sort of lurcher in the politics.

22. He is never too hard for the wise man upon the square, for that is out of his element, and puts him quite by his skill. Nor are wise men ever caught by him, but when they trust him.

23. But as cold and close as he seems, he can and will please all if he gets by it, though it should neither please God nor himself at bottom.

24. He is for every cause that brings him gain, but implacable if disappointed of success.

25. And what he cannot hinder he will be sure to spoil by overdoing it.

26. None so zealous then as he, for that which he cannot abide.

27. What is it he will not or cannot do to hide his true sentiments?

28. For his interest he refuses no side or party; and will take the wrong by the hand when the other won't do, with as good a grace as the right.

29. Nay, he commonly chooses the worst, because that brings the best bribe, his cause being ever money.

30. He fails with all winds, and is never out of his way where anything is to be had.

31. A privateer indeed, and everywhere a bird of prey.

32. True to nothing but himself, and false to all persons and parties to serve his own turn.

33. Talk with him as often as you please, he will never pay you in good coin; for it is either false or clipt.

34. But to give a false reason for anything, let my reader never learn of him, no more than to give a brass half-crown for a good one. Not only because it is not true, but because it deceives the person to whom it is given; which I take to be an immorality.

35. Silence is much more preferable, for it saves the secret as well as the person's honour.

36. Such as give themselves the latitude of saying what they do not mean come to be errant jockeys at more things than one; but in religion and politics it is pernicious.

37. To hear two men talk the reverse of their own sentiments with all the good breeding and appearance of friendship imaginable on purpose to cozen or pump each other, is to a man of virtue and honour one of the melancholiest as well as most nauseous things in the world.

38. But that it should be the character of an able man is to disinherit wisdom and paint out our degeneracy to the life, by setting up fraud, an errant imposter, in her room.

39. The trial of skill between these two is, who shall believe least of what the other says; and he that has the

weakness or good nature to give out first (viz., to believe anything the other says) is looked upon to be tricked.

40. I cannot see the policy any more than the necessity of a man's mind always giving the lie to his mouth; or his mouth ever giving false alarms of his mind. For no man can be long believed that teaches all men to distrust him; and since the ablest have sometimes need of credit, where lies the advantage of their politic cant or banter upon mankind?

41. I remember a passage of one of Queen Elizabeth's great men; as advice to his friend. The advantage, says he, I had upon others at court was that I always spoke as I thought, which being not believed by them I both preserved a good conscience and suffered no damage from that freedom: which as it shows the vice to be older than our times so that gallant man's integrity to be the best way of avoiding it.

42. To be sure it is wise as well as honest neither to flatter other men's sentiments nor dissemble and less contradict our own.

43. To hold one's tongue, or speak truth, or talk only of indifferent things is the fairest conversation.

44. Women that rarely go abroad without vizard masks have none of the best reputation. But when we consider what all this art and disguise are for, it equally heightens the wise man's wonder and aversion. Perhaps it is to betray a father, a brother, a master, a friend, a neighbour, or one's own party.

45. A fine conquest! what noble Grecians and Romans abhorred. As if government could not subsist without knavery, and that knaves were the usefullest props to it; though the basest as well as greatest perversions of the ends of it.

46. But that it should become a maxim shows but too grossly the corruption of the times.

47. I confess I have heard the style of a useful knave, but ever took it to be a silly or a knavish saying; at least an excuse for knavery.

48. It is as reasonable to think a whore makes the best wife as a knave the best officer.

49. Besides, employing knaves encourages knavery instead of punishing it; and alienates the reward of virtue. Or at

least must make the world believe the country yields not honest men enough able to serve her.

50. Art thou a magistrate? Prefer such as have clean characters, where they live, and of estates, to secure a just discharge of their trusts; that are under no temptation to strain points for a fortune: for sometimes such may be found sooner than they are employed.

51. Art thou a private man? Contract thy acquaintance in a narrow compass, and choose those for the subject of it that are men of principles; such as will make full stops where honour will not lead them on; and that had rather bear the disgrace of not being thorough paced men that forfeit their peace and reputation by a base compliance.

52. *The Wise Man.*—The wise man governs himself by the reason of his case, and because what he does is best: best in a moral and prudent, not a sinister sense.

53. He proposes just ends, and employs the fairest and probablest means and methods to attain them.

54. Though you cannot always penetrate his design or his reasons for it yet you shall ever see his actions of a piece, and his performances like a workman. They will bear the touch of wisdom and honour as often as they are tried.

55. He scorns to serve himself by indirect means, or be an interloper in government, since just enterprises never want any just ways to succeed them.

56. To do evil that good may come of it is for bunglers in politics as well as morals.

57. Like those surgeons that will cut off an arm they can't cure, to hide their ignorance and save their credit.

58. The wise man is cautious, but not cunning; judicious, but not crafty; making virtue the measure of using his excellent understanding in the conduct of his life.

59. The wise man is equal, ready, but not officious; has in everything an eye to sure footing. He offends nobody, nor easily is offended, and always willing to compound for wrongs, if not forgive them.

60. He is never captious nor critical; hates banter and jests. He may be pleasant, but not light; he never deals but in substantial ware, and leaves the rest for the toy pates (or shops) of the world; which are so far from being his business that they are not so much as his diversion.

61. He is always for some solid good, civil or moral; as to make his country more virtuous, preserve her peace and liberty, employ her poor, improve land, advance trade, suppress vice, encourage industry and all mechanic knowledge; and that they should be the care of the government and the blessing and praise of the people.

62. To conclude, he is just and fears God, hates covetousness and eschews evil, and loves his neighbour as himself.

63. *Of the Government of Thoughts.*—Man being made a reasonable and so a thinking creature, there is nothing more worthy of his being than the right direction and employment of his thoughts; since upon this depends both his usefulness to the public and his own present and future benefit in all respects.

64. The consideration of this has often obliged me to lament the unhappiness of mankind, that through too great a mixture and confusion of thoughts have been hardly able to make a right or mature judgment of things.

65. To this is owing the various uncertainty and confusion we see in the world, and the intemperate zeal that occasions them.

66. To this also is to be attributed the imperfect knowledge we have of things, and the slow progress we make in attaining to a better; like the Children of Israel that were forty years upon their journey from Egypt to Canaan, which might have been performed in less than one.

67. In fine, it is to this that we ought to ascribe, if not all, at least most of the infelicities we labour under.

68. Clear therefore thy head and rally and manage thy thoughts rightly, and thou wilt save time, and see and do thy business well; for thy judgment will be distinct, thy mind free, and thy faculties strong and regular.

69. Always remember to bound thy thoughts to the present occasion.

70. If it be thy religious duty, suffer nothing else to share in them. And if any civil or temporal affair, observe the same caution, and thou wilt be a whole man to everything, and do twice the business in the same time.

71. If any point over-labours thy mind, divert and relieve it by some other subject of a more sensible or manual nature, rather than what may affect the understanding; for this were

to write one thing upon another, which blots out our former impressions, or renders them illegible.

72. They that are least divided in their care, always give the best account of their business.

73. As therefore thou art always to pursue the present subject till thou hast mastered it, so if it fall out that thou hast more affairs than one upon thy hand, be sure to prefer that which is of most moment, and will least wait thy leisure.

74. He that judges not well of the importance of his affairs, though he may be always busy, he must make but a small progress.

75. But make not more business necessary than is so; and rather lessen than augment work for thyself.

76. Nor yet be over-eager in pursuit of anything; for the mercurial too often happen to leave judgment behind them and sometimes make work for repentance.

77. He that overruns his business leaves it for him that follows more leisurely to take it up; which has often proved a profitable harvest to them that never sowed.

78. It is the advantage that slower tempers have upon the men of lively parts that, though they do not lead, they will follow well, and glean clean.

79. Upon the whole matter, employ thy thoughts as thy business requires, and let that have place according to merit and urgency; giving everything a review and due digestion, and thou wilt prevent many errors and vexations as well as save much time to thyself in the course of thy life.

80. *Of Envy.*—It is the mark of an ill-nature to lessen good actions and aggravate ill ones.

81. Some men do as much begrudge others a good name as they want one themselves; and perhaps that is the reason of it.

82. But certainly they are in the wrong that can think they are lessened because others have their due.

83. Such people generally have less merit than ambition that covet the reward of other men's; and to be sure a very ill-nature that will rather rob others of their due than allow them their praise.

84. It is more an error of our will than our judgment. For we know it to be an effect of our passion not our reason;

and therefore we are the more culpable in our partial estimates.

85. It is as envious as unjust to under rate another's actions, where their intrinsic worth recommends them to disengaged minds.

86. Nothing shows more the folly, as well as fraud of man, than clipping of merit and reputation.

87. And as some men think it an allay to themselves that others have their rights; so they know no end of pilfering to raise their own credit.

88. This envy is the child of pride, and misgives rather than mistakes.

89. It will have charity to be ostentation; sobriety, covetousness; humility, craft; bounty, popularity. In short, virtue must be design, and religion only interest. Nay, the best of qualities must not pass without a *but* to allay their merit and abate their praise. Basest of tempers! and they that have it, the worst of men!

90. But just and noble minds rejoice in other men's success, and help to augment their praise.

91. And indeed they are not without a love to virtue that take a satisfaction in seeing her rewarded, and such deserve to share her character that do abhor to lessen it.

92. *Of Man's Life.*—Why is man less durable than the works of his hands, but because this is not the place of his rest.

93. And it is a great and just reproach upon him that he should fix his mind where he cannot stay himself.

94. Were it not more his wisdom to be concerned about those works that will go with him, and erect a mansion for him where time has power neither over him nor it?

95. It is a sad thing for man so often to miss his way to his best as well as most lasting home.

96. *Of Ambition.*—They that soar too high often fall hard; which makes a low and level dwelling preferable.

97. The tallest trees are most in the power of the winds, and ambitious men of the blasts of fortune.

98. They are most seen and observed, and most envied. Least quiet, but most talked of, and not often to their advantage.

99. Those builders had need of a good foundation that lie so much exposed to weather.

100. Good works are a rock that will support their credit; but ill ones a sandy foundation that yields to calamities.

101. And truly they ought to expect no pity in their fall, that when in power had no bowels for the unhappy.

102. The worst of distempers; always craving and thirsty, restless and hated. A perfect delirium in the mind, insufferable in success, and in disappointments most revengeful.

103. *Of Praise or Applause.*—We are too apt to love praise, but not to deserve it.

104. But if we would deserve it we must love virtue more than that.

105. As there is no passion in us sooner moved or more deceivable, so for that reason there is none over which we ought to be more watchful, whether we give or receive it. For if we give it we must be sure to mean it and measure it too.

106. If we are penurious it shows emulation; if we exceed, flattery.

107. Good measure belongs to good actions; more looks nauseous as well as insincere, besides it is a persecuting of the meritorious who are out of countenance to hear what they deserve.

108. It is much easier for him to merit applause than hear of it. And he never doubts himself more, or the person that gives it, than when he hears so much of it.

109. But to say true there needs not many cautions on this hand, since the world is rarely just enough to the deserving.

110. However, we cannot be too circumspect how we receive praise. For if we contemplate ourselves in a false glass we are sure to be mistaken about our dues; and because we are too apt to believe what is pleasing, rather than what is true, we may be too easily swelled beyond our just proportion by the windy compliments of men.

111. Make ever therefore allowances for what is said on such occasions, or thou exposest as well as deceivest thyself.

112. For an over-value of ourselves gives us but a dangerous security in many respects.

113. We expect more than belongs to us; take all that is given us though never meant us; and fall out with those that are not as full of us as we are of ourselves.

114. In short it is a passion that abuses our judgment and makes us both unsafe and ridiculous.

115. Be not fond therefore of praise, but seek virtue that leads to it.

116. And yet no more lessen or dissemble thy merit than overrate it. For though humility be a virtue, an affected one is none.

117. *Of Conduct in Speech.*—Inquire often, but judge rarely, and thou wilt not often be mistaken.

118. It is safer to learn than teach; and who conceals his opinion has nothing to answer for.

119. Vanity or resentment often engage us, and it is two to one but we come off losers; for one shows a want of judgment and humility as the other does of temper and discretion.

120. Not that I admire the reserved; for they are next to unnatual that are not communicable. But if reservedness be at any time a virtue it is in throngs of ill company.

121. Beware also of affectation in speech; it often wrongs matter, and ever shows a blind side.

122. Speak properly, and in as few words as you can, but always plainly; for the end of speech is not ostentation but to be understood.

123. They that affect words more than matter will dry up that little they have.

124. Sense never fails to give them that have it words enough to make them understood.

125. But it too often happens in some conversations, as in apothecaries' shops, that those pots that are empty or have things of small value in them are as gaudily dressed and flourished as those that are full of precious drugs.

126. This labouring of slight matter with flourished turns of expression is fulsome, and worse than the modern imitation of tapestry and East India goods in stuffs and linens. In short, it is but tawdry talk, and next to very trash.

127. *Union of Friends.*—They that love beyond the world cannot be separated by it.

128. Death cannot kill what never dies.

129. Nor can spirits ever be divided that love and live in the same divine principle, the root and record of their friendship.

130. If absence be not death, neither is theirs.

131. Death is but crossing the world as friends do the seas. They live in one another still.

132. For they must needs be present that love and live in that which is omnipresent.

133. In this divine glass they see face to face; and their converse is free as well as pure.

134. This is the comfort of friends that though they may be said to die, yet their friendship and society are in the best sense ever present, because immortal.

135. *Of Being Easy in Living.*—It is an happiness to be delivered from a curious mind, as well as from a dainty palate.

136. For it is not only a troublesome but slavish thing to be nice.

137. They narrow their own freedom and comforts that make so much requisite to enjoy them.

138. To be easy in living is much of the pleasure of life. But difficult tempers will always want it.

139. A careless and homely breeding is therefore preferable to one nice and delicate.

140. And he that is taught to live upon little owes more to his father's wisdom than he that has a great deal left him does to his father's care.

141. Children can't well be too hardly bred. For besides that it fits them to bear the roughest providences, it is more masculine, active, and healthy.

142. Nay, it is certain that the liberty of the mind is mightily preserved by it. For so it is served, instead of being a servant, indeed a slave, to sensual delicacies.

143. As nature is soon answered, so are such satisfied.

144. The memory of the ancients is hardly in anything more to be celebrated than in a strict and useful institution of youth.

145. By labour they prevented luxury in their young people, till wisdom and philosophy had taught them to resist and despise it.

146. It must be therefore a gross fault to strive so hard for the pleasure of our bodies, and be so insensible and careless of the freedom of our souls.

147. *Of Man's Inconsiderateness and Partiality.*—It is very observable, if our civil rights are invaded or encroached upon, we are mightily touched and fill every place with our resentment and complaint; while we suffer ourselves, our better and nobler selves, to be the property and vassals of sin, the worst of invaders.

148. In vain do we expect to be delivered from such troubles, till we are delivered from the cause of them, our disobedience to God.

149. When he has his dues from us it will be time enough for him to give us ours out of one another.

150. It is our great happiness, if we could understand it, that we meet with such checks in the career of our worldly enjoyments, lest we should forget the Giver, adore the gift, and terminate our felicity here, which is not man's ultimate bliss.

151. Our losses are often made judgments by our guilt and mercies by our repentance.

152. Besides it argues great folly in men to let their satisfaction exceed the true value of any temporal matter. For disappointments are not always to be measured by the loss of the thing, but the over-value we put upon it.

153. And thus men improve their own miseries for want of an equal and just estimate of what they enjoy or lose.

154. There lies a proviso upon everything in this world, and we must observe it at our own peril, viz., to love God above all, and act for judgment, the last I mean.

155. *Of the Rule of Judging.*—In all things reason should prevail. It is quite another thing to be stiff than steady in an opinion.

156. This may be reasonable, but that is ever wilful.

157. In such cases it always happens that the clearer the argument the greater the obstinacy, where the design is not to be convinced.

158. This is to value humour more than truth, and prefer a sullen pride to a reasonable submission.

159. It is the glory of a man to vail to truth; as it is the mark of a good nature to be easily entreated.

160. Beasts act by sense, man should by reason; else he is a greater beast than ever God made. And the proverb is verified, the corruption of the best things is the worst and most offensive.

161. A reasonable opinion must ever be in danger where reason is not judge.

162. Though there is a regard due to education and the tradition of our fathers, truth will ever deserve as well as claim the preference.

163. If like Theophilus and Timothy we have been brought up in the knowledge of the best things, it is our advantage. But neither they nor we lose by trying the truth; for so we learn their as well as its intrinsic worth.

164. Truth never lost ground by inquiry, because she is most of all reasonable.

165. Nor can that need another authority that is self-evident.

166. If my own reason be on the side of a principle, with what can I dispute or withstand it?

167. And if men would once consider one another reasonably, they would either reconcile their differences or more amicably maintain them.

168. Let that therefore be the standard that has most to say for itself; though of that let every man be judge for himself.

169. Reason, like the sun, is common to all; and it is for want of examining all by the same light and measure that we are not all of the same mind. For all have it to that end, though all do not use it so.

170. *Of Formality.*—Form is good, but not formality.

171. In the use of the best of forms, there is too much of that, I fear.

172. It is absolutely necessary that this distinction should go along with people in their devotion; for too many are apter to rest upon what they do than how they do their duty.

173. If it were considered that it is the frame of the mind that gives our performances acceptance we would lay more stress on our inward preparation than our outward action.

174. *Of the Mean Notion we have of God.*—Nothing more shows the low condition man is fallen into than the unsuitable notion we must have of God by the ways we take to please Him.

175. As if it availed anything to Him that we performed so many ceremonies and external forms of devotion, who never meant more by them than to try our obedience, and through them to show us something more excellent and durable beyond them.

176. Doing, while we are undoing, is good for nothing.

177. Of what benefit is it to say our prayers regularly, go to church, receive the sacraments, and may be go to confession

too; ay, feast the priest, and give alms to the poor, and yet lie, swear, curse, be drunk, covetous, unclean, proud, revengeful, vain, and idle at the same time?

178. Can one excuse or balance the other? Or will God think himself well served where His law is violated? Or well used where there is so much more show than substance?

179. It is a most dangerous error for a man to think to excuse himself in the breach of a moral duty by a formal performance of positive worship; and less when of human invention.

180. Our Blessed Saviour most rightly and clearly distinguished and determined this case when He told the Jews that they were his mother, his brethren and sisters who did the will of His Father.

181. *Of the Benefit of Justice.*—Justice is a great support of society, because an insurance to all men of their property. This violated, there is no security, which throws all into confusion to recover it.

182. An honest man is a fast pledge in dealing. A man is sure to have it if it be to be had.

183. Many are so merely of necessity. Others not so only for the same reason. But such an honest man is not to be thanked, and such a dishonest man is to be pitied.

184. But he that is dishonest for gain is next to a robber, and to be punished for example.

185. And indeed there are few dealers but what are faulty, which makes trade difficult, and a great temptation to men of virtue.

186. It is not what they should, but what they can get. Faults or decays must be concealed. Big words given where they are not deserved, and the ignorance or necessity of the buyer imposed upon for unjust profit.

187. These are the men that keep their words for their own ends, and are only just for fear of the magistrate.

188. A politic rather than a moral honesty; a constrained not a chosen justice. According to the proverb, patience per force, and thank you for nothing.

189. But of all injustice that is the greatest that passes under the name of law. A cut purse in Westminster Hall exceeds; for that advances injustice to oppression, where law is alleged for that which it should punish.

190. *Of Jealousy.*—The jealous are troublesome to others, but a torment to themselves.

191. Jealousy is a kind of civil war in the soul, where judgment and imagination are at perpetual jars.

192. This civil dissension in the mind, like that of the body politic, commits great disorders and lays all waste.

193. Nothing stands safe in its way: nature, interest, religion must yield to its fury.

194. It violates contracts, dissolves society, breaks wedlock, betrays friends and neighbours. Nobody is good, and every one is either doing or designing them a mischief.

195. It has a venom that more or less rankles wherever it bites. And as it reports fancies for facts so it disturbs its own house as often as other folks.

196. Its rise is guilt or ill-nature, and by reflection it thinks its own faults to be other men's; as he that is overrun with the jaundice takes others to be yellow.

197. A jealous man only sees his own spectrum when he looks upon other men and gives his character in theirs.

198. *Of State.*—I love service, but not state; one is useful, the other superfluous.

199. The trouble of this, as well as charge, is real; but the advantage only imaginary.

200. Besides, it helps to set us up above ourselves, and augments our temptation to disorder.

201. The least thing out of joint, or omitted, makes us uneasy; and we are ready to think ourselves ill served about that which is of no real service at all. Or so much better than other men, as we have the means of greater state.

202. But this is all for want of wisdom, which carries the truest and most forceable state along with it.

203. He that makes not himself cheap by indiscreet conversation, puts value enough upon himself everywhere.

204. The other is rather pageantry than state.

205. *Of a Good Servant.*—A true and a good servant are the same thing.

206. But no servant is true to his master that defrauds him.

207. Now there are many ways of defrauding a master, as of time, care, pains, respect, and reputation, as well as money.

208. He that neglects his work robs his master, since he is fed and paid as if he did his best; and he that is not as

diligent in the absence as in the presence of his master cannot be a true servant.

209. Nor is he a true servant that buys dear to share in the profit with the seller.

210. Nor yet he that tells tales without doors; or deals basely in his master's name with other people; or connives at other's loiterings, wastings, or dishonourable reflections.

211. So that a true servant is diligent, secret, and respectful. More tender of his master's honour and interest than of his own profit.

212. Such a servant deserves well, and if modest under his merit should liberally feel it at his master's hand.

213. *Of an Immoderate Pursuit of the World.*—It shows a depraved state of mind to cark and care for that which one does not need.

214. Some are as eager to be rich as ever they were to live; for superfluity as for subsistence.

215. But that plenty should augment covetousness is a perversion of providence; and yet the generality are the worse for their riches.

216. But it is strange that old men should excel, for generally money lies nearest them that are nearest their graves; as if they would augment their love in proportion to the little time they have left to enjoy it. And yet their pleasure is without enjoyment, since none enjoy what they do not use.

217. So that instead of learning to leave their great wealth easily, they hold the faster, because they must leave it. So sordid is the temper of some men.

218. Where charity keeps pace with gain, industry is blessed. But to slave to get and keep it sordidly is a sin against Providence, a vice in government, and an injury to their neighbours.

219. Such are they as spend not one-fifth of their income, and, it may be, give not one-tenth of what they spend to the needy.

220. This is the worst sort of idolatry, because there can be no religion in it, nor ignorance pleaded in excuse of it; and that it wrongs other folks that ought to have a share therein.

221. *Of the Interest of the Public in our Estates.*—Hardly anything is given us for ourselves but the public may claim

a share with us. But of all we call ours we are most accountable to God and the public for our estates. In this we are but stewards, and to hoard up all to ourselves is great injustice as well as ingratitude.

222. If all men were so far tenants to the public that the superfluities of gain and expense were applied to the exigencies thereof, it would put an end to taxes, leave never a beggar, and make the greatest bank for national trade in Europe.

223. It is a judgment upon us as well as weakness, though we won't see it, to begin at the wrong end.

224. If the taxes we give are not to maintain pride, I am sure there would be less if pride were made a tax to the government.

225. I confess I have wondered that so many lawful and useful things are excised by laws, and pride left to reign free over them and the public.

226. But since people are more afraid of the laws of man than of God because their punishment seems to be nearest, I know not how magistrates can be excused in their suffering such excess with impunity.

227. Our noble English patriarchs as well as patriots were so sensible of this evil that they made several excellent laws, commonly called sumptuary, to forbid, at least limit the pride of the people; which because the execution of them would be our interest and honour, their neglect must be our just reproach and loss.

228. It is but reasonable that the punishment of pride and excess should help to support the government, since it must otherwise inevitably be ruined by them.

229. But some say it ruins trade, and will make the poor burdensome to the public. But if such trade in consequence ruins the kingdom, is it not time to ruin that trade? Is moderation no part of our duty, and temperance an enemy to government.

230. He is a Judas that will get money by anything.

231. To wink at a trade that effeminates the people and invades the ancient discipline of the kingdom is a crime capital, and to be severely punished instead of being excused by the magistrate.

232. Is there no better employment for the poor than luxury? Miserable nation!

233. What did they before they fell into these forbidden methods? Is there not land enough in England to cultivate and more and better manufactures to be made?

234. Have we no room for them in our plantations, about things that may augment trade, without luxury?

235. In short, let pride pay, and excess be well excised. And if that will not cure the people it will help to keep the kingdom.

236. *The Vain Man.*—But a vain man is a nauseous creature. He is so full of himself that he has no room for anything else, be it never so good or deserving.

237. It is I at every turn that does this, or can do that. And as he abounds in his comparisons, so he is sure to give himself the better of everybody else; according to the proverb, All his geese are swans.

238. They are certainly to be pitied that can be so much mistaken at home.

239. And yet I have sometimes thought that such people are in a sort happy that nothing can put out of countenance with themselves, though they neither have nor merit other people's.

240. But at the same time one would wonder they should not feel the blows they give themselves, or get from others, for this intolerable and ridiculous temper; nor show any concern at that which makes others blush for as well as at them, viz., their unreasonable assurance.

241. To be a man's own fool is bad enough, but the vain man is everybody's.

242. This silly disposition comes of a mixture of ignorance, confidence, and pride; and as there is more or less of the last, so it is more or less offensive or entertaining.

243. And yet perhaps the worst part of this vanity is its unteachableness. Tell it anything and it has known it long ago; and outruns information and instruction, or else proudly puffs at it.

244. Whereas the greatest understandings doubt most, are readiest to learn, and least pleased with themselves; this with nobody else.

245. For though they stand on higher ground and so see farther than their neighbours, they are yet humbled by their prospect, since it shows them something so much higher and above their reach.

246. And truly then it is that sense shines with the greatest beauty when it is set in humility.

247. A humble able man is a jewel worth a kingdom. It is often saved by him, as Solomon's poor wise man did the city.

248. May we have more of them or less need of them.

249. *The Conformist.*—It is reasonable to concur where conscience does not forbid a compliance; for conformity is at least a civil virtue.

250. But we should only press it in necessaries, the rest may prove a snare or temptation to break society.

251. But above all it is a weakness in religion and government where it is carried to things of an indifferent nature, since besides that it makes way for scruples, liberty is always the price of it.

252. Such conformists have little to boast of, and therefore the less reason to reproach others that have more latitude.

253. And yet the latitudinarian that I love is one that is only so in charity, for the freedom I recommend is no scepticism in judgment, and much less so in practice.

254. *The Obligations of Great Men to Almighty God.*—It seems but reasonable that those whom God has distinguished from others by His goodness, should distinguish themselves to Him by their gratitude.

255. For though He has made of one blood all nations, He has not ranged or dignified them upon the level, but in a sort of subordination and dependency.

256. If we look upwards we find it in the heavens where the planets have their several degrees of glory, and so the other stars of magnitude and lustre.

257. If we look upon the earth we see it among the trees of the wood, from the cedar to the bramble; among the fishes, from the leviathan to the sprat; in the air among the birds, from the eagle to the sparrow; among the beasts, from the lion to the cat; and among mankind, from the king to the scavenger.

258. Our great men doubtless were designed by the wise Framer of the world for our religious, moral, and politic planets, for lights and directions to the lower ranks of the numerous company of their own kind, both in precepts and examples; and they are well paid for their pains too who

have the honour and service of their fellow creatures, and the marrow and fat of the earth for their share.

259. But is it not a most unaccountable folly that men should be proud of the providences that should humble them? Or think the better of themselves instead of Him that raised them so much above the level; or of being so in their lives in return of His extraordinary favours?

260. But it is but too near a-kin to us to think no farther than ourselves, either in the acquisition or use of our wealth and greatness, when, alas! they are the preferments of heaven to try our wisdom, bounty, and gratitude.

261. It is a dangerous perversion of the end of Providence to consume the time, power, and wealth He has given us above other men to gratify our sordid passions, instead of playing the good stewards to the honour of our great Benefactor, and the good of our fellow creatures.

262. But it is an injustice too; since those higher ranks of men are but the trustees of heaven for the benefit of lesser mortals, who as minors are entitled to all their care and provision.

263. For though God has dignified some men above their brethren, it never was to serve their pleasures, but that they might take pleasure to serve the public.

264. For this cause doubtless it was that they were raised above necessity or any trouble to live, that they might have more time and ability to care for others. And it is certain where that use is not made of the bounties of Providence, they are embezzled and wasted.

265. It has often struck me with a serious reflection, when I have observed the great inequality of the world, that one man should have such numbers of his fellow creatures to wait upon him who have souls to be saved as well as he; and this not for business but state. Certainly a poor employment of his money, and a worse of their time.

266. But that any one man should make work for so many, or rather keep them from work to make up a train, has a levity or luxury in it very reprovable, both in religion and government.

267. But even in allowable services it has a humbling consideration, and what should raise the thankfulness of the great men to Him that has so much bettered their circum

stances, and moderated the use of their dominion over those of their own kind.

268. When the poor Indians hear us call any of our family by the name of servants, they cry out, What, call brethren servants! We call our dogs servants, but never men. The moral certainly can do us no harm, but may instruct us to abate our height and narrow our state and attendance.

269. And what has been said of their excess may in some measure be applied to other branches of luxury that set ill examples to the lesser world and rob the needy of their pensions.

270. God Almighty touch the hearts of our grandees with a sense of His distinguished goodness, and the true end of it; that they may better distinguish themselves in their conduct to the glory of Him that has thus liberally preferred them, and to the benefit of their fellow creatures.

271. *Of Refining upon other Men's Actions or Interests.*—This seems to be the masterpiece of our politicians, but nobody shoots more at random than those refiners.

272. A perfect lottery and mere haphazard. Since the true spring of the actions of men is as invisible as their hearts; and so are their thoughts too of their several interests.

273. He that judges of other men by himself does not always hit the mark, because all men have not the same capacity nor passions in interest.

274. If an able man refines upon the proceedings of an ordinary capacity, according to his own, he must ever miss it. But much more the ordinary man when he shall pretend to speculate the motives to the able man's actions. For the able man deceives himself by making the other wiser than he is in the reason of his conduct; and the ordinary man makes himself so in presuming to judge of the reasons of the abler man's actions.

275. It is, in short, a wood, a maze, and of nothing are we more uncertain, nor in anything do we oftener befool ourselves.

276. The mischiefs are many that follow this humour, and dangerous. For men misguide themselves, act upon false measures, and meet frequently with mischievous disappointments.

277. It excludes all confidence in commerce; allows of no such thing as a principle in practice; supposes every man to

act upon other reasons than what appear, and that there is no such thing as uprightness or sincerity among mankind. A trick instead of truth.

278. Neither allowing nature or religion, but some worldly fetch or advantage, the true, the hidden motive to all men to act or do.

279. It is hard to express its uncharitableness as well as uncertainty; and has more of vanity than benefit in it.

280. This foolish quality gives a large field, but let what I have said serve for this time.

281. *Of Charity.*—Charity has various senses, but is excellent in all of them.

282. It imports, first, the commiseration of the poor, and unhappy of mankind, and extends a helping hand to mend their condition.

283. They that feel nothing of this are at best not above half of kin to human race; since they must have no bowels, which makes such an essential part thereof, who have no more nature.

284. A man, and yet not have the feeling of the wants or needs of his own flesh and blood! A monster rather! And may he never be suffered to propagate such an unnatural stock in the world.

285. Such an uncharitableness spoils the best gains, and two to one but it entails a curse upon the possessors.

286. Nor can we expect to be heard of God in our prayers that turn the deaf ear to the petitions of the distressed amongst our fellow creatures.

287. God sends the poor to try us as well as he tries them by being such. And he that refuses them a little out of the great deal that God has given him, lays up poverty in store for his own posterity.

288. I will not say these works are meritorious, but dare say they are acceptable and go not without their reward. Though, to humble us in our fulness and liberality too, we only give but what is given us to give as well as use; for if we are not our own, less is that so which God has entrusted us with.

289. Next, charity makes the best construction of things and persons, and is so far from being an evil spy, a backbiter, or a detractor, that it excuses weakness, extenuates mis-

carriages, makes the best of everything, forgives everybody, serves all, and hopes to the end.

290. It moderates extremes, is always for expedients, labours to accommodate differences, and had rather suffer than revenge; and is so far from exacting the utmost farthing, that it had rather lose than seek her own violently.

291. As it acts freely, so zealously too; but it is always to do good, for it hurts nobody.

292. A universal remedy against discord, and a holy cement for mankind.

293. And lastly, it is love to God and the brethren which raises the soul above all worldly considerations; and, as it gives a taste of heaven upon earth, so it is heaven in the fulness of it to the truly charitable here.

294. This is the noblest sense charity has, after which all should press as that more excellent way.

295. Nay, most excellent; for as faith, hope, and charity were the more excellent way that great apostle discovered to the Christians (too apt to stick in outward gifts and church performances), so of that better way he preferred charity as the best part, because it would outlast the rest, and abide for ever.

296. Wherefore a man can never be a true and good Christian without charity, even in the lowest sense of it; and yet he may have that part thereof, and still be none of the apostle's true Christian, since he tells us that though we should give all our goods to the poor, and want charity (in her other and higher senses), it would profit us nothing.

297. Nay, though we had all tongues, all knowledge, and even gifts of prophecy, and were preachers to others, ay, and had zeal enough to give our bodies to be burned, yet if we wanted charity, it would not avail us for salvation.

298. It seems it was his (and indeed ought to be our) *unum necessarium*, or the one thing needful, which our Saviour attributed to Mary in preference to her sister Martha, that seems not to have wanted the lesser parts of charity.

299. Would God this divine virtue were more implanted and diffused among mankind, the pretenders to Christianity especially, and we should certainly mind piety more than controversy, and exercise love and compassion instead of censuring and persecuting one another in any manner whatsoever.

THE ADVICE OF WILLIAM PENN TO HIS CHILDREN

RELATING TO

THEIR CIVIL AND RELIGIOUS CONDUCT

THE ADVICE OF WILLIAM PENN TO HIS CHILDREN

Relating to their Civil and Religious Conduct

CHAPTER I

My Dear Children,—1. Not knowing how long it may please God to continue me amongst you, I am willing to embrace this opportunity of leaving you my advice and counsel with respect to your Christian and civil capacity and duty in this world; and I both beseech you and charge you, by the relation you have to me, and the affection I have always shown to you, and indeed received from you, that you lay up the same in your hearts as well as your heads with a wise and religious care.

2. I will begin with that which is the beginning of all true wisdom and happiness, the holy fear of God.

Children, fear God; that is to say, have a holy awe upon your minds to avoid that which is evil, and a strict care to embrace and do that which is good. The measure and standard of which knowledge and duty is the light of Christ in your consciences, by which, as in John iii. 20, 21, you may clearly see if your deeds, ay and your words and thoughts too, are wrought in God or not (for they are the deeds of the mind, and for which you must be judged); I say with this divine light of Christ in your consciences, you may bring your thoughts, words, and works to judgment in yourselves, and have a right true sound and unerring sense of your duty towards God and man. And as you come to obey this blessed light in its holy convictions, it will lead you out of the world's dark and degenerate ways and works, and bring you unto Christ's way and life, and to be of the number of his true self-denying followers, to take up your cross for His sake, that bore His for yours; and to become the children of the light, putting it on as your holy armour; by which you may see and resist the fiery darts of Satan's temptations, and overcome him in all his assaults.

3. I would a little explain this principle to you. It is called light, John i. 9, iii. 19, 20, 21, and viii. 12; Eph. v. 8, 13, 14; 1 Thes. v. 5; 1 Ep. of John i. 5, 6, 7; Rev. xxi. 23, because it gives man a sight of his sin. And it is also called the quickening spirit; for so he is called; and the Lord from heaven, as 1 Cor. xv. 45, 57, who is called and calls himself the Light of the World, John viii. 12. And why is He called the Spirit? Because He gives man spiritual life. And John xvi. 8, Christ promised to send his Spirit to convince the world of their sins; wherefore that which convinces you and all people of their sins is the spirit of Christ. This is highly prized, Rom. viii., as you may read in that great and sweet chapter, for the children of God are led by it. This reveals the things of God, that appertain to man's salvation and happiness, as 1 Cor. ii. 10, 11, 12. It is the earnest God gives His people, 2 Cor. v. 5. It is the great end and benefit and blessing of the coming of Christ, viz., the shining forth of this light and pouring forth of this spirit. Yea, Christ is not received by them that resist his light and spirit in their hearts; nor can they have the benefit of His birth, life, death, resurrection, intercession, etc., who rebel against the light. God sent His Son to bless us, in turning of us from the evil of our ways. Therefore have a care of evil, for that turns you away from God; and wherein you have done evil, do so no more. But be ye turned, my dear children, from that evil in thought as well as in word or deed, or that will turn you from God, your Creator, and Christ whom He has given you for your Redeemer; who redeems and saves His people from their sins, Tit. ii. 14, not in their sins, read Acts ii. and Heb. viii., and the Christian dispensation will appear to be that of the Spirit, which sin quencheth, hardens the heart against, and bolts the door upon. This holy divine principle is called grace too, 1 Tim. ii. 11, 12, there you will see the nature and office of it, and its blessed effects upon those that were taught of it in the primitive days. And why grace? Because it is God's love and not our desert, his good will, his kindness. He so loved the world that He gave His only begotten Son into the world, that whosoever believeth in Him should not perish, but have everlasting life, John iii. 16, and it is this

Holy Son that, in John i. 14, 16, is declared to be full of grace and truth, and that of His grace we receive grace for grace, that is, we receive of Him the fulness what measure of grace we need. And the Lord told Paul in his great trials, when ready to stagger about the sufficiency of the grace he had received, to deliver him, My grace is sufficent for thee, 2 Cor. xii. 9. O children, love the grace, hearken to this grace, it will teach you, it will sanctify you, it will lead you to the rest and kingdom of God; as it taught the saints of old, first, what to deny, viz., to deny ungodliness and worldly lusts; and then what to do, viz., to live soberly, righteously, and godly in this present world, Tit. ii. 11, 12. And he that is full of grace is full of light, and he that is full of light is the quickening spirit that gives a manifestation of his spirit to everyone to profit with, 1 Cor. xii. 7. And he that is the quickening spirit is the truth. I am the way, the truth, and the life, said He, to his poor followers, John xiv. 6. And if the truth make you free, said He to the Jews, then are you free indeed, John viii. 32, 36. And this truth sheds abroad itself in man and begets truth in the inward parts, and makes false, rebellious, hypocritical man a true man to God again. Truth in the inward parts is of great price with the Lord. And why called truth? Because it tells man the truth of his spiritual state; it shows him his state, deals plainly with him, and sets his sins in order before him. So that, my dear children, the light, spirit, grace, and truth are not divers principles, but divers words or denominations given to one eternal power and heavenly principle in you, though not of you, but of God, according to the manifestation or operation thereof in the servants of God of old time: light to discover and give discerning; spirit to quicken and enliven; grace, to wit, the love of God; truth because it tells man the truth of his condition, and redeems him from the errors of his ways; that as darkness, death, sin, and error are the same, so light, spirit, grace, and truth are the same.

4. This is that which is come by Christ, and a measure of this light, spirit, grace, and truth is given to every man and woman to see their way to go by. This is that which distinguishes Friends from all other societies, as they are found walking in the same, which leads out of vain honours, compliments, lusts, and pleasures of the world.

O my dear children, this is the pearl of price, part with all for it, but never part with it for all the world. This is the gospel leaven, to leaven you, that is, sanctify and season you, in body, soul, and spirit, to God, your heavenly Father's use and service, and your own lasting comfort. Yea, this is the divine and incorruptible seed of the kingdom; of which all truly regenerate men and women, Christians of Christ's making, are born. Receive it into your hearts, give it room there, let it take deep root in you, and you will be fruitful unto God in every good word and work. As you take heed to it and the holy enlightenings and motions of it, you will have a perfect discerning of the spirit of this world in all its appearances in yourselves and others; the motions, temptations, and workings of it, as to pride, vanity, covetousness, revenge, uncleanness, hypocrisy, and every evil way; you will see the world in all its shapes and features, and you will be able to judge the world by it, and the spirit of the world in all its appearances. You will see as I have done that there is much to deny, much to suffer, and much to do. And you will see that there is no power or virtue but in the light, spirit, grace, and truth of Christ to carry you through the world to God's glory and your everlasting peace. Yea, you will see what religion is from above, and what is from below; what is of God's working and of man's making and forcing; also what ministry is of his spirit and giving, and what of man's studying, framing, and imposing. You will, I say, discern the rise, nature, tokens, and fruits of the true from the false ministry, and what worship is spiritual and what carnal, and what honour is of God and what that honour is, which is from below, of men, yea, fallen men, that the Jews and the world so generally love, and which is spoken against in John v. 44; you will see the vain and evil communication that corrupts good manners, the snares of much company and business, and especially the danger of the friendship of this present evil world. And you will also see that the testimony the eternal God hath brought our poor Friends unto, as to religion, worship, truth-speaking, ministry, plainness, simplicity, and moderation in apparel, furniture, food, salutation, as you may read in their writings, from the very beginning, is a true and heavenly testimony of His mind, will, work, and dispensation in this last age of the world to mankind, being the revival of true primitive Christianity: where your most tender father prays that you may be kept, and charges you to watch that you may be preserved in the faith and practice of that blessed testimony; and count it no small mercy from God nor honour to you that you come of parents that counted nothing too dear or near to part with, nor too great to do or suffer, that they might approve themselves to God, and testify their love to His most precious truth in the inward parts in their generation. And I do also charge you, my dear children, to retain in your remembrance those worthy ancients in the work of Christ, which remained alive to your day and memory, and yet remain to your knowledge; more especially that man of God and prince in Israel, the first born and begotten of our day and age of truth, and the first and the great early instrument of God amongst us, George Fox. And what you have heard, seen, and observed of those heavenly worthies, their holy wisdom, zeal, love, labours, and sufferings, and particular tenderness to you, treasure up for your children after you, and tell them what you have heard, seen, and known of the servants and work of God, and progress thereof, as a holy, exemplary, and edifying tradition unto them. And be sure that you forsake not the assembling yourselves with God's people, as the manner of some was, Heb. x. 25, and is at this day, especially among young people, the children of some Friends, whom the love of this present evil world hath hurt and cooled in their love to God and his truth. But do you keep close to meetings, both of worship and business of the church, when of an age and capacity proper for it; and that not out of novelty, formality, or to be seen of men, but in pure fear, love, and conscience to God your Creator, as the public, just, and avowed testimony of your duty and homage to Him. In which be exemplary both by timely coming and a reverent and serious deportment during the assembly; in which be not weary or think the time long till it be over, as some did of the Sabbaths of old time; but let your eye be to Him you come to wait upon and serve, and do what you do as to Him, and He will be your refreshment and reward; for you shall return with the seals and pledges of His love, mercy, and blessings.

5. Above all things, my dear children, as to your communion and fellowship with friends, be careful to keep the unity of

the faith in the bond of peace. Have a care of reflectors, detractors, backbiters, that undervalue and undermine brethren behind their backs, or slight the good and wholesome order of truth, for the preserving things quiet, sweet, and honourable in the church. Have a care of novelties, and airy, changeable people, the conceited, censorious, and puffed up; who at last have always shown themselves to be clouds without rain, and wells without water, that will rather disturb and break the peace and fellowship of the church where they dwell, than not have their wills and ways take place. I charge you, in the fear of the living God, that you carefully beware of all such; mark them as the apostle says, Rom. xvi. 17, and have no fellowship with them; but to advise, exhort, entreat, and finally reprove them, Eph. v. 11. For God is and will be with His people in this holy dispensation we are now under, and which is now amongst us, unto the end of days. It shall grow and increase in gifts, graces, power, and lustre, for it is the last and unchangeable one. And blessed are your eyes if they see it, and your ears if they hear it, and your hearts if they understand it; which I pray that you may to God's glory and your eternal comfort.

6. Having thus expressed myself to you, my dear children, as to the things of God, His truth and kingdom, I refer you to His light, grace, spirit, and truth within you, and the Holy Scriptures of truth without you, which from my youth I loved to read, and were ever blessed to me; and which I charge you to read daily; the Old Testament for history chiefly, the Psalms for meditation and devotion, the prophets for comfort and hope, but especially the New Testament for doctrine, faith, and worship; for they were given forth by holy men of God in divers ages, as they were moved of the Holy Spirit; and are the declared and revealed mind and will of the Holy God to mankind under divers dispensations, and they are certainly able to make the man of God perfect, through faith unto salvation; being such a true and clear testimony to the salvation that is of God, through Christ the second Adam, the Light of the World, the quickening Spirit, who is full of grace and truth, whose light, grace, spirit, and truth bear witness to them in every sensible soul, as they frequently, plainly, and solemnly bear testimony to the light, spirit, grace, and truth, both in Himself and in and to His people,

to their sanctification, justification, redemption, and consolation, and in all men to their visitation, reproof, and conviction in their evil ways. I say having thus expressed myself in general, I refer you, my dear children, to the Light and Spirit of Jesus that is within you, and to the scriptures of truth without you, and such other testimonies to the one same eternal truth as have been born in our day; and shall now descend to particulars that you may more directly apply what I have said in general both as to your religious and civil direction in your pilgrimage upon earth.

CHAPTER II

1. I WILL begin here also with the beginning of time, the morning; so soon as you wake, retire your mind into a pure silence from all thoughts and ideas of worldly things, and in that frame wait upon God to feel His good presence, to lift up your hearts to Him, and commit your whole self into His blessed care and protection. Then rise, if well, immediately; being dressed, read a chapter or more in the Scriptures, and afterwards dispose yourselves for the business of the day; ever remembering that God is present, the overseer of all your thoughts, words, and actions; and demean yourselves, my dear children, accordingly; and do not you dare to do that in His holy all-seeing presence which you would be ashamed a man, yea a child, should see you do. And as you have intervals from your lawful occasions, delight to step home, within yourselves I mean, and commune with your own hearts, and be still; and (as Nebuchadnezzar said on another occasion) one like the Son of God you shall find and enjoy with you and in you; a treasure the world knows not of, but is the aim, end, and diadem of the children of God. This will bear you up against all temptations, and carry you sweetly and evenly through your day's business, supporting you under disappointments, and moderating your satisfaction in success and prosperity. The evening come read again the Holy Scripture, and have your times of retirement before you close your eyes, as in the morning; that so the Lord may be the alpha and omega of every day of your lives. And if God

bless you with families, remember good Joshua's resolution, Josh. xxiv. 15, but as for me and my house, we will serve the Lord.

2. Fear God, show it in desire, refraining, and doing; keep the inward watch, keep a clear soul and a light heart. Mind an inward sense upon doing anything; when you read the Scripture remark the notablest places, as your spirits are most touched and affected, in a common-place book, with that sense or opening which you receive; for they come not by study or in the will of man, no more than the Scripture did; and they may be lost by carelessness and over-growing thoughts and businesses of this life; so in pursuing any other good or profitable book; yet rather meditate than read much. For the spirit of a man knows the things of a man, and with that spirit, by observation of the tempers and actions of men you see in the world, and looking into your own spirit, and meditating thereupon, you will have a deep and strong judgment of men and things. For from what may be, what should be, and what is most profitable or likely to be, you can hardly miss in your judgment of human affairs; and you have a better spirit than your own in reserve for a time of need, to pass the final judgment in important matters.

3. In conversation mark well what others say or do, and hide your own mind, at least till last; and then open it as sparingly as the matter will let you. A just observance and reflection upon men and things give wisdom; those are the great books of learning seldom read. The laborious bee draws honey from every flower. Be always on your watch, but chiefly in company, then be sure to have your wits about you and your armour on; speak last and little, but to the point. Interrupt none, anticipate none, read Prov. x. 8, 13, Be quick to hear, slow to speak; Prov xvii. 27, It gives time to understand and ripens an answer. Affect not words but matter, and chiefly to be pertinent and plain; truest eloquence is plainest; and brief speaking, I mean, brevity and clearness, to make yourselves easily understood by everybody, and in as few words as the matter will admit of, is the best.

4. Prefer the aged, the virtuous, and the knowing; and choose those that excel for your company and friendship, but despise not others.

5. Return no answer to anger, unless with much meekness,

which often turns it away. But rarely make replies, less rejoinders; for that adds fuel to the fire. It is a wrong time to vindicate yourselves, the true ear being then never open to hear it. Men are not themselves and know not well what spirits they are of. Silence to passion, prejudice, and mockery is the best answer, and often conquers what resistance inflames.

6. Learn and teach your children fair writing, and the most useful parts of mathematics, and some business when young, whatever else they are taught.

7. Cast up your income and live on half, if you can one third, reserving the rest for casualties, charities, portions.

8. Be plain in cloths, furniture, and food, but clean, and then the coarser the better, the rest is folly and a snare. Therefore next to sin avoid daintiness and choiceness about your person and houses. For if it be not an evil in itself it is a temptation to it; and may be accounted a nest for sin to brood in.

9. Avoid differences; what are not avoidable refer and keep awards strictly and without grudgings, read Prov. xviii. 17, 18; xxv. 8; Mat. v. 38 to 41; 1 Cor. i. 10 to 13. It is good counsel.

10. Be sure draw your affairs into as narrow a compass as you can, and in method and proportion, time and other requisites proper for them.

11. Have very few acquaintance and fewer intimates, but of the best in their kind.

12. Keep your own secrets, and do not covet others, but if trusted, never reveal them, unless mischievous to somebody; nor then before warning to the party to desist and repent. Prov. xi. 13; ii. 23; xxv. 9, 10.

13. Trust no man with the main chance, and avoid to be trusted.

14. Make few resolutions, but keep them strictly.

15. Prefer elders and strangers on all occasions, be rather last than first in conveniency and respect; but first in all virtues.

16. Have a care of trusting to after games, for then there is but one throw for all; and precipices are ill places to build upon. Wisdom gains time, is beforehand, and teaches to choose seasonably and pertinently; therefore ever strike

while the iron is hot. But if you lose an opportunity it differs in this from a relapse: less caution and more resolution and industry must recover it.

17. Above all, remember your Creator; remember yourselves and your families, when you have them, in the youthful time and forepart of your life; for good methods and habits obtained then will make you easy and happy the rest of your days. Every estate has its snare. Youth and middle-age, pleasure and ambition; old age, avarice; remember, I tell you, that man is a slave where either prevails. Beware of the pernicious lusts of the eye, and the flesh, and the pride of life, 1 John ii. 15, 16, 17, which are not of the Father, but of the world. Get higher and nobler objects for your immortal part, O my dear children, and be not tied to things without you; for then you can never have the true and free enjoyment of yourselves to better things; no more than a slave in Algiers has of his house or family in London. Be free, live at home, in yourselves I mean, where lie greater treasures hid than in the Indies. The pomp, honour, and luxury of the world are the cheats and the unthinking and inconsiderate are taken by them. But the retired man is upon higher ground, he sees and is aware of the trick, condemns the folly, and bemoans the deluded. This very consideration doubtless produced those two passions in the two greatest Gentiles of their time, Democritus and Heraclitus, the one laughing, the other weeping, for the madness of the world, to see so excellent and reasonable a creature as man so meanly trifling and slavishly employed.

18. Choose God's trades before men's, Adam was a gardener, Cain a ploughman, and Abel a grasier or shepherd. These began with the world, and have least of snare and most of use. When Cain became murderer, as a witty man said,[1] he turned a builder of cities and quitted his husbandry. Mechanics as handicrafts are also commendable, but they are but a second brood, and younger brothers. If grace employ you not let nature and useful arts, but avoid curiosity there also, for it devours much time to no profit. I have seen a ceiling of a room that cost half as much as the house; a folly and sin too.

19. Have but few books, but let them be well chosen and

[1] Cowley in his works on agriculture.

well read, whether of religious or civil subjects. Shun fantastic opinions; measure both religion and learning by practice; reduce all to that, for that brings a real benefit to you, the rest is a thief and a snare. And indeed reading many books is but a taking off the mind too much from meditation. Reading yourselves and nature in the dealings and conduct of men is the truest human wisdom. The spirit of a man knows the things of man, and more true knowledge comes by meditation and just reflection than by reading; for much reading is an oppression of the mind, and extinguishes the natural candle; which is the reason of so many senseless scholars in the world.

20. Do not that which you blame in another. Do not that to another which you would not another should do to you. But above all, do not that in God's sight you would not man should see you do.

21. And that you may order all things profitably, divide your day, such a share of time for your retirement and worship of God; such a proportion for your business, in which remember to ply that first which is first to be done; so much time for yourselves, be it for study, walking, visit, etc. In this be first, and let your friends know it, and you will cut off many impertinencies and interruptions, and save a treasure of time to yourselves, which people most unaccountably lavish away. And to be more exact (for much lies in this) keep a short journal of your time, though a day require but a line; many advantages flow from it.

22. Keep close to the meetings of God's people, wait diligently at them to feel the heavenly life in your hearts. Look for that more than words in ministry, and you will profit most. Above all look to the Lord, but despise not instruments, man or woman, young or old, rich or poor, learned or unlearned.

23. Avoid discontented persons, unless to inform or reprove them.

Abhor detraction, the sin of fallen angels and the worst of fallen men.

24. Excuse faults in others, own them in yourselves, and forgive them against yourselves, as you would have your Heavenly Father and judge forgive you. Read Prov. xvii. 9, and Matt. vi. 14, 15. Christ returns and dwells upon that

passage of His prayer, above all the rest, forgiveness, the hardest lesson to man, that of all other creatures most needs it.

25. Be natural; love one another; and remember that to be void of natural affection is a mark of apostasy set by the apostles, 2 Tim. iii. 3. Let not time, I charge you, wear out nature; it may kindred according to custom, but it is an ill one, therefore follow it not. It is a great fault in families at this day. Have a care of it, and shun that unnatural carelessness. Live as near as you can, visit often, correspond oftener, and communicate with kind hearts to one another, in proportion to what the Lord gives you; and do not be close, nor hoard up from one another as if you had no right or claim in one another, and did not descend of one most tender father and mother.

26. What I write is to yours as well as you, if God gives you children. And in case a prodigal should ever appear among them, make not his folly an excuse to be strange or close, and so to expose such a one to more evil. But show bowels as [1] John did to the young man that fell into ill company whom with love he reclaimed, after His example that sends His sun and rain upon all.

27. Love silence, even in the mind; for thoughts are to that as words to the body, troublesome; much speaking as much thinking spends, and in many thoughts as well as words there is sin. True silence is the rest of the mind, and is to the spirit what sleep is to the body, nourishment and refreshment. It is a great virtue; it covers folly, keeps secrets, avoids disputes, and prevents sin. *See* Job xiii. 5; Prov. x. 19; xii. 13; xiii. 3; xviii. 6, 7; xvii. 28.

28. The wisdom of nations lies in their proverbs, which are brief and pithy; collect and learn them, they are notable measures and directions for human life. You have much in little; they save time and speaking; and upon occasion may be the fullest and safest answers.

29. Never meddle with other folks' business, and less with the public, unless called to the one by the parties concerned (in which move cautiously and uprightly) and required to the other by the Lord in a testimony for His name and truth. Remembering that old, but most true and excellent proverb, *Bene qui latuit, bene vixit,* He lives happily that lives hiddenly

[1] Euseb. *Ecc. Hist.* lib. 3, cap. xxiii.

or privately, for he lives quietly. It is a treasure to them that have it. Study it, get it, keep it; too many miss it that might have it. The world knows not the value of it. It doubles man's life by giving him twice the time to himself that a large acquaintance or much business will allow him.

30. Have a care of resentment or taking things amiss, a natural, ready, and most dangerous passion; but be apter to remit than resent, it is more Christian and wise. For as softness often conquers, where rough opposition fortifies, so resentment, seldom knowing any bounds, makes many times greater faults than it finds; for some people have out-resented their wrong so far that they made themselves faultier by it, by which they cancel the debt through a boundless passion, overthrow their interest and advantage, and become debtor to the offender.

31. Rejoice not at the calamity of any, though they be your enemies, Prov. xvii. 5; xxiv. 17.

32. Envy none; it is God that maketh rich and poor, great and small, high and low. Psal. xxxvii. 1; Prov. iii. 31; xxiii. 17; xxiv. 1; 1 Chron. xxii. 11, 12; Ps. cvii. 40, 41.

33. Be intreatable. Never aggravate. Never revile or give ill names. It is unmannerly as well as unchristian. Remember Matt. v. 22, who it was said, He that calls his brother fool, is in danger of hell fire.

34. Be not morose or conceited. One is rude, the other troublesome and nauseous.

35. Avoid questions and strife; it shows a busy and contentious disposition.

36. Add no credit to a report upon conjecture, nor report to the hurt of any. *See* Exod. xxiii. 1; Psal. xv. 3.

37. Beware of jealousy, except it be godly, for it devours love and friendship; it breaks fellowship, and destroys the peace of the mind. It is a groundless and evil surmise.

38. Be not too credulous; read Prov. xiv. 15. Caution is a medium, I recommend it.

39. Speak not of religion, neither use the name of God in a familiar manner.

40. Meddle not with government; never speak of it; let others say or do as they please. But read such book of law as relate to the office of a justice, a coroner, sheriff, and constable; also the doctor and student; some book of

clerkship, and a treatise of wills, to enable you about your own private business only, or a poor neighbour's. For it is a charge I leave with you and yours, meddle not with the public, neither business nor money; but understand how to avoid it, and defend yourselves upon occasion against it. For much knowledge brings sorrow, and much doings more. Therefore know God, know yourselves; love home, know your own business and mind it, and you have more time and peace than your neighbours.

41. If you incline to marry, then marry your inclination rather than your interest. I mean what you love rather than what is rich. But love for virtue, temper, education, and person before wealth or quality, and be sure you are beloved again. In all which be not hasty, but serious; lay it before the Lord, proceed in His fear, and be you well advised. And when married, according to the way of God's people, used amongst Friends, out of whom only choose, strictly keep covenant; avoid occasion of misunderstanding, allow for weaknesses and variety of constitution and disposition, and take care of showing the least disgust or misunderstanding to others, especially your children. Never lie down with any displeasure in your minds, but avoid occasion of dispute and offence; overlook and cover failings. Seek the Lord for one another; wait upon Him together, morning and evening, in His holy fear, which will renew and confirm your love and covenant. Give way to nothing that would in the least violate it. Use all means of true endearment that you may recommend and please one another; remembering your relation and union is the figure of Christ's to His church. Therefore let the authority of love only bear sway your whole life.

42. If God give you children, love them with wisdom, correct them with affection. Never strike in passion, and suit the correction to their age as well as fault. Convince them of their error before you chastise them, and try them, if they show remorse before severity, never use that but in case of obstinacy or impenitency. Punish them more by their understandings than the rod, and show them the folly, shame, and undutifulness of their falts rather with a grieved than an angry countenance, and you will sooner affect their natures, and with a nobler sense, than a servile and rude

chastisement can produce. I know the methods of some are severe corrections for faults, and artificial praises when they do well, and sometimes rewards. But this course awakens passions worse than their faults; for one begets base fear, if not hatred; the other pride and vain glory, both which should be avoided in a religious education of youth; for they equally vary from it and deprave nature. There should be the greatest care imaginable what impressions are given to children. That method which earliest awakens their understandings to love, duty, sobriety, just and honourable things, is to be preferred. Education is the stamp parents give their children; they pass for that they breed them, or less value perhaps, all their days. The world is in nothing more wanting and reprovable, both in precept and example; they do with their children as with their souls, put them out at livery for so much a year. They will trust their estates or shops with none but themselves, but for their souls and posterity they have less solicitude. But do you breed your children yourselves, I mean as to their morals, and be their bishops and teachers in the principles of conversation: as they are instructed so they are likely to be qualified, and your posterity by their precepts and examples which they receive from yours. And were mankind herein more cautious they would better discharge their duty to God and posterity; and their children would owe them more for their education than for their inheritances. Be not unequal in your love to your children, at least in the appearances of it. It is both unjust and indiscreet. It lessens love to parents, and provokes envy amongst children. Let them wear the same clothes, eat of the same dish, have the same allowance as to time and expense. Breed them to some employment, and give all equal but the eldest; and to the eldest a double portion is very well. Teach them also frugality, and they will not want substance for their posterity. A little beginning with industry and thrift will make an estate; but there is great difference between saving and sordid. Be not scanty any more than superfluous; but rather make bold with yourselves, than be straight to others, therefore let your charity temper your frugality and theirs.

What I have written to you I have written to your children and theirs.

43. Servants you will have, but remember, the fewer the better, and those rather aged than young; you must make them such, or dispose of them often. Change is not good, therefore choose well, and the rather because of your children; for children, thinking they can take more liberty with servants than with their parents, often choose the servants' company, and if they are idle, wanton, ill examples, children are in great danger of being perverted. Let them therefore be friends, and such as are well recommended: let them know their business as well as their wages; and as they do the one, pay them honestly the other. Though servants yet remember they are brethren in Christ, and that you also are but stewards and must account to God. Wherefore let your moderation appear unto them, and that will provoke them to diligence for love rather than fear, which is the truest and best motive to service. In short, as you find them so keep, use, and reward them, or dismiss them.

44. Distrust is of the nature of jealousy, and must be warily entertained upon good grounds, or it is injurious to others, and instead of safe, troublesome to you. If you trust little, you will have but little cause to distrust. Yet I have often been whispered in myself of persons and things at first sight and motion that hardly ever failed to be true; though by neglecting the sense, or suffering myself to be argued or importuned from it, I have more than once failed of my expectation. Have therefore a most tender and nice regard to those first sudden and unpremeditated sensations.

45. For your conduct in your business and in the whole course of your life, though what I have said to you, and recommended you to, might be sufficient; yet I will be more particular as to those good and gracious qualifications, I pray God Almighty to season and accomplish you with, to His glory and your temporal and eternal felicity.

CHAPTER III

1. Be humble. It becomes a creature, a depending and borrowed being, that lives not of itself, but breathes in another's air, with another's breath, and is accountable for every moment of time, and can call nothing its own, but is absolutely a tenant at will of the great Lord of heaven and earth. And of this excellent quality you cannot be wanting if you dwell in the holy fear of the omnipresent and all-feeling God; for that will show you your vileness and His excellency, your meanness and His majesty, and withal, the sense of His love to such poor worms in the testimonies He gives of His daily care, mercy, and goodness; that you cannot but be abased, laid low, and humble. I say, the fear and love of God begets humility, and humility fits you for God and men. You cannot step well amiss if this virtue dwell but richly in you; for then God will teach you. The humble He teacheth His ways, and they are all pleasant and peaceable to His children. Yea, He giveth grace to the humble but resisteth the proud, Jam. iv. 6; 1 Pet. v. 5, He regardeth the proud afar off; Psal. cxxxviii. 6, They shall not come near Him, nor will He hear them in the day of their distress. Read Prov. xi. 2; xv. 33; xvi. 18, 19. Humility seeks not the last word, nor first place; she offends none, but prefers others, and thinks lowly of herself; is not rough or self-conceited, high, loud, or domineering; blessed are they that enjoy her. Learn of me, said Christ, for I am meek and lowly in heart. He washed His disciples' feet, John xiii., indeed himself was the greatest pattern of it. Humility goes before honour, Prov. xviii. 12. There is nothing shines more clearly through Christianity than humility; of this the Holy Author of it is the greatest instance. He was humble in His incarnation; for He that thought it no robbery to be equal with God, humbled Himself to become a man; and many ways made Himself of no reputation. As first in His birth or descent, it was not of the princes of Judah, but a virgin of low degree, the espoused of a carpenter; and so she acknowledges in her heavenly anthem, or ejaculation, Luke i. 47, 48, 52,

speaking of the great honour God had done her: And my spirit hath rejoiced in God my Saviour, for He hath regarded the low estate of His hand-maiden; He has put down the mighty from their seats, and exalted them of low degree. Secondly, He was humble in His life. He kept no court but in deserts and mountains and in solitary places; neither was He served in state, His attendants being of the mechanic size. By the miracles He wrought we may understand the food He ate, viz., barley bread and fish; and it is not to be thought there was any curiosity in dressing them. And we have reason to believe his apparel was as moderate as His table. Thirdly, He was humble in His sufferings and death. He took all affronts patiently, and in our nature triumphed over revenge. He was despised, spit upon, buffeted, whipped, and finally crucified between thieves, as the greatest malefactor; yet He never reviled them, but answered all in silence and submission, pitying, loving, and dying for those by whom he was ignominiously put to death. O Mirror of Humility! Let your eyes be continually upon it, that you may see yourselves by it. Indeed his whole life was one continued great act of self-denial. And because He needed it not for Himself, He must needs do it for us; thereby leaving us an example that we should follow His steps, 1 Pet. ii. 21. And as He was we should be in this world according to the beloved disciple, 1 John ii. 6. So what He did for us was not to excuse but excite our humility. For as He is like God, we must be like Him, and that the froward, the contentious, the revengeful, the striker, the dueller, etc., cannot be said to be of that number, is very evident. And the more to illustrate this virtue I would have you consider the folly and danger of pride, its opposite. For this it was that threw the angels out of heaven, man out of paradise, destroyed cities and nations, was one of the sins of Sodom, Ezek. xvi. 49, the destruction of Assyria and Israel, Isa. iii. 16, and the reason given by God for His great vengeance upon Moab and Ammon, Zeph. ii. 9, 10. Besides, pride is the vainest passion that can rule in man, because he has nothing of his own to be proud of, and to be proud of another's shows want of wit and honesty too. He did not only not make himself, but is born the nakedest and most helpless of almost all creatures. Nor can he add to his days or stature, or so much as make one hair of his head white or black. He is so absolutely in the power of another, that as I have often said, he is at best but a tenant at will of the great Lord of all, holding life, health, substance, and everything at His sovereign disposal; and the more man enjoys the less reason he has to be proud, because he is the more indebted and engaged to thankfulness and humility.

Wherefore avoid pride as you would avoid the devil; remembering you must die, and consequently those things must die with you that could be any temptation to pride; and that there is a judgment follows, at which you must give an account both for what you have enjoyed and done.

2. From humility springs meekness. Of all the rare qualities of wisdom, learning, valour, etc., with which Moses was endued, he was denominated by his meekness. This gave the rest a lustre they must otherwise have wanted. The difference is not great between these excellent graces; yet the Scripture observes some. God will teach the humble His way, and guide the meek in judgment. It seems to be humility perfectly digested, and from a virtue become a nature. A meek man is one that is not easily provoked, yet easily grieved; not peevish or testy, but soft, gentle, and inoffensive. O blessed will you be, my dear children, if this grace adorn you! There are divers great and precious promises to the meek in Scripture. That God will clothe the meek with salvation; and blessed are they for they shall inherit the earth, Psal. xxxvii. 11; Mat. v. 5. Christ presses it in His own example, Learn of me for I am meek, etc., Mat. xi. 29. And requires His to become as little children in order to salvation, Mat. xviii. 3, and a meek and quiet spirit is of great price with the Lord, 1 Pet. iii. 4. It is a fruit of the spirit, Gal. v. 22, 23, exhorted to Eph. iv. 2; Col. iii. 12; Tit. iii. 2, and many places more to the same effect.

3. Patience is an effect of a meek spirit, and flows from it. It is a bearing and suffering disposition; not choleric or soon moved to wrath, or vindictive; but ready to hear and endure too, rather than be swift and hasty in judgment or action. Job is as much famed for this as was Moses for the other virtue: without it there is no running the Christian race, or obtaining the heavenly crown; without it there can be no experience of the work of God, Rom. v. 3, 4, 5. For

patience worketh, saith the apostle, experience; nor hope of an eternal recompense, for experience worketh that hope. Therefore, says James, Let patience have its perfect work, Jam. i. 4. It is made the saints' excellency; here is the patience of the saints, Rev. xiii. 10. It is joined with the kingdom of Christ, Rev. i. 9. Read Luke xxi. 19. In patience possess your souls. Rom. xii. 12; xv. 4; 2 Cor. vi. 4; 1 Thes. v. 14. Be patient towards all men, Tit. ii. 2; Heb. vi. 12; x. 36, which shows the excellency and necessity of patience, as that does the true dignity of a man. It is wise and will give you great advantage over those you converse with on all accounts. For passion blinds men's eyes, and betrays men's weakness; patience sees the advantage and improves it. Patience inquires, deliberates, and brings to a mature judgment; through your civil as well as Christian course you cannot act wisely and safely without it; therefore I recommend this blessed virtue to you.

4. Show mercy whenever it is in your power, that is forgive, pity, and help, for so it signifies. Mercy is one of the attributes of God, Gen. xix. 19; Exod. xx. 6; Psal. lxxxvi. 15; Jer. iii. 12. It is exalted in Scripture above all His works, and is a noble part of His image in man. God hath recommended it, Hos. xii. 6, Keep mercy and judgment and wait on the Lord. God hath shown it to man, and made it His duty, Mic. vi. 8, He hath showed thee, O man, what is good, and what doth the Lord require of thee, but to do justly, and to love mercy, and to walk humbly, or to humble thyself to walk with thy God: a short but ample expression of God's love and man's duty; happy are you if you mind it. In which you see mercy is one of the noblest virtues. Christ has a blessing for them that have it, blessed are the merciful, Mat. v., for they shall find mercy; a strong motive indeed. In Luke vi. 35, 36, he commands it. Be you merciful as your Father is merciful. He bid the Jews that were so over-righteous, but so very unmerciful, learn what this meaneth: I will have mercy and not sacrifice, Matt. ix. 13. He hit them in the eye. And in his parable of the Lord and His servants, he shows what will be the end of the unmerciful steward, Mat. xviii. 34, 35, that having been forgiven much by his Master, would not forgive a little to his fellow-servant. Mercy is a great part of God's law, Exod. xxiii. 4, 5. It is

a material part of God's true fast, Isa. lviii. 6, 7. It is a main part of God's covenant, Jer. xxxi. 34; Heb. viii. 12. And the reason and rule of the last judgment, Matth. xxv. 31, to the end: pray read it. It is a part of the undefiled religion, Jam. i. 27; iii. 17. Read Prov. xiv. 21, 22. But the merciful man's mercy reaches farther, even to his beast; then surely to man, his fellow-creature, he shall not want it. Wherefore, I charge you, oppress nobody, man nor beast. Take no advantage upon the unhappy, pity the afflicted, make their case your own, and that of their wives and poor innocent children the condition of yours, and you cannot want sympathy, bowels, forgiveness, nor a disposition to help and succour them to your ability. Remember, it is the way for you to be forgiven, and helped in time of trial. Read the Lord's Prayer, Luke xi. Remember the nature and goodness of Joseph to his brethren; follow the example of the Good Samaritan, and let Edom's unkindness to Jacob's stock, Obad. 10-16, and the heathen's to Israel, Zach. i. 21; ii. 8, 9, be a warning to you. Read also Prov. xxv. 21, 22; Rom. xii. 19, 20.

5. Charity is a near neighbour to mercy. It is generally taken to consist in this, not to be censorious, and to relieve the poor. For the first, remember you must be judged, Matth. vii. 1. And for the last, remember you are but stewards. Judge not, therefore, lest you be judged. Be clear yourselves before you fling the stone. Get the beam out of your own eye; it is humbling doctrine, but safe. Judge, therefore, at your own peril. See it be righteous judgment, as you will answer it to the Great Judge. This part of charity also excludes whisperings, backbiting, tale-bearing, evil-surmising, most pernicious follies and evils, of which beware. Read 1 Cor. xiii. For the other part of charity, relieving the poor, it is a debt you owe to God. You have all you have or may enjoy, with the rent-charge upon it. The saying is, that he who gives to the poor, lends to the Lord. But it may be said, not improperly, the Lord lends to us to give to the poor. They are at least partners by providence with you, and have a right you must not defraud them of. You have this privilege, indeed, when, what, and to whom; and yet, if you heed your guide, and observe the object, you will have a rule for that too.

I recommend little children, widows, infirm and aged persons chiefly to you. Spare something out of your own belly rather than let theirs go pinched. Avoid that great sin of needless expense on your persons and on your houses, while the poor are hungry and naked. My bowels have often been moved to see very aged and infirm people, but especially poor helpless children, lie all night in bitter weather at the thresholds of doors in the open streets for want of better lodging. I have made this reflection, If you were so exposed, how hard would it be to endure? The difference between our condition and theirs has drawn from me humble thanks to God, and great compassion and some supply to those poor creatures. Once more be good to the poor. What do I say? Be just to them and you will be good to yourselves. Think it your duty, and do it religiously. Let the moving passage, Matth. xxv. 35, to the end, live in your minds: I was an hungry, and thirsty, and naked, sick, and in prison, and you administered unto Me, and the blessing that followed. Also what He said to another sort, I was an hungry, and thirsty, and naked, and sick, and in prison, and you administered not unto Me; for a dreadful sentence follows to the hard-hearted world. Woe be to them that take the poor's pledge, Ezek. xviii. 12, 13, or eat up the poor's right. O devour not their part! Less lay it out in vanity, or lay it up in bags, for it will curse the rest. Hear what the Psalmist says, Psal. xli., Blessed is he that considereth the poor, the Lord will deliver him in time of trouble: The Lord will preserve and keep him alive, and he shall be blessed upon the earth: And thou wilt not deliver him into the will of his enemies. The Lord will strengthen him upon the bed of languishing: Thou wilt make all his bed in his sickness. This is the reward of being faithful stewards and treasurers for the poor of the earth. Have a care of excuses, they are, I know, ready at hand, but read Prov. iii. 27, 28, Withhold not good from them to whom it is due, when it is in the power of thine hand to do it. Say not unto thy neighbour go, and come again, and to-morrow I will give, when thou hast it by thee. Also bear in mind Christ's doctrine, Matth. v. 42, Give to him that asketh thee, and from him that would borrow of thee, turn not thou away. But above all remember the poor woman that gave her mite; which Christ preferred above all, because she gave all, but it was to God's treasury, Mark xii. 42, 43, 44.

6. Liberality or bounty is a noble quality in man, entertained of few, yet praised of all, but the covetous dislike it because it reproaches their sordidness. In this she differs from charity, that she has sometimes other objects, and exceeds in proportion. For she will cast her eye on those that do not absolutely want, as well as those that do; and always outdoes necessities and services. She finds out virtue in a low degree, and exalts it. She eases their burden that labour hard to live. Many kind and generous spells such find at her hand that do not quite want, whom she thinks worthy. The decayed are sure to hear of her. She takes one child and puts out another to lighten the loads of overcharged parents, more to the fatherless. She shows the value of services in her rewards, and is never debtor to kindnesses; but will be creditor on all accounts. Where another gives sixpence the liberal man gives his shilling; and returns double the tokens he receives. But liberality keeps temper too; she is not extravagant any more than she is sordid; for she hates niggard's feasts as much as niggard's fasts; and as she is free, and not starched, so she is plentiful, but not superfluous and extravagant. You will hear of her in all histories, especially in Scripture, the wisest as well as the best of books. Her excellency and her reward are there. She is commanded and commended, Deut. xv. 3, 4, 7, 8, and Psal. xxxvii. 21, 26. The righteous showeth mercy and giveth, and the good man is merciful and ever lendeth. He shows favour and lendeth and disperseth abroad, Psal. cxii. 5, 9. There is that scattereth, and yet increaseth; and there is that withholdeth more than is meet, but it tendeth to poverty. The liberal soul shall be fat, Prov. xi. 24, 25. The bountiful eye shall be blessed, Prov. xxii. 9. The churl and liberal man are described and a promise to the latter that his liberality shall uphold him, Isa. xxxii. 78. Christ makes it a part of His religion and the way to be the children of the highest (read Luke vi. 34, 35) to lend and not receive again, and this to enemies as well as friends; yea to the unthankful and to the evil; no exception made, no excuse admitted. The apostle Paul, 2 Cor. ix. 5 to x., enjoines it, threatens the straight-handed and promises the open-hearted a liberal reward.

Wheresoever therefore, my dear children, liberality is required of you, God enabling of you, sow not sparingly nor grudgingly, but with a cheerful mind, and you shall not go without your reward; though that ought not to be your motive. But avoid ostentation, for that is using virtue to vanity, which will run you to profuseness, and that to want; which begets greediness, and that avarice, the contrary extreme. As men may go westward until they come east, and travel until they and those they left behind them, stand Antipodes, up and down.

7. Justice or righteousness is another attribute of God, Deut. xxxii. 4; Psal. ix. 7, 8; v. 8; Dan. ix. 7. Of large extent in the life and duty of man. Be just therefore in all things, to all; to God as your Creator; render to Him that which is His, your hearts, for that acknowledgment He has reserved to Himself, by which only you are entitled to the comforts of this and a better life. And if He has your hearts you have Him for your treasure, and with Him all things requisite to your felicity. Render also to Cæsar that which is his, lawful subjection; not for fear only, but conscience sake. To parents, a filial love and obedience. To one another, natural affection. To all people in doing as you would be done by. Hurt no man's name or person. Covet no man's property in any sort. Consider well of David's tenderness to Saul when he sought his life to excite your duty; and Ahab's unjust covetousness and murder of Naboth to provoke your abhorrence of injustice. David, though anointed king, took no advantages, he believed and therefore did not make haste, but left it to God to conclude Saul's reign, for he would not hasten it. A right method and a good end, my dear children, God has shown it you, and requires it of you.

Remember the tenth commandment, it was God gave it, and that will judge you by it. It comprehends restitution as well as acquisition, and especially the poor man's wages, Lev. xix. 13; Deut. xxiv. 14, 15; Jer. xxii. 13; Amos. v. 11; Mal. iii. 5. Samuel is a great and good example of righteousness, 1 Sam. xii. 3. He challenged the whole house of Israel whom he had oppressed or defrauded. The like did the apostle to the Corinthians, 2 Cor. vii. 2. He exhorted the Christians to be careful that they did not defraud, 1 Thes.

iv. 6, for this reason, that God was the avenger of the injured. But as bad as it was there must be no going to law amongst Christians, 1 Cor. vi. 7. To your utmost power, therefore, owe no one anything but love, and that in prudence as well as righteousness; for justice gives you reputation, and adds a blessing to your substance. It is the best security you can have for it.

I will close this head with a few Scriptures to each branch. To your superiors: Submit to every ordinance of man, for the Lord's sake, Pet. ii. 13. Obey those that have rule over you, Heb. xiii. 17. Speak not evil of dignities, Jude viii; 2 Pet. ii. x. My son, fear thou the Lord and the king, and meddle not with them that are given to change, Prov. xxiv. 21. To your parents: Honour your father and your mother, that the days may be long in the land, which the Lord your God shall give you, Exod. xx. 12. Children, obey your parents, it is the first command with promise, Ephes. vi. 1, 2. Great judgments follow those that disobey this law, and defraud their parents of their due. Whoso robbeth his father or his mother and saith it is no transgression, the same is the companion of a destroyer, Prov. xxviii. 24. Or such would destroy their parents if they could. It is charged by the prophet Ezekiel upon Jerusalem as a mark of her wicked state, In thee have thy princes set lightly by father or mother, oppressed strangers, and vexed fatherless and widows, Ezek. xxii. 6, 7. To thy neighbour, hear what God's servants taught: To do justice and judgment is more acceptable to the Lord than sacrifice, Prov. xxi. 3. Divers weights and measures are alike abomination unto the Lord, Levit. xix. 36; Deut. xxv. 13 to 16 inclusive; Prov. xi. 1; xx. 10, 23. Read Prov. xxii. 16, 22, 23; xxiii. 10, 11. Peruse the 6th of Micah; also Zech. viii. 16, 17. And especially Psalm xv. As a short but full measure of life, to give acceptance with God.

I have said but little to you of distributing justice, or being just in power or government; for I should desire you may never be concerned therein, unless it were upon your own principles, and then the less the better, unless God require it from you. But if it ever be your lot, know no man after the flesh; know neither rich not poor, great nor small, nor kindred, nor stranger, but the cause according to your understanding and conscience, and that upon deliberate inquiry and information. Read Exod. xxiii. from 1 to 10; Deut. i. 16, 17; xvi. 19, 20; xxiv. 17; 2 Sam. xxiii. 3; Jer. xxii. 3, 4; Prov. xxiv. 23; Lam. iii. 35, 36; Hos. xii. 6; Amos viii. 4, 5, 6, 7, 8; Zeph. ii. 3; iii. 1, 3; Zech. vii. 9, 10; Jer. v. 4, 5, 6; viii. 6, 7. Which show both God's commands and complaints, and man's duty in authority; which, as I said before, waive industriously at all times, for privacy is freed from the clamour, danger, incumbrance, and temptation that attend stations in government. Never meddle with it, but for God's sake.

8. Integrity is a great and commendable virtue. A man of integrity is a true man, a bold man, and a steady man; he is to be trusted and relied upon. No bribes can corrupt him, no fear daunt him; his word is slow in coming, but sure. He shines brightest in the fire, and his friend hears of him most when he most needs him. His courage grows with danger, and conquers opposition by constancy. As he cannot be flattered or frighted into that he dislikes, so he hates flattery and temporising in others. He runs with truth, and not with the times; with right and not with might. His rule is straight; soon seen but seldom followed. It has done great things. It was integrity preferred Abel's offering, translated Enoch, saved Noah, raised Abraham to be God's friend and father of a great nation, rescued Lot out of Sodom, blessed and increased Jacob, kept and exalted Joseph, upheld and restored Job, honoured Samuel before Israel, crowned David over all difficulties, and gave Solomon peace and glory while he kept it. It was this preserved Mordecai and his people, and signally defended Daniel among the lions, and the children in the flames, that it drew from the greatest king upon earth, and an heathen too, a most pathetical confession to the power and wisdom of the God that saved them, and which they served. Thus is the Scripture fulfilled, The integrity of the upright shall guide them, Prov. xi. 3. O my dear children! fear, love, and obey this great, holy, and unchangeable God, and you shall be happily guided and preserved through your pilgrimage to eternal glory.

9. Gratitude or thankfulness is another virtue of great lustre, and so esteemed with God and all good men. It is an owning of benefits received, to their honour and service

that confer them. It is indeed a noble sort of justice, and might in a sense be referred as a branch to that head; with this difference though, that since benefits exceed justice, the tie is greater to be grateful than to be just; and consequently there is something baser and more reproachful in ingratitude than injustice. So that though you are not obliged by legal bonds or judgments to restitution with due interest, your virtue, honour, and humanity are naturally pledges for your thankfulness; and by how much the less you are under external ties, esteem your inward ties so much the stronger. Those that can break them would know no bounds: for make it a rule to you, the ungrateful would be unjust too, but for fear of the law. Always own therefore the benefits you receive, and then to choose when they may most honour or serve those that conferred them. Some have lived to need the favours they have done, and should they be put to ask where they ought to be invited? No matter if they have nothing to show for it, they show enough when they show themselves to those they have obliged. And such see enough to induce their gratitude when they see their benefactors in adversity; the less law the more grace and the stronger tie. It is an evangelical virtue, and works as faith does, only by love. In this it exactly resembles a Christian state, we are not under the law, but under grace, and it is by grace and not by merit that we are saved. But are our obligations the less to God that He heaps His favours so undeservedly upon us? Surely no. It is the like here; that which we receive is not owed or compelled, but freely given, so no tie; but choice, a voluntary goodness without bargain or condition, but has this therefore no security? Yes, certainly, the greatest; a judgment written and acknowledged in the mind; he is his to the altar with a good conscience. But how long? As long as he lives. The characters of gratitude, like those of friendship, are only defaced by death, else indelible. A friend loveth at all times, says Solomon, Prov. xvii. 17; xxvii. 10. And thine own friend and thy father's friend forsake not. It is injustice which makes gratitude a precept. There are three sorts of men that can hardly be grateful, the fearful man, for in danger he loses his heart with which he should help his friend; the proud man, for he takes that virtue for a reproach. He that unwillingly remembers he owes anything to God will not readily remember he is beholden to man. History lays it to the charge of some of this sort of great men that uneasy to see the authors of their greatness have not been quiet till they have accomplished the ruin of those that raised them. Lastly, the covetous man is as ill at it as the other two. His gold has spoiled his memory, and won't let him dare be grateful, though perhaps he owes the best part, at least the beginning of it, to another's favour. As there is nothing more unworthy in a man, so nothing in man so frequently reproached in Scripture. How often does God put the Jews in mind for their forgetfulness and unthankfulness, for the mercies and favours they received from Him. Read Deut. xxxii. 15. Jesurun waxed fat and kicked against God, grew unmindful, forgot and forsook his rock that had done mighty things for him. Thus Moses, Deut. xxxi. 16, 17. Also Judg. x. 11, 12, 13, and 1 Sam. viii. 8. David likewise in his lxxviii., cv., cvi. Psalms gives a history of God's love to Israel, and their ingratitude. So Isa. xvii. 1 to 11. Likewise Jer. ii. 31, 32; v. 7 to 20; xv. 6; xvi. 10, 11, 12, 20, 21; xviii. 15; Hos. viii. 9. It is a mark of apostacy from Christianity by the apostle, 2 Tim. iii. 2.

10. Diligence is another virtue useful and laudable among men. It is a discreet and understanding application of oneself to business; and avoids the extremes of idleness and drudgery. It gives great advantages to men. It loses no time, it conquers difficulties, recovers disappointments, gives dispatch, supplies want of parts; and is that to them which a pond is to a spring; though it has no water of itself it will keep what it gets, and is never dry. Though that has the heels, this has the wind; and often wins the prize. Nor does it only concern handicrafts and bodily affairs, the mind is also engaged and grows foul, rusty, and distempered without it. It belongs to you throughout your whole man; be no more santering in your minds than in your bodies. And if you would have the full benefit of this virtue, do not balk it by a confused mind. Shun diversions; think only of the present business till that be done. Be busy to purpose; for a busy man and a man of business are two different things. Lay your matters right, and diligence succeeds them, else pains is lost. How laborious are some to no purpose? Consider your end well, suit your means to it, and then

diligently employ them, and you arrive where you would be with God's blessing. Solomon praises diligence very highly. First, it is the way to wealth. The diligent hand makes rich, Prov. x. 4. The soul of the diligent shall be made fat, xiii. 4. There is a promise to it, and one of another sort to the sluggard, xxiii. 21. Secondly, it prefers men, verse 29. Seest thou a man diligent in his business he shall stand before kings. Thirdly, it preserves an estate: Be thou diligent to know the state of thy flocks, and look well to thy herd; for riches are not for ever, xxvii. 23, 24. There is no living upon the principal, you must be diligent to preserve what you have, whether it be acquisition or inheritance; else it will consume. In short, the wise man advises, whatsoever thy hand finds to do, do it with thy might, Eccl. ix. 10. As it mends a temporal state, no spiritual one can be got or kept without it. Moses earnestly presses it upon the Israelites, Deut. iv. 9 and vi. 7. The apostle Paul commends it in the Corinthians and Titus to them for that reason, 2 Cor. viii. 7, 22. So he does Timothy to the Philippians on the same account, and urges them to work out their salvation, Phil. ii. 12, 20, 21. Peter also exhorts the churches to that purpose: Wherefore the rather, brethren, says he, give diligence to make your calling and election sure: for if you do these things you shall never fail, 2 Pet. i. 10 and in iii. 13, 14. Wherefore, beloved, seeing that you look for such things (the end of the world and last judgment) be diligent that you may be found of Him in peace, without spot and blameless. Thus diligence is an approved virtue. But remember that is a reasonable pursuit or execution of honest purposes, and not an overcharging or oppressive prosecution to mind or body of most lawful enterprises. Abuse it not therefore to ambition or avarice. Let necessity, charity, and conveniency govern it, and it will be well employed, and you may expect prosperous returns.

11. Frugality is a virtue too, and not of little use in life, the better way to be rich, for it has less toil and temptation. It is proverbial, a penny saved is a penny got. It has a significant moral; for this way of getting is more in your own power and less subject to hazard, as well as snares, free of envy, void of suits, and is beforehand with calamities. For many get that cannot keep, and for want of frugality spend

what they get, and so come to want what they have spent. But have a care of the extreme: want not with abundance, for that is avarice, even to sordidness. It is fit you consider children, age, and casualties, but never pretend those things to palliate and gratify covetousness. As I would have you liberal but not prodigal; and diligent, but not drudging; so I would have you frugal, but not sordid. If you can, lay up one half of your income for those uses, in which let charity have at least the second consideration; but not Judas's, for that was in the wrong place.

12. Temperance I must earnestly recommend to you, throughout the whole course of your life. It is numbered amongst the fruits of the spirit, Gal. xxii. 23, and is a great and requisite virtue. Properly and strictly speaking, it refers to diet; but in general may be considered as having relation to all the affections and practices of men. I will therefore begin with it in regard to food, the sense in which it is customarily taken. Eat to live, and not live to eat, for that is below a beast. Avoid curiosities and provocations; let your chiefest sauce be a good stomach, which temperance will help to get you. You cannot be too plain in your diet, so you are clean; nor too sparing, so you have enough for nature. For that which keeps the body low, makes the spirit clear, as silence makes it strong. It conduces to good digestion, that to good rest, and that to a firm constitution. Much less feast any, except the poor, as Christ taught, Luke xiv. 12, 13. For entertainments are rarely without sin; but receive strangers readily. As in diet so in apparel, observe, I charge you, an exemplary plainness. Choose your clothes for their usefulness not the fashion, and for covering and not finery, or to please a vain mind in yourselves or others. They are fallen souls that think clothes can give beauty to man. The life is more than raiment, Matth. vi. 25. Man cannot mend God's work, who can give neither life nor parts. They show little esteem for the wisdom and power of their Creator that under-rate his workmanship (I was going to say His image) to a tailor's invention. Gross folly and profanity! But do you, my dear children, call to mind who they were of old that Jesus said took so much care about what they should ear, drink, and put on. Were they not Gentiles, Heathens, a people without God in the world? Read Matth. vi., and

when you have done that peruse those excellent passages of the apostle Paul and Peter, 1 Tim. ii. 9, 10, and 1 Pet. iii. 3, 5, where if you find the exhortation to women only conclude it was effeminate, and a shame then for men to use such arts and cost upon their person. Follow you the example of those primitive Christians, and not voluptuous Gentiles that perverted the very order of things. For they set lust above nature, and the means above the end, and preferred vanity to conveniency. A wanton excess that has no sense of God's mercies, and therefore cannot make a right use of them, and less yield the returns they deserve. In short, these intemperances are great enemies to health and to posterity; for they disease the body, rob children, and disappoint charity, and are of evil example; very catching as well as pernicious evils. Nor do they end there. They are succeeded by other vices, which made the apostle put them together in his epistle to the Galatians, v. 20, 21. The evil fruits of this part of intemperance are so many and great that upon a serious reflection I believe there is not a country, town, or family almost, that does not labour under the mischief of it. I recommend to your perusal the first part of *No Cross no Crown*, and of the *Address to Protestants*, in which I am more particular in my censure of it. As are the authorities I bring in favour of moderation. But the virtue of temperance does not only regard eating, drinking, and apparel; but furniture, attendance, expense, gain, parsimony, business, diversion, company, speech, sleeping, watchings, and every passion of the mind, love, anger, pleasure, joy, sorrow, resentment, are all concerned in it. Therefore bound your desires, learn your will's subjection, take Christ for your example as well as guide. It was He that led and taught a life of faith in Providence, and told His disciples the danger of the cares and pleasures of this world; they choked the seed of the kingdom, stifled and extinguished virtue in the soul, and rendered man barren of good fruit. His sermon upon the Mount is one continued divine authority in favour of a universal temperance. The apostle, well aware of the necessity of this virtue, gave the Corinthians a seasonable caution. Know ye not, says he, that they which run in a race run all, but one receiveth the prize? So run that ye may obtain. And every man that striveth for mastery (or seeketh victory) is temperate in all things (he acts discreetly and with a right judgment). Now they do it to obtain a corruptible crown, but we an incorruptible. I therefore so run as not uncertainly; so fight I, not as one that beateth the air: but I keep under my body, and bring it into subjection; lest that by any means, when I have preached to others, I myself should become a castaway, 1 Cor. ix. 25, 27. In another chapter he presses the temperance almost to indifferency: but this I say, brethren, the time is short: it remaineth then that both they that have wives be as though they had none; and those that weep as though they wept not; and they that rejoice as though they rejoiced not; and they that use this world as not abusing it. And all this is not without reason. He gives a very good one for it. For, saith he, the fashion of the world passeth away: but I would have you without carefulness, 1 Cor. vii. 29-32. It was for this cause he pressed it so hard upon Titus to warn the elders of that time to be sober, grave, temperate, Tit. ii. 2, not eager, violent, obstinate, tenacious, or inordinate in any sort. He makes it an indispensable duty in pastors of churches, that they be not self-willed, soon angry, given to wine or filthy lucre, but lovers of hospitality, of good men, sober, just, holy, temperate, Tit. i. 7, 8. And why so? Because against these excellent virtues there is no law, Gal. v. 23.

I will shut up this head (being touched upon in divers places of this advice) with this one most comprehensive passage of the apostle, Philip. iv. 5. Let your moderation be known unto all men, for the Lord is at hand. As if He had said, Take heed! Look to your ways! Have a care what ye do! For the Lord is near you, even at the door; He sees you, He marks your steps, tells your wanderings, and He will judge you. Let this excellent, this home and close sentence live in your minds. Let it ever dwell upon your spirits, my beloved children, and influence all your actions, ay, your affections and thoughts. It is a noble measure, sufficient to regulate the whole; they that have it are easy as well as safe. No extreme prevails; the world is kept at arm's end; and such have power over their own spirits, which gives them the truest enjoyment of themselves and what they have: a dominion greater than that of empires. O may this virtue be yours! You have grace from God for that end, and it is sufficient; employ it and you cannot miss of temperance, nor therein of the truest happiness in all your conduct.

13. I have chosen to speak in the language of the Scripture, which is that of the Holy Ghost, the spirit of truth and wisdom, that wanted no art of direction of man to speak by and express itself fitly to man's understanding. But yet that blessed principle, the eternal word I begun with to you, and which is that light, spirit, grace, and truth, I have exhorted you to in all its holy appearances or manifestations in yourselves, by which all things were at first made, and man enlightened to salvation, is Pythagoras's great light and salt of ages, Anaxagoras's divine mind, Socrates's good spirit, Timæus's unbegotten principle and author of all light, Hieron's God in man, Plato's eternal, ineffable, and perfect principle of truth, Zeno's maker and father of all, and Plotin's root of the soul: who as they thus styled the eternal word, so the appearance of it in man wanted not very significant words. A domestic God, or God within, says Hieron, Pythagoras, Epictetus, and Seneca; genius, angel, or guide, says Socrates and Timæus; the light and spirit of God, says Plato; the divine principle in man, says Plotin; the divine power and reason, the infallible immortal law in the minds of men, says Philo; and the law and living rule of the mind, the interior guide of the soul, and everlasting foundation of virtue, says Plutarch. Of which you may read more in the first part of the *Christian Quaker*, and in the *Confutation of Atheism*, by Dr. Cudworth. These were some of those virtuous Gentiles commended by the apostle, Rom. ii. 13, 14, 15, that though they had not the law given to them as the Jews had, with those instrumental helps and advantages, yet doing by nature the things contained in the law, they became a law unto themselves.

WILLIAM PENN.

A TENDER VISITATION

A TENDER VISITATION

In the Love of God that overcometh the World, to all People in the High and Low Dutch Nations who hunger and thirst after Righteousness, and desire to know and worship God in Truth and in Sincerity; containing a Plain Testimony to the Ancient and Apostolic Life, Way, and Worship that God is reviving and exalting in the Earth, in His Spirit and Truth

Friends,—In that love wherewith God the Father of all mercy and our Lord Jesus Christ hath loved and visited my soul, I likewise love and visit you; wishing in the same love that you with all the saints might come to experience what is the knowledge, faith, hope, worship, and service that is of and from God, and which alone is truly acceptable unto Him: and that you might so run that you may obtain: and that you being armed with the spiritual weapons may so fight as you may gain the prize and inherit the crown; so that the great God, the Lord of heaven and earth; He who shall judge the quick and the dead; He may be known by you to be your God, and you may know yourselves to be His children; born not of blood, nor of the will of the flesh, nor of the will of man, but born again of His holy and incorruptible seed; by the word of God, born of His spirit, and joined unto Him in an everlasting covenant; that while you live here you may not live to yourselves, but to the glory of God: and when you have finished your course here below, you may lay down your heads in peace, and enter into everlasting rest with the faithful; here all tears shall be wiped away from your eyes, and everlasting joy and gladness shall be the portion of your inheritance.

Let me therefore, friends, speak freely and be openhearted unto you, and consider you my words in the fear of God, for I am pressed in spirit to write to you.

First, have you all turned yourselves to God, who was the

teacher of Adam, while in his innocency; who was the teacher of the Israelites through His prophets, and of the true Christians through His Son Jesus; through whom He speaks His will in the hearts of all true Christians: if not, then are you yet erring from His spirit, and going astray from the Lord, who is the teacher of the new covenant?

Secondly, know you the end and design of the coming of Christ? Are you come to an inward experience of what the same is? Hearken to the words of His beloved disciple, who has said, for this purpose the Son of God was manifested that He might (put an end to sin, and) destroy the works of the devil. Do you know this by your own experience? Ah! deceive not yourselves; where, pray, does sin dwell? And where are the works of the devil? Are they not in the hearts of men and women? Is not that the seat of wickedness, the tabernacle of sin, the temple of the devil? Have not men there worshipped his spirit? Have not men there bowed down before him? And are not all such born of his evil seed? Must not Christ, who is the seed of God, bruise his head, there destroy his work, and take his kingdom from him? The soul which by Satan is defiled and kept in captivity, must not Christ redeem it, purify it, and save it? That it may be changed and seasoned with the divine seed, and so come to bear the holy image of the same; to that end that Christ may come to dwell in a pure heart, and that God may be worshipped in His own evangelical temple, in His own spirit in man and woman? What of these things are you truly come to know? And what have you yet felt hereof? Christ is therefore come into the world, even for that very end is He called Jesus, viz., that He should save His people from their sins: and to that end has John directed all to Him by these words, behold the Lamb of God which taketh away the sin of the world.

Look now to yourselves, O inhabitants of Christendom! whether He has taken away your sins, and what those sins are. Examine and try yourselves by His holy light from what evil things you are now redeemed, which you were before subject unto; for Christ saves no man from the wrath of God whom He hath not first redeemed from sin, for the wages of sin is death, and whatsoever men sow that they shall reap in the great and last day of judgment.

To whom then do you live, my friends, and in what life?

Do you live in the life of God and Christ wherein the saints of old did live, whose lives were hid with Christ in God; and who did live because Christ lived in them? Is the old wine and also the old bottles put away? Is the old man with all his deeds put off? The old evil and corrupt ground which brings forth all evil and corrupt fruits, is that burnt up by the fire of God? For His word is like a fire; the old heavens, the old service of God, peace, gladness, and the old worship which altogether are as dead in the fallen nature, are they rolled up as a scroll, and vesture, and melted through the strong heat of the burning and judging spirit of God? Are you become as new bottles, which receive the new wine of the kingdom of God, which endures for ever? Have you, my friends, put on the new man, which after God is created in righteousness and in true holiness? Can you feel that there is brought forth in you the new heaven and the new earth wherein righteousness dwelleth? Consider, you who truly and sincerely seek to know the Lord and His works in you, and spend not your money for that which is not bread, nor your labour for that which satisfieth not, nor will profit anything in the day of account, that your souls be not deceived, but that you may be saved in the day of the Lord.

Come you that are weary and heavy laden, and you that hunger and thirst after righteousness and desire to walk in the purity and righteousness of the saints: be it known unto you that Jesus Christ who can discharge, ease, help, and save you all, He is near you, and stands at the door of your hearts, and that He waits to be gracious to you; He knocks that you may open unto Him: it is He who has visited you with His saving light, whereby He has manifested your state and condition to you and begotten a holy feeling in you; whereby you are become weary of your evil doings, and raises up a holy thirst in you after better things. Now then, if you desire and expect ever to be filled and satisfied from Him, then must you receive Him as He is revealed, and as His holy will is made known in your hearts; and keep yourselves under His holy judgments and reproofs: for the reproofs of instruction are the way of eternal life. Love therefore that which reproves you for evil, and turn from those evils for which you are reproved; for Zion shall be redeemed through judgment, and her converts with righteousness. Love, I say, the judgments of Christ, and submit thereunto, and wait for Him, to feel Him yet more and more, that you thus may say with one of old, in the way of Thy judgment, O Lord, have we waited for Thee: and with our souls have we desired Thee in the night season; and with our spirits within us will we seek Thee early: for when Thy judgments are in the earth the inhabitants of the world will learn righteousness: for judgment, said Christ, am I come into this world: that is, as a holy light, to make manifest; and as a righteous judge to condemn all unrighteousness of men: and all those that love His reproofs and willingly suffer His chastisings and fatherly rebukes, they shall see judgment brought forth unto victory, and that the prince of this world, the corrupt root, the corrupt nature, ground, or origin in you, as well as the evil fruits and ungodly works thereof, shall be judged. And when this is done, and is fulfilled, then you shall know what it is to sing His high praises in truth and righteousness: then you shall come to sing the song of the Lamb; and know that you by that Lamb are redeemed and saved.

But it may be some will ask, who is able to perform so great and blessed a work? Fear not, you that seek the kingdom of God, and His righteousness, with all your hearts: for God has laid help upon one that is mighty, viz., upon Jesus Christ, and He shall make your sins known unto you, and redeem you from all unrighteousness, if you will walk in His light, as His beloved disciple speaks, saying, if we walk in the light, as He is in the light, we have fellowship one with another, and the blood of Jesus Christ cleanseth us from all sin. And therefore, friends, if you will be saved by the blood of Christ, then must you leave and forsake all which the light of Christ does condemn in you; yea, you must watch against your own thoughts, words, and deeds, that you at unawares may not be overcome by the enemy of your souls: for he comes as a thief in the night to destroy you. Do not live nor act so as to grieve the Holy Spirit of God; but turn your minds from all evil, in thoughts, words, and deeds; yea, if you love the light of Christ then bring your deeds every day to the light and see whether they are wrought in God or no: for all things that are reproved or justified are made manifest by the light; for whatsoever doth make manifest is light;

and that light burns as an oven against all unrighteousness; yea, it is like a refiner's fire: for it is the fiery part of the baptism of Christ, and therefore it is called the brightness of His coming, the consuming spirit of His mouth, whereby that wicked one shall be revealed, and burnt up, and rooted out; the thorns and briars shall be burned up and devoured, and the filthiness both of flesh and spirit purged away. If now your sins are become a burthen to you; if you thereby are wearied, and if you heartily desire that they may be weakened in you, and at last conquered also; then let the holy watch of Jesus be sincerely and earnestly kept in your hearts; which watch is the light; for in darkness is no safe nor true watching. Watch therefore with the light of Christ wherewith you are enlightened; watch (I say) against every unfruitful thought, word, and work of darkness: stand upon your guard in the blessed light, and be you armed therewith like the saints of old, that you may discern the enemy, and resist him when and howsoever he does appear and approach unto you; that so he may not overcome you; but that you may obtain victory over him: for when he sees his allurements ineffectual, his snares discovered and broken (as this is done in the light of Christ), then is he weakened in his attempts, and your souls grow stronger to resist him, until at last he be wholly defeated and conquered. For this was the way of the ancients who were more than conquerors, who walking after the light and spirit of Jesus were redeemed from condemnation, which will come upon all those that live after the flesh. O this light and this grace bringeth salvation! For it teacheth us to deny ungodliness and worldly lusts, which bring condemnation, and to live soberly, righteously, and godly in this present world. And this is the only living way to the everlasting rest and peace of God. This was the teacher of the saints, this was Paul's refuge and comfort in his greatest temptations. My grace (said the Lord) is sufficient for thee. And as it has been in time past, so is it in this our day to all them that come to receive it, embrace it, and love it, and who are willing to be guided by it, and follow it; and to them said the Lord, depart you from all evil ways, from all vain uses and customs, and from the vanities of this world. Receive you my counsel, which is the living oracle, or the voice of God, and the fountain of all wisdom; and do not hew out to yourselves cisterns, broken cisterns, that can hold no water.

Thirdly, are your preachers and teachers sent by God or by men? How are they come to be your teachers? Consider of this seriously: are they of those that have accompanied with Jesus? Are they instructed and sanctified by Him? Are they born again? Have they received their commissions, and are they sent forth by Him? Are they true and faithful witnesses? Have they heard, seen, tasted, and handled that which they speak and deliver unto you? Is it the living word which they preach unto you? Or do they by their own spirit and understanding, in their own time and will, explain and interpret those matters which the saints of old and the primitive Christians spake forth as they were moved by the Holy Ghost? If it be so, then have they not received such work or such victory through the Holy Spirt in themselves as the saints had experience of.

Fourthly, do your preachers turn your minds to the light of Christ (that is the life in Him), which shines in your hearts; which alone discovers sin to the creature, and shows every man what the Lord doth require of him? Do they direct you to that light which did lead the saints of old; and by their believing in the light made them children of light; wherein the nations of them that are saved shall walk? Do they turn you (I say) to this light, to this grace and spirit in yourselves, which cometh by Jesus Christ? Does your knowledge, feeling, experience, and worship consist in the revelations and works of this blessed principle of God's begetting in you? So that your faith and hope consist not in word only (though they may all be true in words), nor in the education of an outward religious persuasion by vain teachers; but that your faith and hope are grounded and builded upon the power of the living God, who gives victory over the world unto all those who in their hearts believe in the light of Jesus. And this blessed hope purifies the heart and fortifies the soul.

Fifthly, when you come to your meetings, both preachers and people, what do you do? Do you then gather together bodily only, and kindle a fire compassing yourselves about with the sparks of your own kindling, and so please yourselves, and walk in the light of your own fire, and in the sparks which you have kindled; as those did in the time of old, whose portion it was to lie down in sorrow? Or rather, do you sit down in true silence, resting from your own will and workings, and waiting upon the Lord, fixed with your minds in that light, wherewith Christ has enlightened you, until the Lord breathes life in you, refresheth you, and prepares you, and your spirits, and souls to make you fit for His service, that you may offer unto Him a pure and spiritual sacrifice? For that which is born of the flesh, is flesh; and he that soweth to his flesh shall of the flesh reap corruption: for flesh and blood cannot inherit the kingdom of God: but he that soweth to the spirit shall of the spirit reap life eternal through Christ who has quickened him.

What have you felt then, my friends, of this work in your hearts? Has Christ there appeared? What has He done for you? Have you bowed down before Him, and received Him in your hearts? Is He formed in you? Do you live no more, but does Christ live in you? For if you know not Christ to be in you, then are you yet reprobates, though you confess Him in words: as the apostle said of old.

All you therefore that hunger and thirst after the righteousness of God's kingdom, which is an everlasting blessed kingdom, turn in, my friends, and come to Christ, who stands at the door of your hearts and knocks. He is the light of the world, and it concerns all true servants of the Lord to direct all men to this light; else have they not a right discerning, nor true sight or taste of the things of God, viz., to turn men from darkness to light, from the kingdom of Satan to the power and kingdom of God; from the dark inventions and human traditions of men to Christ, the great light of God, the high priest and holy prophet, whom all men must hear and out of whose mouth the law of the spirit of life must be received. By this He judges men in righteousness, and in Him are hid all the treasures of wisdom and knowledge. This is the high priest of all true Christians, and their chief treasure.

Happy, therefore, are all those that receive Him in their hearts, those that know Him to be their light, their guide, their king, their law-giver, their bishop, and their heavenly shepherd, who follow Him through all things, and through all persecutions and sufferings, and that steadfastly love His cross (the power of God) and with all gladness embrace the reproach thereof; who have experienced that without Christ they can do nothing; and therefore wait for His divine power, strength, and wisdom to govern and guide them. For such can receive no testimony from any preachers, except that testimony which is given from the Holy Unction, in and through them; because men without Christ can do nothing, as He has said: for men cannot preach, men cannot pray, men cannot sing as it ought to be; yea, men without Him can do nothing to the praise and glory of God: for it is only the Son of God that glorifies the Father through His children.

And therefore let him kindle the fire with the pure coals from His holy altar; and do you not offer to Him in your self-will. No, Jesus did not do His own will, but the will of His Father. So let us not do our own, but His will; He has done nothing but what His Father had made known unto Him; and we must all witness what Christ has declared unto us, and what He has wrought in us, or else we should be false witnesses. Woman, said Christ to His mother, mine hour is not yet come: so that He did wait His Father's time, in whose hands the times and seasons are. We must wait, but God orders, and happy are those that do His will. My sheep, said Christ, hear my voice, and follow me; but they will not hear the voice of strangers. Now those that speak, if their voices and conversations are not with the life, the power, and with the spirit of Christ, they are strange voices (I pray you observe well); and Christ's sheep will not sit under such voices nor under such shepherds, who do but steal the words of the prophets and apostles, but do not experience them, nor succeed them in their spirits and conversations; for Christ's sheep do discern those that so teach from His, for He has given them that spiritual gift to see them; which is not to be had nor found in the crafty wisdom of the world with all its human learnings, arts, and sciences; but stands in the innocent nature of the true sheep; and for them it is like natural, viz., souls that are become harmless and are arrived at the state of a little child; for to such doth God reveal His secrets; because by the work of regeneration they are become His own begotten; and to such belongs the kingdom of God, and the knowledge of the mysteries thereof.

Wherefore, pray take notice, how it is with you. Is sin revealed? Yes. Through what? By the light of Christ.

But is sin likewise judged? Have you submitted yourselves to His light? And are you therewith united? Is your old self-righteousness thereby judged? And are thereby all your false judgments judged? Is the Prince of this World judged in you? Does Christ go before you? And does He give you eternal life? Examine and search yourselves, for thus He deals with His sheep: I go before them, they follow Me, and behold I give them life eternal. Does Christ go before you and lead you in all your worship, which you do as your bounden duty to God? Do you wait for His leadings? Is it the religion of Christ wherein you walk? Read His holy Sermon on the Mount. Or else do you go before Him, and do you climb up another way before He stirs in you, before He moves you, before He gives you power and ability to approach His throne? Ah! true silence before the Lord is better abundantly than forward prayers and self-willed orders, or any traditional and formal performances: for consider that it is life eternal to know God. Now, no man can know Him who has not heard His voice: and no man can hear His voice who is not silent in himself, and waits not patiently for Him, that He may hear what God will speak to his soul through Christ Jesus, the great, holy, and heavenly high priest of God, to mankind, who is the heavenly prophet also unto all them that believe in His name. But, my friends, do you know the fellowship of His holy life, of His blessed cross, death, and resurrection? Do you confess Him inwardly in yourselves as well as outwardly before men? If so, then has He given you life eternal. Again, if you feel not in you life and immortality brought to light then are you yet in your sins, and know not the Lamb of God who taketh away the sins of the world. For as many as received Him to them gave He power to become the children of God. And they know by the witness of God in themselves that they are of God, as said the beloved disciple John, and the whole world lieth in wickedness.

Beloved friends, beware, therefore, of idolatry and worshipping of images, I mean the worship of inward images, which is an inward idolatry; for if you show a great aversion against all outward idolatry, yet if you worship God after the imaginations you have of God, and which you conceive in your own minds, without the inspiration of the Almighty, you worship images of your own framing, and so come to commit idolatry. And therefore take heed that your worship does not consist in your own imaginations and self-conceits of God; and do not bow down to such (which is indeed to yourselves), and then think or presume that you are bowing down to God and Christ; when, on the contrary, it is nothing else but a mere picture of your own making. And this is the great abomination and loss of poor Christendom, viz., that the spirit which deceives man sits in the place of God, and is worshipped as God by those that know not the true and living God, who is as a consuming fire, and as everlasting burnings in the soul against sin, righteousness, and judgment of the world.

Now He that revealeth the Father is the Son, the true light. For He has said, no man knoweth the Father, but the Son, and He to whom the Son will reveal Him. How has Christ revealed the Father unto you? Are you come to Jesus? If so, then you have known the Godly sorrow, the true mourning, and that repentance which men need never to repent of. But if you have not known this day of judgment and contrition then are you not come to Christ. Wherefore come you to Jesus, viz., to His appearance in you, by His divine light and spirit, which every way discovers and judges the world's nature, spirit, and image in you. For to Him is all judgment committed, and He will reveal the Father; yea, He that has seen the Son has likewise seen the Father; for He is in the Father, and the Father is in Him. If now the manifestation of Jesus in you, as well of the Father as of the Son, is the foundation of your knowledge, so that God and Christ, whom to know is life eternal, are become the holy object of your worship; then are you real worshippers in His spirit and truth; then are you come out from the workmanship, from the will and imaginations of your own spirits, and from all human worship, and are come to the worship of the spirit of the living God, and to live in Him, be led and moved by Him in all Godly performances, for the spirit of man only knows the things of man, but the spirit of God knows and reveals the things of God. And this worship of His kingdom and Church has Christ raised up again in these our days, which was set up by Christ sixteen hundred years ago. And in this worship have the true followers worshipped the Father, before the great apostasy from the spirit and power of the Lord broke in upon the primitive ages of the Church. And after such a glorious manner shall it be restored; yea, so it is already with many thousands whom God, through the appearance of Christ in the heart, has gathered, both in our and other countries, whereby He has judged them as men in the flesh (in their fleshly lusts, in their fleshly worships) that they might live unto God and Christ, who quickened them by the death of the cross, and justified them as men in the spirit risen from the dead.

Glory be therefore to God, who lives and reigns on high, that that dark and sorrowful night is vanishing, and that the sun-rising of the eternal day has already appeared, and is arising more and more over the nations in the world; in which day Babylon, the mother of harlots [false worshippers], shall come in remembrance before the God of the whole earth, viz., that Babylon, which has followed merchandising with the Scripture, and with the souls of men, and has persecuted the spiritual seed, the children of God, and faithful witnesses of Jesus (although clothed in sackcloth) because they would not receive her mark, and her fine linen too, nor submit to her fleshly birth, invention, profession, worship, and dominion.

This Babylon lives but too much yet in every one, of all sorts of people or professors, by whom the truth is held in unrighteousness; when they see not through the light of the spirit of Christ, and when their knowledge and worship of God is not received and performed by that same blessed spirit; there, I say, is Babylon, that is, confusion: Oh, come out of her, my people! saith the Lord, and I will receive you.

He that calls God his Father and is not born of God; He that calls Christ Lord, and not by the holy spirit; but meanwhile is serving another master: those that attribute to themselves the words of the regenerated, their revelations and experiences, when they are yet unregenerated, and have no part therein, but endeavour in all these things to make themselves a fair covering—they shall experience in the day of the Lord that it shall profit them nothing: for woe to those, said the Lord, that cover with a covering, and not of my spirit; that take counsel, but not of me. Let therefore all those that are yet in Babylon hasten out of her speedily, and you that are in the suburbs of that great city hasten you away; yea, make haste, with all speed! Prepare yourselves to meet the

Lamb, your bridegroom; who comes now to you (who are mourning, hungering, and thirsting after Him) to lead you out of your bewildered states to His saving light and blessed appearance: for now He sees you, and now He calls you, and knocks at your doors to come in unto you: and therefore open ye unto Him, and let Him in; let Him no longer lie in the manger, nor at your doors; but rather give Him your hearts, and let Him reign over you as a king, for He has bought us with His own precious blood, and is therefore worthy that we serve and honour Him, and that He reign over us; and that He be our king and law-giver, who gave His own life for us that we should not perish, but have everlasting life in Him. He has laid down His life for you, and can you not lay down your sins for His sake; yea, for your own sakes? Consider that He descended from the glory of His Father to bring you to glory; and can you not depart from the withering glory of this world that you may inherit His glory, which is everlasting? It is that wrong, false self in man which only hinders it, it is that only which objects against it, that consults and endeavours to avoid the cross.

This self has in all times been desirous to be in great esteem, and has therefore in all ages hindered men from doing the will of God on earth, as it is in heaven: but where self is disannulled, and men have had no great esteem for the selfish part, but have humbled themselves to the death of the cross of Christ that He might deliver them from the wrath to come, and give them an inheritance in the kingdom of His Father, there the will of God will be done on earth as it is in heaven, and therein will the heavenly Father be glorified. On the contrary, those that live in sin they are in communion with the devil, and drink his cup of unrighteousness: which, however it is sweet in the mouth, is afterwards bitter in the belly. And though it be sweet here for a time it shall afterwards be crabbed and distasteful. Again, the cup of Christ is here bitter in the mouth, but sweet hereafter in the belly. Here sour, but hereafter pleasant. You, said He, shall weep and lament, but the world shall rejoice: but observe the end hereof, your sorrow shall be turned into joy, but their rejoicing into weeping.

And this is therefore the word of truth, no man shall enjoy the cup of blessing or drink out of the cup of salvation but he that has first drank of the cup of tribulation; he that has first known his fellowship with the sufferings of Christ and of His holy mystical cross: for those that suffer with Him shall reign with Him, and no cross, no crown.

Lean then upon His breast, for so does the bride in spirit. Trust in Him and not in man, nor in yourselves, for He will guide you best, because He is given you of God to be your heavenly guide. And if it should be in a way under the cross (which way is proper to Him), yet it is notwithstanding a way of joy and pleasantness, and all His holy paths are peace to those that love Him. O therefore feel His holy drawings, and wait in His light upon His holy movings in your souls! Stand still and see His salvation wrought in you by His own arm: that you may know Him to be Jesus indeed, viz., a Saviour as well from your sins here, as from the wrath to come; and that He may preserve you from vain thoughts, vain words, and vain conversations, yea, from the voluntary worship of this world and from the slavish fear of man. To the end that He may work His own work in you, and make you conformable to His own blessed image; and that you may be made free by the Lord through the power of His everlasting gospel, which is now again sounded forth by His own angel to the inhabitants of the earth, calling with a loud voice, fear God, and give glory to Him, for the hour of His judgment is come. And you must feel this judgment in your hearts, that the prince of this world, with all his evil seed, with all his wrong plants and appearances, may be judged in you; and that you may be witnesses upon earth for God and the Lamb that sits upon the throne against all darkness of men and devils; nay, against death, hell, and the grave; and that God may bless you with all sorts of blessings in Christ Jesus.

But yet I find myself pressed in spirit to give you one warning more, viz., that you would not longer use vain words (though true in themselves), because they are worth nothing, for they take God's name in vain that use it without life and power: and I entreat all those that endeavour to know God and come to the true life of His dear Son, that you make no profession of worship without the feeling, preparing, and ordering of the true and overcoming power of God: for such worship is not of God, and such professors are poor, lean, naked, and miserable people; yea, they are only as chaff among the corn: and therefore beware you of that woman Jezabel, the false prophetess, of whom the early Christians were warned, who has the words, but not the life of the Son of God: her preaching tends to death, she makes a talk of the sound and fame of wisdom (but will not afterwards harbour her, when she cries in her streets), she awakens none, she brings no man to God; she does not build up in the heavenly work nor administer the right spiritual bread to the soul: for Christ only is the bread which gives life eternal, and those that will eat of this bread must first come to Him; let Him into their hearts as Lord and Master, to provide and order His to His praise, and as such must He be received when He appears in their souls even as a refiner's fire and as a fuller's soap to purify and refine from all unrighteousness; yea, to reveal unto men their sins, and destroy the same with the brightness of His coming, and with the spirit of His mouth in which no deceit is found. He is that light in the brightness of His coming which you must love and whose testimony you must keep, and He is the quickening spirit whose breath of His mouth revives the soul and destroys the sin that slays it: for all those that come to receive Him in this office, in this way, and in this work, shall also know that He is the Lamb of God, which taketh away the sin of the world, the spiritual passover, the heavenly bread, the true vine which bringeth forth the new wine of the kingdom, the blessed olive tree; yea, the tree of life and eternal salvation, which grows in the midst of the paradise of God, whose leaves are for the healing of the nations.

This is a salutation to you all from the holy and fervent love which God has poured into my heart and soul; who am in a travail to help the nations to be gathered to Christ, the light and salvation thereof, that Zion may be the joy and Jerusalem the praise of the whole earth. Amen, amen.

A SUMMONS OR CALL TO CHRISTENDOM

A SUMMONS OR CALL TO CHRISTENDOM

In an Earnest Expostulation with Her to prepare for the Great and Notable Day of the Lord that is at the Door.

Awake, O Christendom! Awake, and come to judgment, for the great and notable day of the Lord is drawing apace upon thee; prepare to meet Him, thou and thy children, for the hour of His judgment hasteneth upon you as travail on a woman with child, in which all your works shall be tried, and that by fire, for the day of the Lord shall burn as an oven, and all the proud, and all that do wickedly, shall be as stubble. Yea, by fire and by sword will the Lord God Almighty plead with all flesh; with all fleshly worshippers and workers who live after the flesh to fulfil the lusts thereof, and with the spirit of judgment, and the spirit of burning, that is, with spiritual judgment and burning, will He visit all ranks and regions upon the earth: yea, His holy terrors shall take hold of the rebellious, and anguish and distress shall fill the souls of the guilty. The faces of nations shall gather paleness, and their knees smite together because of the anger of God that is kindling against them, and His fierce wrath that is revealing from heaven against all the ungodly, but more especially against the children of the mystery of iniquity. It is in this day that the kindreds of the earth shall mourn with a great lamentation.

O Christendom! thou hast long sat as a queen that should never know sorrow; great have been thy pretences, and large thy profession of God, Christ, spirit, and scriptures; come, let me expostulate with thee and thy children in the fear and presence of Him that shall bring every word and work to judgment. God is pure, and the pure in heart only see Him. Now, are you pure? Do you see Him? God is a spirit, and none can worship Him aright but such as come to His spirit, and obey it. Do you so? Christ is the gift of God, have you received Him into your hearts? Does He rule there? Then have you eternal life abiding in you. If not, you are not true Christians. The spirit of truth leadeth into all truth; and the children of God are born of it, and led by it. But are you led into all the holy ways of truth, born of this eternal spirit? Then you follow not the spirit of this world; nor do your own wills, but the will of God. You profess the holy Scriptures; but what do you witness and experience? What interest have you in them? Can you set to your seal they are true by the work of the same spirit in you that gave them forth in the holy ancients? What is David's roarings and praises to thee that livest in the lusts of this world? What is Paul's and Peter's experiences to thee that walkest after the flesh?

O you that are called Christians, give ear a little unto me, for I am pressed in spirit to write to you. Read with patience and consider my words; for behold what I have to say unto you concerneth your eternal good.

God hath so loved the world that He hath sent His only begotten Son into the world that those that believe on Him should have eternal life. And this Son is Christ Jesus, the true light that lighteth everyone coming into the world; and they that abide not in Him, the light, dwell in darkness, in sin, and are under the region and shadow of death. Yea, dead in sin and see not their own states, neither perceive the sad conditions of their own souls. They are blind to the things of God's kingdom, and insensible of true and spiritual life and motion, what it is to live to God. And in that state are alienated from God without true judgment and living knowledge; and under the curse. For in Jesus Christ, the light of the world, are hid all the treasures of wisdom and knowledge, redemption, and glory; they are hid from the worldly Christian, from all that are captivated by the spirit and lusts of the world: and whoever would see them (for therein consist the things that belong to their eternal peace) must come to Christ Jesus the true light in their consciences, bring their deeds to Him, love Him and obey Him; whom God hath ordained a light to lighten the Gentiles, and for His salvation to the ends of the earth. Light and salvation are joined together, and none can come to salvation but as they come first to the light, and submit to the manifestation of it which leadeth to salvation. For the nations of them that are saved shall walk in the light of the Lamb, Christ Jesus. Light and justification are also joined together: if we walk in the light as God is in the light, the blood of Jesus Christ His Son cleanseth us from all sin. And light and life eternal are joined together. For in the Word (that was with God in the beginning, and was God, by whom all things were made, that were made) was life, and the life was the light of men. And this is the testimony of Jesus, I am the light of the world; he that followeth Me shall not abide in darkness, but have the light of life; yea, it is eternal life to believe in Him, in Christ the light, to receive, embrace, and to follow Him. And that was the true light (saith the same beloved disciple) which lighteth every man that cometh into the world. Now this light shineth in darkness, in the children of darkness, in their dark hearts, in their black souls, and defiled consciences, but in this darkness they comprehend it not. Neither can man know the nature and benefit of it whilst he rebelleth against it; for the virtue and excellency of it is shut up and hid from the children of disobedience. To as many as received Him of old gave He power to become the children of God; and they that did His will knew His doctrine to be of God, and of power and efficacy to their salvation.

But this is the great condemnation of the world at this day, that though God hath sent His son a light into the hearts of all men and women to manifest and reprove their evil deeds, and to save them; yet they love darkness, they love the lusts and imaginations of their vain hearts better than this holy light that is given unto them for salvation. They choose Barabbas rather than Jesus. Yea, they have set up other lights than Christ Jesus, God's great light; and other prophets than Christ, God's great prophet; and other priests than Jesus, the high priest of the new covenant: but they are dark lights, false prophets, and blind priests. All that came before me, saith Christ, are thieves and robbers. And all that pray, preach, sing, worship, etc., and not by the light and spirit of Jesus, they go before Christ, before Christ cometh, before He prepareth their hearts, and toucheth their lips with a coal from His heavenly altar; and perform worship in their own will, time, and power, and stay not for

His leadings. And therefore all such rob Christ of His office, who is the leader of the true Christians; their heavenly high priest, to anoint them, and offer up their sacrifice to God for them; and prophet, to let them see and know by His light in their hearts what they ought to do according to the new and everlasting covenant; I will write My law in their hearts, and put My spirit in their inward parts, and they shall be all taught of Me, saith the Lord.

Now this is the question to the whole world called Christians. Do you see with this divine light? Have you searched your hearts with it? And are you anointed by this high priest with His holy unction that leadeth into all truth? Doth this heavenly prophet give you vision and reveal the Father to you? Is He your eye, your head, your wisdom? Do you live, move, and have your life and being in Him, in praying, preaching, and singing, yea, in your whole conversation? Are you renewed into his life and image? And have you heard His voice, and seen His shape? Are you witnesses of His holy rebukes, His pure judgments, the shame and death of His cross? Is He the fountain of your knowledge? The author of your faith? O consider! Are you of those that have spoke with Jesus? That have been taught in the school of His holy cross? Students in His heavenly academy? O have you drunk of His cup, and been baptised with His baptism? Tell me in the fear of the Lord God, you that call yourselves Christians, doth He go before you and lead you as a master teacheth His disciples, and a captain leadeth His soldiers? And do you follow Him in all the weighty things of this life? And doth He order your minds, and rule your affections? If not you are thieves and robbers; for you rob Christ of His office. For God hath appointed Him to be the leader and ruler of all people; yea, it is God's decree; and those that He leadeth not in their thoughts, words, and works shall never come to God; for all must come to God by Him, that is, by His light and spirit ruling in their hearts, which sanctifieth, regenerateth, and converteth the soul to God.

And the cause of the confusion and contention that is about religion in Europe at this day is that men have deserted this true light and holy spirit, and so are degenerated from the life and power of pure and unspotted religion, and have attempted to comprehend Christ's doctrines without Christ's light, and to know the things of God without the spirit of God. And being thus miserably erred by wicked works from the one spirit of truth they have wandered into the fallible conceits and opinions of men. And in this state one party hath contended against another. From words they have fallen to blows, and the strongest hath oppressed the weakest. And not knowing what spirit they were of have called light darkness, and darkness light; putting the sheep's skin upon the wolf, and the wolf's skin upon the poor sheep of Christ, endeavouring by carnal weapons to enforce their opinions, and to extort conformity by worldly laws and punishments to their persuasions. All this is out of the light, life, and doctrine of Christ Jesus, and in the spirit of darkness, confusion, strife, and bloodshed, which are of the devil. All which babel must and shall come down by the light, power, and spirit of Jesus now rising in the world; and hell, death, and the grave shall not be able to hinder it: for the set time, the appointed time of the Father is come, and the judgment is begun.

O ye that are called Roman Catholics, tell me, are you truly Catholic, that is, of a universal spirit? Then you will not persecute, but love all, and be tender to all. Are you truly Roman, and successors of that ancient apostolic Church? Then you walk not after the flesh, but after the spirit, yea, the spirit of Christ dwelleth in you, and you are led by the spirit of God, and can call Him Father in truth and righteousness, and the word of God in the heart is your teacher, and not the traditions of men; for so the Romans of old time were instructed. O consider, if you are true successors you must follow them in the same nature, spirit, and life. For in that only standeth the Christian succession, to wit, in Christ. And every branch, person, or church that abideth not in this great vine is rejected for the fire. Therefore deceive not yourselves, as the Jews of old did, with crying, the temple of the Lord, the temple of the Lord; and saying, we have Abraham to our father, and to us belong the fathers, covenants, law, priesthood, and chair of Moses. For as the apostle said of old, so say I to you: His servants you are to whom you obey, and He that committeth sin is of the devil. So that Christ's successors are they that take up His cross, follow Him, and that abide in His holy doctrine, that keep

His commandments, and themselves unspotted from the world. And those that follow the lust of the eye, the lust of the flesh, and pride of life, are not of Christ, nor of the Father, but of the world; subjects to the prince of the power of the air, and successors of Sodom, Gomorrah, Egypt, Tyre, Sidon, and persecuting Jerusalem; and not of the harmless, self-denying, holy, suffering spouse of Christ Jesus, that is ruled in all things by her husband, her head, her Lord. O search and try with the light of Jesus, if you are not degenerated from primitive simplicity and purity? For great are the abominations of all sects that flow like a deluge throughout your countries! Repent and turn to the ancient apostolical spirit and life, that you may enter into the rest of God.

O you that call yourselves Evangelists or Gospellers, are you Evangelical? Are you saved from the lusts and pleasures and dead worships of the world by the mighty power of God, which is the gospel, and led by an evangelical spirit? If not, you are not yet redeemed, you are not yet under grace, which is the gospel state: for you are not taught by it, but rebel against it; how then are you true gospellers, men of gospel liberty, men of deliverance and redemption; to whom immortality is brought to light (as it is to all that truly know and receive the blessed gospel) that are yet subjects and servants to sin? How can you sing the song of the Lamb, that are not delivered by the Lamb; but by your vain conversations crucify the Lamb, and do despite to the spirit of grace, and that every day? The true Gospellers are those that receive the angel's message, who is the great preacher of the everlasting gospel, viz., fear God, give glory to His name, for the hour of His judgment is come, and no more worship the beast. Do you fear God in truth and in sincerity? Then are you fearful of offending the Lord, and tender of God's glory; then are your hearts kept clean, then are you wise to salvation; and so you can glorify God indeed: otherwise your prayers and praises are not evangelical in God's sight.

But tell me, O ye Gospellers, is the hour of His judgment come to you? Is it begun at your houses yet? How do you feel it? Hath it broke your hearts? Hath it contrited your spirits? Have ye known the godly sorrow? The chastisement of the Lord and rebukes of the Almighty?

Hath His pure eternal word divided yet betwixt your soul and spirit, the joints and marrow? Have you ever been weary and heavy laden with sin; hath it been a burden to you? Did you ever cry out in the agony of your spirit yet, men and brethren, what shall we do to be saved? O! who shall deliver us from the body of sin here, and the wrath to come! (The travail of the holy ancients.) If not, you are yet strangers to Christ and His kingdom. And if you die in that state, where He is gone you shall never come. For Sion, God's city, must be redeemed through judgments, and her converts through righteousness. Yea, the house of God cannot escape it; wherefore, said one of old, if judgment begin at the house of God, where shall the sinner and ungodly appear? O woe to them that live without the judgments of the Lord! Woe to them that cast His reproofs behind their backs, and live in earthly pleasures, fatting up themselves in their lusts and pleasures as for the day of slaughter, and treasuring up wrath against the day of wrath. O the ancient saints lived not thus; they wrought out their salvation with fear and trembling; yea, they gave all diligence to make their calling and election sure. Which way do you work out yours? Habakkuk, that holy prophet, his lips quivered, and his belly trembled, that his soul might rest in the day of trouble. Is this your state? Or are you not rather worshippers of the beast at this day, lovers of the worldly, sensual, voluptuous life, walking in the lusts of the eye, the lusts of the flesh, and pride of life; like rebellious Israel of old, forgetting God days without number? But this know, that all that forget God shall be turned into hell.

Oh! what is become of the Fatherly visitation made to your progenitors, those good beginnings sown in persecutions and martyrdom? Have you answered the loving kindness of God therein? Have you advanced in the way of righteousness? Are you become a holy nation, and a peculiar people to God, zealous of good works? But have you not betaken yourselves to the wisdom and learning of this world to make ministers, and deserted the spirit of the Lord, and fled to the power and policy of this world to defend and protect you, and not to the name of the Lord, which hath always been the strong tower of the righteousness? Nay, are you not divided one against another, and turned persecutors for religion, yourselves denying that liberty to others you took for yourselves? Ah! where is the royal law of doing as you would be done unto.

Thus have you decayed and degenerated into a worldly clergy and a carnal people, holding and maintaining reformed words in an unreformed spirit, yea, are not the same evils, pride, passion, malice, wars, bloodshed, persecution, deceit, fleshly lusts, wantonness, vain pleasures and sports, yea, all manner of worldly-mindedness to be found in you that were in the persecutors of your forefathers, and against which your most serious and best ancestors faithfully testified? So that the difference now is about words and sentences, and not about the life, nature, and spirit of pure and undefiled religion. And men are to be known now by their denominations and subscriptions to certain human creeds, man-made faiths and forms, and not by the spirit and image of Christ Jesus, by the nature of the true sheep, and by that holy unction that was the bond of the heavenly fellowship of the saints of old.

And you that are called reformed, with the rest of the subdivided sects, what better are you for your names? Are ye regenerated yet? Are you reformed from the lusts of the eye, the lusts of the flesh, and the pride of life; from the devil and all his works? Are you born of the incorruptible seed that liveth and abideth for ever? And are you come out of the corruptible things, and doth Christ lead you? Is the government of your souls upon His shoulders? Tell me, is it the new birth, that which is born of God through many tribulations, the new man created in Christ Jesus, that calleth God Father in your prayers, and that maketh mention of Him in your preachings? Or is it the first birth of the earth, earthly, the old man, the corrupt and unregenerated nature, that which born of the flesh, that is to say, of the seed of the evil one, the father of all the fleshly lusts, inventions, imaginations, and traditions of men, that taketh pleasure in the vain and wicked sports and pleasures of this apostate world, that forget God, and turn His grace into wantonness; reproaching, nicknaming, and persecuting the children of regeneration with scornful names and cruel punishments, calling God Father as the Jews did; and crucifying Christ afresh by a vain conversation at the same time.

O you degenerated Christians of all sorts, yea, all the several sects in Christendom that have deserted your first love, and degenerated from the life and power of primitive godliness, with the light of Christ Jesus in your hearts examine yourselves. God hath lighted your candle, search and try yourselves; see how it standeth with you as to your eternal condition before you go hence and be no more in this world. Consider, are you in the true faith of Christ or no? For without true faith none can please God; and without pleasing Him no man can be saved. The devils believe, yea, and tremble too; that is more than thousands called Christians do, and so far they are short of the very devils. Have you faith? Let us try it in the name of God. What is it for faith? Doth it overcome the world? Doth it live and depend upon God? Can it forsake country and kindred? Turn out Ishmael? Offer up Isaac? Live a pilgrim, a stranger in the world? Doth it work by that love which can forsake all for Christ's name's sake? Doth it fight against the devil? Resist his fiery darts? Overcome his assaults and temptations? And finally purify the soul to God's use? Is this your faith, O you carnal, outside Christians? No such matter; for you live in the flesh, fulfilling the lusts thereof; and your care is what you shall eat, drink, and put on, and how you shall get the mammon, friendship, and glory of this world. Examine yourselves and prepare, for the day of the Lord hasteneth upon you. And have a care lest you partake of the plagues that God hath prepared for Babylon; she that calleth herself the Lamb's bride and is a harlot committing fornication throughout all nations and sects, that is, those that by a lying spirit have had their hearts seduced from God and His holy fear, yet in words professed to be His people; who call themselves Jews, but are not; Christians, and are not, but of the synagogue of Satan; being strangers to the circumcision in spirit, and the baptism that is with fire and with the Holy Ghost. With fire to consume the fleshly nature; and with the Holy Ghost to beget the heavenly nature in man. O the downfall of this great city, and the desolation of this false church through all the sects in Christendom, is come and coming! Yea, in one day shall it be accomplished, even in the day of the appearance of Christ, who is the second Adam, the Lord from heaven, who by the brightness of His coming, and by the breath of His mouth in the hearts of nations shall reveal and destroy this great antichrist, this man of sin in man that sitteth in the place of God, yea, exalted above all that is called God, requiring conformity to all his inventions and injunctions upon pain of life, liberty, and estate. Nor are any suffered to buy or sell in this great city but such as will receive his mark.

Woe to you all in the name of the Lord that call God your Father and are not born of Him; that name His name, and hate to be reformed. That call Jesus Lord, and not by the Holy Ghost; who take His pure name into your mouths and depart not from iniquity. I say to you on God's behalf, as God said to the Jews of old; your prayers, your sacrifices, and your solemn assemblies, etc., in an unconverted state, are abomination to the Lord. No matter for your names, your pretences, your creeds, if you live without God in the world; that is, without His holy awe in your hearts, without a divine sense of His presence in your souls, and know not that godly sorrow that worketh unfeigned repentance, the only way to eternal life. Your worship God loatheth. A dog's neck, swine's blood, yea, to bless an idol or kill a man is altogether as acceptable with the Lord. O! God is wrath with the feigned worships as well as common ungodliness of the world. Come to Christ's spirit, be led of it, and do not your own wills but the will of Christ Jesus; and then you shall know the true worship. For the true ministry and worship of God stand not in the will, wisdom, or appointment of men, nor can they be performed by unregenerated men; but in the leadings of His eternal spirit, by whom all the faithful offer up themselves an acceptable sacrifice to God, not to live unto themselves, but to Him that hath purchased them. It is true Christ Jesus died for the ungodly, but not that they should continue ungodly, but take up His daily cross and follow Him. Christ (saith Peter) suffered for us, leaving us an example that we should follow His steps. As He was in this world so we should be, not conformable to the rudiments, fashions, and customs of this world that pass away; but transformed and renewed in our minds by the grace that He hath given us: which grace bringeth salvation to all that obey it, teaching such to deny all ungodliness, and worldly lusts, and to live soberly, righteously, and godly in this present evil world: because without holiness none shall ever see the Lord: that is God's decree.

Wherefore be you not deceived, O you formal and titular Christians; God will not be mocked: such as you sow, such shall you reap at the hand of the Lord. Yea, for every idle word shall you give an account in the day of judgment. Think not with yourselves you have Christ to your Saviour, and you are reconciled to God through Christ, and that God looketh not upon you as you are in yourselves, but as in Christ; whilst you walk not after the spirit, but after the flesh. For the wages of sin is death; but the gift of God is eternal life, through Jesus Christ our Lord. To whom? Not to them that despise His light in their hearts, that grieve His spirit, and by a worldly conversation go on to crucify Him; and who follow not Jesus in the way of tribulation and regeneration. God is of purer eyes than to behold iniquity; and He looketh upon men and women to be what they really are, and not what they imagine themselves to be. Behold He cometh, and His reward is with Him, and He will reward all according to their works. Sinners, while such, can no more come into Christ than into God; for God is in Christ, and Christ is in God: Christ is holy, harmless, pure, and undefiled, and separate from sinners. And if ever you would have God look upon you to be in Christ you must come into Christ. And you can never come into Christ, the new and heavenly man, that is undefiled and separated from sinners, till you come out of sin, and the author of it, the devil, the old man of sin, and leave your wicked deeds of darkness.

Therefore be ye separate from every evil way: Christ, the immaculate Lamb of God, came not only to save men from wrath, but from sin, which is the cause of wrath. Behold the Lamb of God, saith John, which taketh away the sins of the world. Not their sin that will not believe in Him, but the sins of those that are weary and heavy laden, that wait, hunger, thirst, and cry for His salvation; whom God hath given for a light to lighten the Gentiles, and for His salvation to the ends of the earth. O you that are called by His sacred name, repent, repent! Prepare, prepare to meet the Lord, who is coming in the way of His judgments to visit the inhabitants of the earth; and put away the evil of your doings, and turn to Him that He may receive you.

But woe in the name of the Lord to all that rebel against the light of Christ Jesus, who serve another master, and follow another captain, and obey the prince of the power of the air, who reigneth in the hearts of the children of disobedience. Yea, woe unto all who are covered with a covering, and not of my spirit; that take counsel, and not of Me, saith the Lord: who gather sticks and kindle a fire of their own, and compass themselves about in the sparks which they have kindled; for this shall they have at My hand, they shall lie down in sorrow.

Woe from God to all the will-worshippers who worship, but not in the spirit and in the truth; their worship is not available. He that worships God aright is turned to the spirit, and is taught and led by the spirit. And such as have received the spirit of Christ are not led by their own spirits, nor by the spirits of this world, nor according to the inventions and traditions of men: neither do they conform themselves to the customs and fashions of this world, nor will they bow to the glory of this world, or the God of it. But having seen Him, whom they have pierced with their vain conversation in times past, they mourn and are in great bitterness because they have done despite to His holy spirit of grace, that strove so long with them for their redemption. And being called by His spiritual call in their hearts to come out of Babylon, the great city of will-worship, confusion, and darkness that is in the earth, do cheerfully resign up all to follow Him in the narrow way of self-denial, as His holy disciples did of old. And such have learned by good experience that without Christ they can do nothing: though in these days scarcely anything is done with Him or by Him. For He is resisted in His spiritual appearance in the consciences of those that make a profession of Him with their mouths, and therefore He doth not many mighty works in them. Yea, He is smitten, spit upon, crowned with thorns, pierced, and crucified of all false Christians through their rebellion and wickedness.

O woe from the great and just God that made heaven and earth, upon all people that work iniquity and forget God! Woe to you kings and princes that have crucified the Lord of life and glory; yea, you have crucified Him in yourselves, and helped to crucify Him in others. He lieth slain at this day in your streets. For you have not ruled for God as you ought to have done, but for yourselves to please your own lusts; and have not sought the glory of the Lord, nor the prosperity of His work in the earth, so much as the greatness of your own names, and to enlarge your worldly dominions, often oppressing the poor, and persecuting conscientious dissenters; but suffering almost all manner of vice and vanity to go unpunished. How doth the lust of the eye, the lust of the flesh, and the pride of life reign in your territories? Are not your courts the very schools of vanity and nurseries of worldly lusts and pleasures which war against the soul and lead to eternal destruction? O! you have much to answer for before the great God at the day of His terrible tribunal, who have power in your hands to chase away wickedness and to reform the world. It is written, a king upon his throne of judgment scattereth all evil with his eye. O! that the kings and princes of the world knew this throne of true judgment! That they had this godlike majesty, that they would purge their lands of evil doers, that they and their people might escape the wrath and vengeance of God, that is ready to be poured forth upon them!

And woe to you nobles of the earth that spend your estates in pleasures, and your days in vanity, that like those of old drink wine in bowls, and stretch yourselves upon couches of ivory, that invent musical instruments for your mirth, but remember not the afflictions of Joseph, neither consider of your latter end. What pride, lust, and excess lie at your doors! What spoil and waste do you make in the world! You live as if you should never die, caring only what you should eat, what you should drink, and what you should put on; how you should trim, perfume, and beautify your poor mortal selves, and at which plays and sports you should divert and spend away that troublesome and melancholy thing called time (as you esteem it), instead of redeeming the time, because the days are evil, and preparing for the eternal judgment. Is this the way to glory? Did Jesus give you this example? O! He is crucified by these things! This is far from the true nobility and Christian honour that cometh from above.

Woe to you judges of the earth who pervert judgment for a reward, that oppress the poor, and despise the cause of the needy, who regard the mighty and the rich in judgment, and delay justice for the fear or favour of man. That subject the laws to your wills, and righteous rules to your passions and interest. Repent and be just, for God, the just God, the great judge of heaven and earth, shall judge you all according to your works. And dreadful shall that day of His reckoning and tribunal be to all the workers of iniquity. But especially to unjust and corrupt judges.

And woe to you lawyers that refuse no cause for money, but will plead even against law, truth, and justice for advantage, teaching your tongues to advocate for a lie, and your mouths for gain to plead the cause of unrighteousness; raising unreasonable wealth unto yourselves by the folly, ignorance, and contention of the people. O the equivocation, deceit, falsehood, and iniquity that is in your profession, in which you let your consciences out to hire at every summons, for all sorts of causes. Insomuch that it is the money and not the cause that prevaileth. And the worst cause most commonly is most desired, because the client, doubtful of his success, is usually the most liberal to you. This also is for judgment.

And woe to you merchants and traders that have not the Lord's fear before your eyes, whose God is gold and gain, that neither buy nor sell with regard to His just principle in your consciences, that use vain and deceitful words, and that are not come to the just measure and the righteous balance, but use frauds for advantage: that neither eye the Lord's providence by sea nor His care by land; but day and night cast about how to raise to yourselves a great name and estate to exalt your nests and rank your families among the rich and the noble of the earth! The Lord will also plead with you. Repent, and fear before God.

Woe to you farmers and countrymen that reward the Lord evil for good, who giveth you increase of all things in their proper seasons, yet you discern not His hand, you regard not His care; you live without God in the world: yet no life is fuller of the Lord's providence, who preserveth and prospereth your flocks, who increaseth your wine, your corn, and your grass; instead of remembering His goodness with reverence, and in your harvests praising Him with fear, you sacrifice to your lusts, and rejoice only in your fullness; making merry at your harvests without the fear of God, or looking to Him that giveth you the increase. Repent and fear before the God of the whole earth.

But above all others. Woe to you Scribes, Pharisees, and hypocrites, you priests and pastors who have taken a charge that God never gave you; who run, and He never sent you; who say, thus saith the Lord, and He never spoke to you, or by you. That steal the words of the prophets and apostles, and with them make merchandise to the people, not knowing the pure word of God in your hearts, to be as a hammer, a fire, a sword, to destroy sin, and to purge, redeem, and reconcile you to God; but boast in other men's lines, and speak things made ready to your hands. That teach for hire, and divine for money; who seek honour of men, and love the uppermost places at feasts. Who speak peace to the wicked, and sow pillows under their elbows for reward: pleasers of men more than pleasers of God. Woe to you in the name of the Lord that counterfeit His commission and deceive the people, requiring their money for that which is not bread, and their labour for that which doth not profit. At your doors lieth the blood of souls in which you have traded. O you physicians of no value, whom have you cured? Where is the seal of your ministry? Is it not an abominable cheat that you take money to cure, yet cannot cure; that have no medicine to cure; and at last maintain that the disease is incurable? You are they that will neither enter into the kingdom yourselves nor suffer others. For whenever we have seen your delusions, and deserted your assemblies, presently a packet of letters must be sent to Damascus. The magistrate must be called upon to be jailer and hangman for the priest. What wars, changes, and persecutions ever befell the world since you had a being, in which you have not been at head or tail? O your practices shall more and more come to light: and the day hasteneth that your very name and calling (as now held) shall be had in abhorrence by the nations. O you numerous offspring of the great false prophet that hath been a liar from the beginning; hereby is it known that God hath never sent you that you have not profited the people; they are God's words by the prophet Jeremy. Weep and howl for the day of your great calamity hasteneth upon you! Your father and mother are come into remembrance before the Lord, the hour of their judgment is at the door. God will fill you the cup of His fury, you shall drink it at His hand.

O! I cannot but cry aloud to you all, of all ranks and qualities, from the highest to the lowest that walk not after the spirit, but after the flesh, daily fulfilling the lusts thereof; that you would repent and be saved. O how hath Christ's religion been profaned, and His holy name blasphemed by the lewd life of professed Christians! The very heathens are scandalised, and the nations round about have you in scorn and derision. Arise, O God, for Thy Name's sake! O what tremendous oaths and lies! What revenge and murders, with drunkenness and gluttony! What pride and luxury! What chamberings and wantonness! What fornications, rapes, and adulteries! What masks and revels! What lustful ornaments and enchanting attires! What proud customs and vain complements! What sports and pleasures! What plays and romances! What intrigues and pastimes! Again, what falseness and treachery! What avarice and oppression! What flattery and hypocrisy! What malice and slander! What contention and law-suits? What wars and bloodshed! What plunders, fires, and desolations! And it is not only committed by Christians in general one against another, but by Christians of the same faith, sect, and church one against another; praying to the same God to destroy one another; and singing psalms to God when they have wickedly destroyed one another. O the rapes, fires, murders, and rivers of blood that lie at the doors of professed Christians! If this be godly, what is devilish? If this be Christian, what is Paganish? What is anti-Christian, but to make God a party to their wickedness? O profanation! O blasphemy! What need is there of any other demonstration, that Christendom is foully apostatised from the doctrine and example of Christ Jesus and His true followers, who saith, if ye love Me, keep My commandments. By this shall all men know that ye are My disciples, if ye have love one to another. And John said, whosoever doth not love his brother is not of God, and whosoever hateth his brother is a murderer; and ye know that no murderer hath eternal life abiding in him. And it is not to be supposed that they kill one another in love: for murder is not the effect of love and brotherly kindness, but of malice, envy, and revenge. O

Christendom! how art thou and thy children degenerated from God, and fallen from the doctrine of Christ, whose holy name thou professest! Thou art become a city full of uncleanness, committing whoredom under every green tree; following other lovers than Jesus, whose spouse thou professest to be. O thou rebellious city, thou cage of unclean birds, thou and thy children have filled the earth with the stink of your abominations!

O how expert have you been in these impieties! How ingenious to work wickedness, and how fruitful in your inventions to gratify the lust of the eye, the lust of the flesh, and the pride of life! O how hath the heathen nature as an evil leaven prevailed, and leavened the great body of Christians at this day, as if the end of Christ's coming into the world had been to furnish us with a new profession, but not to give us a new nature; to learn men to talk, and not to live; to cry hosanna, but in works to crucify Him. What did the heathens that Christians have not done? Yea, the same lusts, vanities, and impieties that reigned among them are to be found improved among Christians. So that it is Paganism made free of the Christian profession, or heathenism Christianised. And not to conform to the heathen in the Christian is not to be a Christian but a heathen. O the ignorance as well as wickedness of the present Christian world! Verily, the Christian life is oppressed under this mass of darkness and impiety, found in the conversations of apostate Christians, even as Christ was grieved and burdened with the darkness and obstinacy of the apostate Jews. And as the hard-heartedness of the false Jews crucified Him outwardly, so hath the hard-heartedness of the false Christians crucified Him inwardly: which hath fulfilled what is recorded in the Apocalypse, viz., that the Lord was crucified in Sodom and Egypt spiritually so called: for the false Christians are the spiritual Sodom and Egypt, who love and live in Sodom's sins, and Egypt's lusts and pleasures. Yea, they are of the race of them that stoned the prophets and crucified the Lord of glory: of the same nature and spirit. O the blood of Jesus lieth at their doors shed, spilt, and trod under foot of them, and will one day cry for eternal vengeance against them if they repent not with unfeigned sorrow, and turn to the Lord with their whole hearts: certainly, woe, anguish, and tribulation shall be their portion for ever! That which they have grieved shall grieve them; and that which they have bruised and resisted shall reject and torment them; yea, it shall be a never-dying worm, and an endless pain to them. O woe to the worker of iniquity in that day! Woe to the slothful servant! Woe to the mocker and scoffer! Woe to the drunkard and unclean person! Woe to them that spend their days in vanity and their lives in earthly pleasures! Woe to the proud Pharisee and disdainful Scribe! Woe to the fearful and unbelieving! Woe to idolaters and liars! Yea, and woe from God to all the cruel persecutors of the innocent lambs and sheep of Jesus, for their pure conscience to Him! For they shall have their part in the lake that burneth with fire and brimstone, which is the second death.

O that you might escape this great damnation! And I testify to you in the word of the Lord, that God giveth unto you all a day of visitation in which you may escape the wrath to come. For this end God hath sent His son a light into your hearts; it is He which manifesteth all your thoughts, words, and deeds unto you; it is He which checks and reproveth you; yea, it is He which expostulateth and striveth with you; it is He that knocketh at your doors and awakeneth you to judgment. Who condemneth every unfruitful thought, word, and work in you. Repent, I exhort you, turn to Him, hear His voice, and harden not your hearts; but while it is to-day, and the light shineth, and the spirit striveth, O humble yourselves, hear His judgments, love His reproofs. And though His word be as a fire in your hearts, and though you are even scorched within you, because of the heat thereof, yet bear the indignation of the Lord in that you have sinned against Him. Wait, watch, and walk in the light of the Lord Jesus, that in His blood you may feel remission of sins, and sanctification unto life eternal. That you may no more walk after the flesh to fulfil the lusts thereof, but in the spirit of holiness; that you may be sealed unto the day of redemption. O the peace, the joy, the pleasure, and the undeclarable comfort that is daily met with in the holy and righteous way of the Lord.

O this riseth powerfully in my soul that His form hath no comeliness in it, that will please flesh; His way and worship is most remote from it. Flesh and blood have no share in

His worship; the will and runnings of man have no part in His way. It is neither at the mountain where one sort runneth; not at Jerusalem whither another sort goeth; but in spirit within the veil, hid from flesh and blood. Yea, there it is that His worship is known and performed. Any form is more pleasant than this: His visage is more marred than any man's. All will-worship, all human invention, findeth acceptance where He cannot find a place to lay His head on. O this is a bitter cup to the creature; few will drink it! They are hard to be persuaded to sit still and patiently to wait for the salvation of God, to let Him work all their works in them and for them. They know not what it is to have the mouth in the dust, to have all flesh silent before the Lord, that the voice of God may be heard; that He may prepare them, and that the will of God may be brought forth in them. O this mystery of iniquity, how hath it wrought, and how doth it yet work! It claimeth a right to the living child; but she hath no right to it: she is the womb of death, and can bring forth no living fruit to God. All nations have drunk her cup. But the hour of her judgment is come. She is seen, disveiled, and condemned by the living spirit of God, that is felt, and received, and obeyed by a remnant who are gathered from the mouths of idol shepherds, and all the errings and strayings of false prophets that have no vision; and are come to the Lord to know His law in their hearts, and fear and spirit to be in their inward parts, and are taught and led by Him. And these follow the Lamb, and are His host this day that fight under His banner with His holy testimony against the whore, false prophet, and beast. And behold they shall prevail. For greater is He that is in them than he that is in the world.

O this is a great mystery, but a greater truth. Moses the servant is externally more comely than He. Yea, the prophets were as pleasant singers and as delightful instruments of music; their visions, sights, and glorious prophecies of the last days and new covenant times were (says one of them of old) as a pleasant song. But the Son, the substance, when He came, no beauty, no excellency, no comeliness. What is the matter? The way is narrow for flesh and blood; there is a cross must be taken up, a bitter cup drunk, and a baptism, yea, of blood gone through. Man must die to his own will, affections, imaginations, and carnal conceptions; he must wait and watch, yea, continually. His own religion and righteousness is as odious as his sin and iniquity, yea, in a sense more dangerous. It is no outside will do; not that which pleaseth the busy, active will and mind of the creature; that gratifieth the external senses, that have prevailed against the soul: O no, it is a hidden life, a hidden temple, a hidden worship, and that in God's time; yea, a hidden manna, a hidden supper, not discernible by the vain sects of this world. Of this tabernacle is Jesus builder; of this covenant and worship is He author; of this altar is He priest. To this did He gather His of old, and to this is He gathering the nations. And the bride saith, come, and the spirit saith, come; and He saith, come. And blessed are they that come and see how good He is.

But such who, like Sodom of old, go on to grieve the spirit of the Lord, to rebel against His light, and vex God's just lot, that liveth in the midst of them, persisting in their lusts and abominations, God's angel shall smite them with blindness. The day of their visitation shall pass away, and the forbearance of God shall be at an end, and fire from heaven shall devour them. Which with my soul I fervently and tenderly desire you may all escape, whom God hath taught to hate your sin, deny your glory, and separate from all your false worships by His own light, spirit, and truth, and to follow His dear Son in the way of regeneration, whose love to me hath taught me to love all mankind, and to seek their salvation.

W. PENN.

AMSTERDAM, *the 20th of the 8th month*, 1677.

A BRIEF ACCOUNT OF THE RISE AND PROGRESS OF THE PEOPLE CALLED QUAKERS

A BRIEF ACCOUNT OF THE RISE AND PROGRESS OF THE PEOPLE CALLED QUAKERS

In which their Fundamental Principle, Doctrines, Worship, Ministry, and Discipline are plainly declared, etc.

AN EPISTLE TO THE READER

Reader,—This following account of the people called Quakers, etc., was written in the fear and love of God. First, as a standing testimony to that ever blessed truth in the inward parts with which God in my youthful time visited my soul, and for the sense and love of which I was made willing in no ordinary way to relinquish the honours and interests of the world. Secondly, as a testimony for that despised people that God has in His great mercy gathered and united by His own blessed spirit in the holy profession of it; whose fellowship I value above all worldly greatness. Thirdly, in love and honour to the memory of that worthy servant of God, G. Fox, the first instrument thereof, and therefore styled by me the great and blessed apostle of our day. As this gave birth to what is here presented to thy view in the first edition of it, by way of preface to G. F.'s excellent journal; so the consideration of the present usefulness of the following account of the people called Quakers (by reason of the unjust reflections of some adversaries that once walked under the profession of Friends) and the exhortations that conclude it, prevailed with me to consent that it should be republished in a smaller volume; knowing also full well that great books, especially in these days, grow burthensome, both to the pockets and minds of too many; and that there are not a few that desire (so it be at an easy rate) to be informed about this people that have been so much everywhere spoken against. But, blessed be the God and Father of our Lord Jesus Christ, it is upon no worse grounds than it was said of old time of the primitive Christians; as I hope will appear to every sober and considerate reader. Our business after all the ill-usage we have met with being the realities of religion, an effectual change before our last and great change. That all may come to an inward, sensible, and experimental knowledge of God through the convictions and operations of the light and spirit of Christ in themselves; the sufficient and blessed means given to all, that thereby all may come savingly to know the only true God and Jesus Christ whom He hath sent to enlighten and redeem the world: which knowledge is indeed eternal life. And that thou, Reader, mayest obtain it is the earnest desire of him that is ever thine in so good a work,

W. P.

CHAPTER I

CONTAINING A BRIEF ACCOUNT OF DIVERS DISPENSATIONS OF GOD IN THE WORLD TO THE TIME HE WAS PLEASED TO RAISE THIS DESPISED PEOPLE CALLED QUAKERS.

DIVERS have been the dispensations of God since the creation of the world unto the sons of men; but the great end of all of them has been the renown of His own excellent name in the creation and restoration of man: man, the emblem of himself as a God on earth, and the glory of all His works. The world began with innocency: all was then good that the good God had made: and as He blessed the works of His hands, so their natures and harmony magnified Him their Creator. Then the morning stars sang together for joy, and all parts of His works said Amen to His law. Not a jar in the whole frame; but man in paradise, the beasts in the field, the fowl in the air, the fish in the sea, the lights in the heavens, the fruits of the earth; yea, the air, the earth, the water, and fire worshipped, praised, and exalted His power, wisdom, and goodness. O holy Sabbath, O holy day to the Lord!

But this happy state lasted not long. For man, the crown and glory of the whole, being tempted to aspire above his place unhappily yielded against command and duty, as well as interest and felicity, and so fell below it; lost the divine image, the wisdom, power, and purity He was made in. By which, being no longer fit for paradise, he was expelled that garden of God, his proper dwelling and residence, and was driven out as a poor vagabond from the presence of the Lord to wander in the earth, the habitation of beasts.

Yet God that made him had pity on him; for He seeing man was deceived, and that it was not of malice or an original presumption in him, but through the subtilty of the serpent (who had first fallen from his own state, and by the mediation of the woman, man's own nature and companion, whom the serpent had first deluded) in His infinite goodness and wisdom found out a way to repair the breach, recover the loss, and restore fallen man again by a nobler and more excellent Adam, promised to be born of a woman; that as by means of a woman the evil one had prevailed upon man, by a woman also He should come into the world who would prevail against him and bruise his head, and deliver man from his power. And which in a signal manner, by the dispensation of the Son of God in the flesh, in the fulness of time was personally and fully accomplished by Him and in Him as man's Saviour and Redeemer.

But His power was not limited in the manifestation of it to that time; for both before and since His blessed manifestation in the flesh He has been the light and life, the rock and strength of all that ever feared God; was present with them in their temptations, followed them in their travels and afflictions, and supported and carried them through and over the difficulties that have attended them in their earthly pilgrimage. By this Abel's heart excelled Cain's, and Seth obtained the pre-eminence, and Enoch walked with God. It was this that strove with the old world, and which they rebelled against, and which sanctified and instructed Noah to salvation.

But the outward dispensation that followed the benighted state of man after his fall, especially among the patriarchs, was generally that of angels; as the Scriptures of the Old Testament do in many places express, as to Abraham, Jacob, etc. The next was that of the law by Moses, which was also delivered by angels, as the apostle tells us. This dispensation was much outward, and suited to a low and servile state;

called therefore by the apostle Paul that of a schoolmaster, which was to point out and prepare that people to look and long for the Messiah, who would deliver them from the servitude of a ceremonious and imperfect dispensation by knowing the realities of those mysterious representations in themselves. In this time the law was written on stone, the temple built with hands, attended with an outward priesthood and external rites and ceremonies, that were shadows of the good things that were to come, and were only to serve till the seed came, or the more excellent and general manifestation of Christ, to whom was the promise, and to all men only in Him, in whom it was yea and Amen, even life from death, immortality, and eternal life.

This the prophets foresaw, and comforted the believing Jews in the certainty of it; which was the top of the Mosaical dispensation, and which ended in John's ministry, the forerunner of the Messiah, as John's was finished in Him, the fulness of all. And then God that at sundry times and in divers manners had spoken to the fathers by His servants the prophets, spoke to men by His Son Christ Jesus, who is heir of all things; being the gospel day, which is the dispensation of sonship; bringing in thereby a nearer testament and a better hope; even the beginning of the glory of the latter days, and of the restitution of all things; yea, the restoration of the kingdom unto Israel.

Now the spirit that was more sparingly communicated in former dispensations began to be poured forth upon all flesh, according to the prophet Joel, and the light that shined in darkness, or but dimly before, the most gracious God caused to shine out of darkness, and the day star began to arise in the hearts of believers, giving unto them the knowledge of God in the face (or appearance) of His Son Christ Jesus.

Now the poor in spirit, the meek, the true mourners, the hungry and thirsty after righteousness, the peacemakers, the pure in heart, the merciful, and persecuted came more especially in remembrance before the Lord, and were sought out and blessed by Israel's true shepherd. Old Jerusalem with her children grew out of date, and the New Jerusalem into request, the mother of the sons of the gospel day. Wherefore no more at old Jerusalem nor at the mountain of Samaria will God be worshipped above other places; for behold He is by His own Son declared and preached a spirit, and that He will be known as such, and worshipped in the spirit and in the truth! He will now come nearer than of old time, and He will write His law in the heart, and put His fear and spirit in the inward parts, according to His promise. Then signs, types, and shadows flew away, the day having discovered their insufficiency in not reaching to the inside of the cup, to the cleansing of the conscience; and all elementary services were expired in and by Him that is the substance of all.

And to this great and blessed end of the dispensation of the Son of God did the apostles testify, whom He had chosen and anointed by His spirit, to turn the Jews from their prejudice and superstition, and the Gentiles from their vanity and idolatry to Christ's light and spirit that shined in them; that they might be quickened from the sins and trespasses in which they were dead to serve the living God in the newness of the spirit of life, and walk as children of the light and of the day, even the day of holiness. For such put on Christ, the light of the world, and make no more provision for the flesh to fulfil the lusts thereof. So that the light, spirit, and grace that come by Christ and appear in man were that divine principle the apostles ministered from and turned people's minds unto, and in which they gathered and built up the churches of Christ in their day. For which cause they advise them not to quench the spirit, but to wait for the spirit, and speak by the spirit, and pray by the spirit, and walk in the spirit too, as that which approved them, the truly begotten children of God; born not of flesh and blood, or of the will of man, but of the will of God; by doing His will and denying their own; by drinking of Christ's cup, and being baptised with His baptism of self-denial; the way and path that all the heirs of life have ever trod to blessedness. But alas! even in the apostles' days those bright stars of the first magnitude of the gospel light, some clouds foretelling an eclipse of this primitive glory began to appear, and several of them gave early caution of it to the Christians of their time, that even then there was, and yet would be more and more, a falling away from the power of godliness, and the purity of that spiritual dispensation by such as sought to make a fair show in the flesh, but with whom the offence of the cross ceased. Yet with this comfortable conclusion that they saw beyond it a more glorious time than ever to the true Church. Their sight was true, and what they foretold to the churches, gathered by them in the name and power of Jesus, came to pass. For Christians degenerated apace into outsides, as days and meats, and divers other ceremonies. And which was worse, they fell into strife and contention about them; separating one from another, then envying and, as they had power, persecuting one another to the shame and scandal of their common Christianity, and grievous stumbling and offence of the heathen; among whom the Lord had so long and so marvellously preserved them. And having got at last the worldly power into their hands by kings and emperors embracing the Christian profession, they changed, what they could, the kingdom of Christ, which is not of this world, into a worldly kingdom; or at least styled the worldly kingdom that was in their hands the kingdom of Christ, and so they became worldly and not true Christians. The human inventions and novelties, both in doctrine and worship, crowded fast into the church; a door opened thereunto by the grossness and carnality that appeared then among the generality of Christians, who had long since left the guidance of God's meek and heavenly spirit, and given themselves up to superstition, will-worship, and voluntary humility. And as superstition is blind, so it is heady and furious, for all must stoop to its blind and boundless zeal or perish by it; in the name of the spirit persecuting the very appearance of the spirit of God in others, and opposing that in others which they resisted in themselves, viz., the light, grace, and spirit of the Lord Jesus Christ; but always under the notion of innovation, heresy, schism, or some such plausible name. Though Christianity allows of no name or pretence whatever for persecuting of any man for matters of mere religion, being in its very nature meek, gentle, and forbearing; and consists of faith, hope, and charity, which no persecutor can have whilst he remains a persecutor; in that a man cannot believe well, or hope well, or have a charitable or tender regard to another whilst he would violate his mind or persecute his body for matters of faith or worship towards his God.

Thus the false church sprang up and mounted the chair. But though she lost her nature she would needs keep her good name of the Lamb's-bride, the true church, and mother of the faithful: constraining all to receive her mark, either in their forehead or right hand; that is, publicly or privately. But indeed and in truth she was mystery Babylon, the mother of harlots, mother of those that with all their show and outside of religion were adulterated and gone from the spirit, nature, and life of Christ, and grown vain, worldly, ambitious, covetous, cruel, etc., which are the fruits of the flesh and not of the spirit.

Now it was that the true church fled into the wilderness, that is, from superstition and violence, to a retired, solitary, and lonely state; hidden and, as it were, out of sight of men though not out of the world. Which shows that her wanted visibility was not essential to the being of a true church in the judgment of the Holy Ghost; she being as true a church in the wilderness, though not as visible and lustrous, as when she was in her former splendour of profession. In this state she made many attempts to return, but the waters were yet too high, and her way blocked up, and many of her excellent children in several nations and centuries fell by the cruelty of superstition, because they would not fall from their faithfulness to the truth.

The last age did set some steps towards it, both as to doctrine, worship, and practice. But practice quickly failed; for wickedness flowed in a little time as well among the professors of the reformation as those they reformed from; so that by the fruits of conversation they were not to be distinguished. And the children of the reformers, if not the reformers themselves, betook themselves very early to earthly policy and power, to uphold and carry on their reformation that had been begun with spiritual weapons; which I have often thought has been one of the greatest reasons the reformation made no better progress as to the life and soul of religion. For whilst the reformers were lowly and spiritually minded, and trusted in God, and looked to Him, and lived in His fear, and consulted not with flesh and blood, nor sought deliverance in their own way, there were daily added to the church such as one might reasonably say should be saved. For they were not so careful to be safe from persecution as to be faithful and inoffensive under it; being more concerned to spread the truth by their faith and patience in tribulation than to get the worldly power out of their hands that inflicted those sufferings upon them. And it will be well if the Lord suffer them not to fall by the very same way they took to stand.

In doctrine they were in some things short; in other things, to avoid one extreme they ran into another. And for worship there was for the generality more of man in it than of God. They owned the spirit, inspiration, and revelation indeed, and grounded their separation and reformation upon the sense and understanding they received from it in the reading of the Scriptures of truth. And this was their plea, the Scripture is the text, the spirit the interpreter, and that to everyone for himself. But yet there was too much of human invention, tradition, and art that remained both in praying and preaching; and of worldly authority, and worldly greatness in their ministers; especially in this kingdom, Sweden, Denmark, and some parts of Germany. God was therefore pleased in England to shift us from vessel to vessel: and the next remove humbled the ministry so that they were more strict in preaching, devout in praying, and zealous for keeping the Lord's day, and catechising of children and servants, and repeating at home in their families what they had heard in public. But even as these grew into power they were not only for whipping some out, but others into the temple. And they appeared rigid in their spirits rather than severe in their lives, and more for a party than for piety. Which brought forth another people that were yet more retired and select.

They would not communicate at large or in common with others; but formed churches among themselves of such as could give some account of their conversion, at least, of very promising experiences of the work of God's grace upon their hearts; and under mutual agreements and covenants of fellowship they kept together. These people were somewhat of a softer temper, and seemed to recommend religion by the charms of its love, mercy, and goodness, rather than by the terrors of its judgments and punishments; by which the former party would have awed people into religion.

They also allowed greater liberty to prophecy than those before them; for they admitted any member to speak or pray as well as their pastor, whom they always chose, and not the civil magistrate. If such found anything pressing upon them to either duty, even without the distinction of clergy or laity, persons of any trade had their liberty, be it never so low and mechanical. But alas! even these people suffered great loss. For tasting of worldly empire and the favour of princes, and the gain that ensued, they degenerated but too much. For though they had cried down national churches and ministry, and maintenance too, some of them when it was their own turn to be tried fell under the weight of worldly honour and advantage, got into profitable parsonages too much, and outlived and contradicted their own principles. And, which was yet worse, turned, some of them, absolute persecutors of other men for God's sake, that but so lately came themselves out of the furnace; which drove many a step farther, and that was into the water: another baptism, as believing they were not scripturally baptised; and hoping to find that presence and power of God in submitting to this watery ordinance, which they desired and wanted.

These people also made profession of neglecting, if not renouncing and censuring not only the necessity, but use of all human learning, as to the ministry; and all other qualifications to it, besides the helps and gifts of the spirit of God, and those natural and common to men. And for a time they seemed like John of old, a burning and a shining light to other societies.

They were very diligent, plain, and serious; strong in Scripture, and bold in profession; bearing much reproach and contradiction. But that which others fell by proved their snare. For worldly power spoiled them too; who had enough of it to try them what they would do if they had more. And they rested also too much upon their watery dispensation instead of passing on more fully to that of the fire and Holy Ghost, which was His baptism, who came with a fan in His hand that He might thoroughly (and not in part only) purge His floor and take away the dross and the tin of His people, and make a man finer than gold. Withal, they grew high, rough, and self-righteous, opposing farther attainment; too much forgetting the day of their infancy and littleness, which gave them something of a real beauty; insomuch that many left them, and all visible churches and societies, and wandered up and down as sheep without a shepherd, and as doves without their mates; seeking their beloved but could not find Him (as their souls desired to know Him) whom their souls loved above their chiefest joy.

These people were called seekers by some, and the family of love by others; because as they came to the knowledge of one another they sometimes met together not formally to pray or preach at appointed times or places in their own wills, as in times past they were accustomed to do; but waited together in silence, and as anything rose in any one of their minds that they thought savoured of a divine spring, they sometimes spoke. But so it was that some of them, not keeping in humility and in the fear of God, after the abundance of revelation, were exalted above measure; and for want of staying their minds in a humble dependance upon Him that opened their understandings to see great things in His law, they ran out in their own imaginations, and mixing them with those divine openings brought forth a monstrous birth to the scandal of those that feared God, and waited daily in the temple not made with hands for the consolation of Israel; the Jew inward, and circumcision in spirit.

This people obtained the names of ranters, from their extravagant discourses and practices. For they interpreted Christ's fulfilling of the law for us to be a discharging of us from any obligation and duty the law required of us, instead of the condemnation of the law for sins past upon faith and repentance. And that now it was no sin to do that which before it was a sin to commit; the slavish fear of the law being taken off by Christ, and all things good that man did, if He did but do them with the mind and persuasion that it was so. Insomuch that divers fell into gross and enormous practices; pretending in excuse thereof that they could without evil commit the same act which was sin in another to do; thereby distinguishing between the action and the evil of it by the discretion of the mind and intention in the doing of it. Which was to make sin superabound by the aboundings of grace, and to turn from the grace of God into wantonness; a securer way of sinning than before. As if Christ came not to save us from our sins, but in our sins; not to take away sin, but that we might sin more freely at His cost, and with less danger to ourselves. I say this ensnared divers, and brought them to an utter and lamentable loss as to their eternal state; and they grew very troublesome to the better sort of people, and furnished the looser with an occasion to profane.

CHAPTER II

OF THE RISE OF THIS PEOPLE, THEIR FUNDAMENTAL PRINCIPLE, AND DOCTRINE, AND PRACTICE IN TWELVE POINTS RESULTING FROM IT. THEIR PROGRESS AND SUFFERINGS. AN EXPOSTULATION WITH ENGLAND THEREUPON

It was about that very time, as you may see in G. F.'s Annals, that the eternal, wise, and good God was pleased in His infinite love to honour and visit this benighted and bewildered nation with His glorious dayspring from on high; yea, with a most sure and certain sound of the word of light and life, through the testimony of a chosen vessel to an effectual and blessed purpose, can many thousands say, Glory be to the name of the Lord for ever.

For as it reached the conscience and broke the heart and brought many to a sense and search, so that which people had been vainly seeking without, with much pains and cost, they by this ministry found within where it was they wanted what they sought for, viz., the right way to peace with God. For they were directed to the light of Jesus Christ within them as the seed and leaven of the kingdom of God; near all, because in all, and God's talent to all. A faithful and true witness, and just monitor in every bosom. The gift and grace of God, to life and salvation that appears to all, though few regard it. This the traditional Christian, conceited of himself, and strong in his own will and righteousness, overcome with blind zeal and passion, either despised as a low and common thing, or opposed as a novelty, under many hard names and opprobrious terms, denying in his ignorant and angry mind any fresh manifestations of God's power and spirit in man in these days, though never more needed to make true Christians. Not unlike those Jews of old that rejected the Son of God at the very same time that they blindly professed to wait for the Messiah to come; because, alas! He appeared not among them according to their carnal mind and expectation.

This brought forth many abusive books, which filled the greater sort with envy, and lesser with rage; and made the way and progress of this blessed testimony straight and narrow indeed to those that received it. However, God owned His own work, and this testimony did effectually reach, gather, comfort, and establish the weary and heavy laden, the hungry and thirsty, the poor and needy, the mournful and sick of many maladies, that have spent all upon physicians of no value, and waited for relief from heaven; help only from above: seeing, upon a serious trial of all things, nothing else would do but Christ Himself; the light of His countenance, a touch of His garment, and help from His hand; who cured the poor woman's issue, raised the centurion's servant, the widow's son, the ruler's daughter, and Peter's mother. And like her they no sooner felt His power and efficacy upon their souls but they gave up to obey Him in a testimony to His power; and that with resigned wills and faithful hearts, through all mockings, contradictions, beatings, prisons, and many other jeopardies that attended them for His blessed name's sake.

And truly they were very many and very great; so that in all human probability they must have been swallowed up quick of the proud and boisterous waves that swelled and beat against them, but that the God of all their tender mercies was with them in His glorious authority; so that the hills often fled and the mountains melted before the power that filled them; working mightily for them as well as in them, one ever following the other. By which they saw plainly, to their exceeding great confirmation and comfort, that all things were possible with Him with whom they had to do. And that the more that which God required seemed to cross man's wisdom, and expose them to man's wrath, the more God appeared to help and carry them through all to His glory.

Insomuch that if ever any people could say in truth, thou art our sun and our shield, our rock and sanctuary; and by thee we have leaped over a wall, and by thee we have run through a troop, and by thee we have put the armies of the aliens to flight, these people had right to say it. And as God had delivered their souls of the wearisome burdens of sin and vanity, and enriched their poverty of spirit, and satisfied their great hunger and thirst after eternal righteousness, and filled them with the good things of His own house, and made them stewards of His manifold gifts; so they went forth to all quarters of these nations to declare to the inhabitants thereof what God had done for them; what they had found, and where and how they had found it, viz., the way to peace with God. Inviting all to come and see, and taste for themselves, the truth of what they declared unto them.

And as their testimony was to the principle of God in man, the precious pearl and leaven of the kingdom, as the only blessed means appointed of God to quicken, convince, and sanctify man; so they opened to them what it was in itself, and what it was given to them for: how they might know it from their own spirit, and that of the subtle appearance of the evil one; and what it would do for all those whose minds should be turned off from the vanity of the world, and its lifeless ways and teachers, and adhere to His blessed light in themselves, which discovers and condemns sin in all its appearances, and shows how to overcome it if minded and obeyed in its holy manifestations and convictions: giving power to such to avoid and resist those things that do not please God, and to grow strong in love, faith, and good works. That so man, whom sin hath made as a wilderness, overrun with briars and thorns, might become as the garden of God, cultivated by His divine power, and replenished with the most virtuous and beautiful plants of God's own right-hand planting to His eternal praise.

But these experimental preachers of glad tidings of God's truth and kingdom could not run when they list, or pray or preach when they pleased, but as Christ their Redeemer prepared and moved them by His own blessed spirit, for which they waited in their services and meetings, and spoke as that gave them utterance; and which was as those having authority, and not like the dreaming, dry, and formal Pharisees. And so it plainly appeared to the serious-minded, whose spiritual eye the Lord Jesus had in any measure opened: so that to one was given the word of exhortation, to another the word of reproof, to another the word of consolation, and all by the same spirit, and in the good order thereof, to the convincing and edifying of many.

And truly they waxed strong and bold through faithfulness; and by the power and spirit of the Lord Jesus became very fruitful; thousands, in a short time, being turned to the truth in the inward parts, through their testimony, in ministry and sufferings. Insomuch as in most countries, and many of the considerable towns of England, meetings were settled, and daily there were added such as should be saved. For they were diligent to plant and to water, and the Lord blessed their labours with an exceeding great increase; notwithstanding all the opposition made to their blessed progress by false rumours, calumnies, and bitter persecutions; not only from the powers of the earth, but from every one that listed to injure and abuse them: so that they seemed indeed to be as poor sheep appointed to the slaughter, and as a people killed all the day long.

It were fitter for a volume than a preface, but so much as to repeat the contents of their cruel sufferings from professors as well as from profane, and from magistrates as well as the rabble: that it may be said of this abused and despised people they went forth weeping and sowed in tears, bearing testimony to the precious seed, even the seed of the kingdom, which stands not in words, the finest, the highest that man's wit can use, but in power: the power of Christ Jesus, to whom God the Father hath given all power in heaven and in earth that He might rule angels above and men below. Who impowered them, as their work witnesseth, by the many that were turned, through their ministry, from darkness to the light, and out of the broad into the narrow way of life and peace; bringing people to a weighty, serious, and godlike conversation; the practice of that doctrine which they taught.

And as without this secret divine power there is no quickening and regenerating of dead souls, so the want of this generating and begetting power and life is the cause of the little fruit that the many ministries that have been and are in the world bring forth. O that both ministers and people were sensible of this! My soul is often troubled for them, and sorrow and mourning compass me about for their sakes. O that they were wise! O that they would consider and lay to heart the things that truly and substantially make for their lasting peace!

Two things are to be considered, the doctrine they taught and the example they led among all people. I have already touched upon their fundamental principle, which is as the corner stone of their fabric: and indeed, to speak eminently and properly, their characteristic or main distinguishing point or principle, viz., the light of Christ within, as God's gift for man's salvation. This, I say, is as the root of the goodly tree of doctrines that grew and branched out from it, which I shall now mention in their natural and experimental order.

First, repentance from dead works to serve the living God. Which comprehends three operations. First, a sight of sin. Secondly, a sense and godly sorrow for sin. Thirdly, an amendment for the time to come. This was the repentance they preached and pressed, and a natural result from the principle they turned all people unto. For of light came sight; and of sight came sense and sorrow; and of sense and sorrow came amendment of life. Which doctrine of repentance leads to justification; that is, forgiveness of the sins that are past, through Christ the alone propitiation, and the sanctification or purgation of the soul, from the defiling nature and habits of sin present, by the spirit of Christ in the soul; which is justification in the complete sense of that word: comprehending both justification from the guilt of the sins that are past, as if they had never been committed, through the love and mercy of God in Christ Jesus; and the creatures being made inwardly just through the cleansing and sanctifying power and spirit of Christ revealed in the soul; which is commonly called sanctification. But that none can come to know Christ to be their sacrifice that reject Him as their sanctifier. The end of His coming being to save His people from the nature and defilement as well as guilt of sin; and that therefore those that resist His light and spirit make His coming and offering of none effect to them.

From hence sprang a second doctrine they were led to declare, as the mark of the price of the high calling to all true Christians, viz., perfection from sin, according to the Scriptures of truth; which testify it to be the end of Christ's coming, and the nature of His kingdom, and for which His spirit was and is given, viz., to be perfect as our heavenly Father is perfect, and holy because God is holy. And this the apostles laboured for, that the Christians should be sanctified throughout in body, soul, and spirit, but they never held a perfection in wisdom and glory in this life or from natural infirmities or death as some have with a weak or ill mind imagined and insinuated against them.

This they called a redeemed state, re-generation, or the new birth. Teaching everywhere according to their foundation, that without this work were known there was no inheriting the kingdom of God.

Thirdly, this leads to an acknowledgment of eternal rewards and punishments, as they have good reason; for else of all people certainly they must be the most miserable; who, for above forty years, have been exceeding great sufferers for their profession; and, in some cases, treated worse than the worst of men; yea, as the refuse and off-scouring of all things.

This was the purport of their doctrine and ministry; which, for the most part is what other professors of Christianity pretend to hold in words and forms, but not in the power of godliness; which, generally speaking, has been long lost by men's departing from that principle and seed of life that is in man, and which man has not regarded, but lost the sense of; and in and by which He can only be quickened in His mind to serve the living God in newness of life. For as the life of religion was lost, and the generality lived and worshipped God after their own wills, and not after the will of God, nor the mind of Christ, which stood in the works and fruits of the holy spirit; so that which they pressed was not notion, but experience; no formality, but godliness; as being sensible in themselves through the work of God's righteous judgments, that without holiness no man shall ever see the Lord with comfort.

Besides these general doctrines, as the larger branches, there sprang forth several particular doctrines that did exemplify and farther explain the truth and efficacy of the general doctrine before observed, in their lives and examples, as:

I. Communion and loving one another. This is a noted mark in the mouth of all sorts of people concerning them. They will meet, they will help and stick one to another, whence it is common to hear some say, look how the Quakers love and take care of one another. Others, less moderate, will say, the Quakers love none but themselves. And if loving one another, and having an intimate communion in religion, and constant care to meet to worship God and help one another be any mark of primitive Christianity, they had it, blessed be the Lord, in an ample manner.

II. To love enemies. This they both taught and practised. For they did not only refuse to be revenged for injuries done them, and condemned it as of an unchristian spirit, but they did freely forgive; yea, help and relieve those that had been cruel to them, when it was in their power to have been even with them. Of which many and singular instances might be given: endeavouring, through faith and patience, to overcome all injustice and oppression, and preaching this doctrine as Christians for others to follow.

III. Another was the sufficiency of truth-speaking according to Christ's own form of sound words, of yea, yea, and nay, nay, among Christians, without swearing; both from Christ's express prohibition to swear at all, Mat. v., and for that they being under the tie and bond of truth in themselves, there was no necessity for an oath; and it would be a reproach to their Christian veracity to assure their truth by such an extraordinary way of speaking; simple and uncompounded answers, as yea and nay (without asseverations, attestations, or supernatural vouchers), being most suitable to evangelical righteousness. But offering at the same time to be punished to the full for false speaking, as others for perjury, if ever guilty of it. And hereby they exclude with all true, all false and profane swearing; for which the land did and doth mourn, and the great God was and is not a little offended with it.

IV. Not fighting, but suffering, is another testimony peculiar to this people: they affirm that Christianity teacheth people to beat their swords into ploughshares, and their spears into pruning hooks, and to learn war no more, that so the wolf may lie down with the lamb, and the lion with the calf, and nothing that destroys be entertained in the hearts of people: exhorting them to employ their zeal against sin, and turn their anger against Satan, and no longer war one against another; because all wars and fightings come of men's own hearts' lusts, according to the apostle James, and not of the meek spirit of Christ Jesus, who is captain of another warfare, and which is carried on with other weapons. Thus as truth-speaking succeeded swearing, so faith and patience succeeded fighting in the doctrine and practice of this people. Nor ought they for this to be obnoxious to civil government, since if they cannot fight for it neither can they fight against it; which is no mean security to any state. Nor is it reasonable that people should be blamed for not doing more for others than they can do for themselves. And, Christianity set aside, if the costs and fruits of war were well considered, peace with all its inconveniences is generally preferable. But though they were not for fighting, they were for submitting to government; and that not only for fear but for conscience sake; where government doth not interfere with conscience; believing it to be an ordinance of God, and where it is justly administered a great benefit to mankind. Though it has been their lot through blind zeal in some and interest in others to have felt the strokes of it with greater weight and rigour than any other persuasion in this age; whilst they of all others, religion set aside, have given the civil magistrate the least occasion of trouble in the discharge of his office.

V. Another part of the character of this people was, and is, they refuse to pay tithes or maintenance to a national ministry; and that for two reasons: the one is they believe all compelled maintenance even to gospel ministers to be unlawful, because expressly contrary to Christ's command, who said, freely you have received, freely give: at least, that the maintenance of gospel ministers should be free, and not forced. The other reason of their refusal is because those ministers are not gospel ones, in that the Holy Ghost is not their foundation, but human arts and parts. So that it is not matter of humour or sullenness, but pure conscience towards God, that they cannot help to support national ministries where they dwell, which are but too much and too visibly become ways of worldly advantage and preferment.

VI. Not to respect persons was and is another of their doctrines and practices, for which they were often buffeted and abused. They affirmed it to be sinful to give flattering titles, or to use vain gestures and complements of respect.

Though to virtue and authority they ever made a difference; but after their plain and homely manner, yet sincere and substantial way: well remembering the examples of Mordecai and Elihu; but more especially the command of their Lord and Master Jesus Christ, who forbade His followers to call men Rabbi, which implies Lord or Master; also the fashionable greetings and salutations of those times; that so self-love and honour to which the proud mind of man is incident in his fallen estate might not be indulged but rebuked. And though this rendered their conversation disagreeable, yet they that will remember what Christ said to the Jews, how can you believe in me who receive honour one of another? will abate of their resentment, if His doctrine has any credit with them.

VII. They also used the plain language of thee and thou to a single person whatever was His degree among men. And indeed the wisdom of God was much seen in bringing forth this people in so plain an appearance. For it was a close and distinguishing test upon the spirits of those they came among; showing their insides and what predominated notwithstanding their high and great profession of religion. This among the rest sounded so harsh to many of them, and they took it so ill, that they would say, Thou me, thou my dog! If thou thou'st me, I'll thou thy teeth down thy throat; forgetting the language they use to God in their own prayers, and the common style of the Scriptures, and that it is an absolute and essential propriety of speech. And what good, alas! had their religion done them, who were so sensibly touched with indignation for the use of this plain, honest, and true speech?

VIII. They recommended silence by their example, having very few words upon all occasions. They were at a word in dealing: nor could their customers with many words tempt them from it, having more regard to truth than custom, to example than gain. They sought solitude; but when in company they would neither use nor willingly hear unnecessary as well as unlawful discourses: whereby they preserved their minds pure and undisturbed from unprofitable thoughts and diversions. Nor could they humour the custom of good-night, good-morrow, good-speed; for they knew the night was good, and the day was good, without wishing of either; and that in the other expression the holy name of

God was too lightly and unthankfully used, and therefore taken in vain. Besides, they were words and wishes of course, and are usually as little meant as are love and service in the custom of cap and knee; and superfluity in those as well as in other things was burdensome to them; and therefore they did not only decline to use them, but found themselves often pressed to reprove the practice.

IX. For the same reason they forbore drinking to people or pledging of them, as the manner of the world is. A practice that is not only unnecessary, but they thought evil in the tendencies of it, being a provocation to drink more than did people good, as well as that it was in itself vain and heathenish.

X. Their way of marriage is peculiar to them; and shows a distinguishing care above other societies professing Christianity. They say that marriage is an ordinance of God, and that God only can rightly join man and woman in marriage. Therefore they use neither priest or magistrate: but the man or woman concerned take each other as husband and wife in the presence of divers credible witnesses, promising to each other, with God's assistance, to be loving and faithful in that relation till death shall separate them. But antecedent to this, they first present themselves to the monthly meeting for the affairs of the church where they reside; there declaring their intentions to take one another as husband and wife if the said meeting have nothing material to object against it. They are constantly asked the necessary questions, as in case of parents or guardians, if they have acquainted them with their intention, and have their consent, etc. The method of the meeting is to take a minute thereof and to appoint proper persons to inquire of their conversation and clearness from all others, and whether they have discharged their duty to their parents or guardians; and to make report thereof to the next monthly meeting, where the same parties are desired to give their attendance. In case it appears they have proceeded orderly, the meeting passes their proposal, and so records it in their meeting book. And in case the woman be a widow and hath children due care is then taken that provision also be made by her for the orphans before the meeting pass the proposals of marriage; advising the parties concerned to appoint a convenient time and place, and to give fitting notice to their relations, and such friends and neighbours as they desire should be the witnesses of their marriage; where they take one another by the hand, and by name promise reciprocally love and fidelity after the manner before expressed. Of all which proceedings a narrative in way of certificate is made, to which the said parties first set their hands, thereby making it their act and deed; and then divers relations, spectators, and auditors set their names as witnesses of what they said and signed. And this certificate is afterwards registered in the record belonging to the meeting where the marriage is solemnised. Which regular method has been, as it deserves, adjudged in courts of law a good marriage; where is has been by cross and ill people disputed and contested for want of the accustomed formalities of priest and ring, etc., ceremonies they have refused: not out of humour, but conscience reasonably grounded; inasmuch as no Scripture example tells us that the priest had any other part of old time than that of a witness among the rest before whom the Jews used to take one another: and therefore this people look upon it as an imposition to advance the power and profits of the clergy. And for the use of the ring, it is enough to say that it was a heathenish and vain custom, and never in practice among the people of God, Jews, or primitive Christians. The words of the usual form, as with my body I thee worship, etc., are hardly defensible. In short, they are more careful, exact, and regular than any form now used; and it is free of the inconveniencies with which other methods are attended: their care and checks being so many, and such, as that no clandestine marriages can be performed among them.

X. It may not be unfit to say something here of their births and burials, which make up so much of the pomp and solemnity of too many called Christians. For births, the parents name their own children; which is usually some days after they are born, in the presence of the midwife, if she can be there, and those that were at the birth, who afterwards sign a certificate for that purpose prepared of the birth and name of the child or children; which is recorded in a proper book, in the monthly meeting to which the parents belong; avoiding the accustomed ceremonies and festivals.

XI. Their burials are performed with the same simplicity.

If the body of the deceased be near any public meeting place, it is usually carried thither for the more convenient reception of those that accompany it to the burying-ground. And it so falls out sometimes that while the meeting is gathering for the burial some or other has a word of exhortation for the sake of the people there met together. After which the body is born away by young men, or else those that are of their neighbourhood, or those that were most of the intimacy of the deceased party: the corpse being in a plain coffin, without any covering or furniture upon it. At the ground they pause some time before they put the body into its grave, that if any there should have anything upon them to exhort the people they may not be disappointed, and that the relations may the more retiredly and solemnly take their last leave of the body of their departed kindred, and the spectators have a sense of mortality, by the occasion then given them to reflect upon their own latter end. Otherwise they have no set rites or ceremonies on those occasions. Neither do the kindred of the deceased ever wear mourning; they looking upon it as a worldly ceremony and piece of pomp; and that what mourning is fit for a Christian to have, at the departure of a beloved relation or friend, should be worn in the mind, which is only sensible of the loss: and the love they had to them, and remembrance of them, to be outwardly expressed by a respect to their advice and care of those they have left behind them, and their love of that they loved. Which conduct of theirs, though unmodish or unfashionable, leaves nothing of the substance of things neglected or undone: and as they aim at no more, so that simplicity of life is what they observe with great satisfaction; though it sometimes happens not to be without the mockeries of the vain world they live in.

These things to be sure gave them a rough and disagreeable appearance with the generality; who thought them turners of the world upside down, as indeed, in some sense, they were: but in no other than that wherein Paul was so charged, viz., to bring things back into their primitive and right order again. For these and such like practices of theirs were not the result of humour, or for civil distinction, as some have fancied, but a fruit of inward sense, which God through His holy fear had begotten in them. They did not consider how to contradict the world or distinguish themselves as a party from others; it being none of their business, as it was not their interest: no, it was not the result of consultation or a framed design by which to declare or recommend schism or novelty. But God having given them a sight of themselves they saw the whole world in the same glass of truth; and sensibly discerned the affections and passions of men, and the rise and tendency of things: what it was that gratified the lust of the flesh, the lust of the eye, and the pride of life, which are not of the Father, but of the world. And from thence sprang in the night of darkness and apostacy, which hath been over people through their degeneration from the light and spirit of God, these and many other vain customs which are seen by the heavenly day of Christ that dawns in the soul to be either wrong in their original, or by time and abuse hurtful in their practice. And though these things seemed trivial to some, and rendered these people stingy and conceited in such persons' opinions, there was and is more in them than they were or are aware of.

It was not very easy to our primitive friends to make themselves sights and spectacles, and the scorn and derision of the world; which they easily foresaw must be the consequence of so unfashionable a conversation in it. But here was the wisdom of God seen in the foolishness of these things. First, that they discovered the satisfaction and concern that people had in and for the fashions of this world, notwithstanding their high pretences to another; in that any disappointment about them came so very near them as that the greatest honesty, virtue, wisdom, and ability were unwelcome without them. Secondly, it seasonably and profitably divided conversation; for this making their society uneasy to their relations and acquaintance, it gave them the opportunity of more retirement and solitude; wherein they met with better company, even the Lord God their Redeemer; and grew strong in His love, power, and wisdom, and were thereby better qualified for His service. And the success abundantly showed it. Blessed be the name of the Lord.

And though they were not great and learned in the esteem of this world (for then they had not wanted followers upon their own credit and authority) yet they were generally of the most sober of the several persuasions they were in, and of the most repute for religion; and many of them of good capacity, substance, and account among men.

And also some among them wanted not for parts, learning, or estate; though then as of old not many wise or noble, etc., were called, or at least received the heavenly call, because of the cross that attended the profession of it in sincerity. But neither do parts or learning make men the better Christians, though the better orators and disputants; and it is the ignorance of people about the divine gift that causes that vulgar and mischievous mistake. Theory and practice, speculation and enjoyment, words and life, are two things. O it is the penitent, the reformed, the lowly, the watchful, the self-denying and holy soul that is the Christian! And that frame is the fruit and work of the spirit, which is the life of Jesus: whose life though hid in the fulness of it in God the Father, is shed abroad in the hearts of them that truly believe, according to their capacity. O that people did but know this to cleanse them, to circumcise them, to quicken them, and to make them new creatures indeed! recreated or regenerated after Christ Jesus unto good works; that they might live to God and not to themselves; and offer up living prayers and living praises to the living God through His own living spirit, in which He is only to be worshipped in this gospel day.

O that they that read me could but feel me! For my heart is affected with this merciful visitation of the Father of lights and spirits to this poor nation and the whole world through the same testimony. Why should the inhabitants thereof reject it? Why should they lose the blessed benefit of it? Why should they not turn to the Lord with all their hearts and say from the heart, speak, Lord, for now thy poor servants hear? O that thy will may be done; thy great, thy good, and holy will, in earth as it is in heaven! Do it in us, do it upon us, do what thou wilt with us; for we are Thine, and desire to glorify Thee our Creator, both for that and because Thou art our Redeemer; for Thou art redeeming us from the earth; from the vanities and pollutions of it, to be a peculiar people unto Thee. O this were a brave day for England, if so she could say in truth! But alas, the case is otherwise; for which some of thine inhabitants, O land of my nativity! have mourned over thee with bitter wailing and lamentation. Their heads have been indeed as waters, and their eyes as fountains of tears, because of thy transgression and stiffneckedness; because thou wilt not hear, and fear, and return to the rock, even thy rock, O England! From whence thou art hewn. But be thou warned, O land of great profession, to receive Him into thy heart. Behold, at that door it is He hath stood so long knocking! but thou wilt yet have none of Him. O be thou awakened lest Jerusalem's judgments do swiftly overtake thee, because of Jerusalem's sins that abound in thee. For she abounded in formality, but made void the weighty things of God's law, as thou daily dost.

She withstood the Son of God in the flesh, and thou resisteth the Son of God in the spirit. He would have gathered her as a hen gathereth her chickens under her wings, and she would not; so would He have gathered thee out of thy lifeless profession, and have brought thee to inherit substance; to have known His power and kingdom: for which He often knocked within by His grace and spirit; and without, by His servants and witnesses. But on the contrary, as Jerusalem of old persecuted the manifestation of the Son of God in the flesh and crucified Him, and whipt and imprisoned His servants; so hast thou, O land! crucified to thyself afresh the Lord of life and glory and done despite to His spirit of grace, slighting the fatherly visitation, and persecuting the blessed dispenser of it by thy laws and magistrates. Though they have early and late pleaded with thee in the power and spirit of the Lord, in love and meekness, that thou mightest know the Lord, and serve Him, and become the glory of all lands.

But thou hast evilly entreated and requited them, thou hast set at nought all their counsel, and wouldst have none of their reproof, as thou shouldst have had. Their appearance was too straight, and their qualifications were too mean for thee to receive them; like the Jews of old that cried, Is not this the carpenter's son, and are not His brethren among us; which of the scribes of the learned (the orthodox) believed in Him? Prophesying their fall in a year or two, and making and executing of severe laws to bring it to pass: endeavouring to terrify them out of their holy way or destroy them for abiding faithful to it. But thou hast seen how many governments that rose against them, and determined their downfall, have been overturned and extinguished, and that they are still preserved, and become a great and a considerable people among the middle sort of thy numerous inhabitants. And notwithstanding the many difficulties without and within which they have laboured under since the Lord God eternal first gathered them, they are an increasing people; the Lord still adding unto them in divers parts such as shall be saved if they persevere to the end. And to thee, O England! were they, and are they lifted up as a standard, and as a city set upon a hill, and to the nations round about thee, that in their light thou mayst come to see light, even in Christ Jesus, the light of the world, and therefore thy light and life too, if thou wouldst but turn from thy many evil ways and receive and obey it. For in the light of the Lamb must the nations of them that are saved walk, as the Scripture testifies.

Remember, O nation of great profession! How the Lord has waited upon thee since the dawning of reformation, and the many mercies and judgments by which He has pleaded with thee; and awake and arise out of thy deep sleep, and yet hear His word in thy heart, that thou mayst live.

Let not this thy day of visitation pass over thy head, nor neglect thou so great salvation as is this which is come to thy house, O England! For why shouldst thou die? O land that God desires to bless! Be assured it is He that has been in the midst of this people, in the midst of thee, and not a delusion, as thy mistaken teachers have made thee believe. And this thou shalt find by their marks and fruits, if thou wilt consider them in the spirit of moderation.

CHAPTER III

OF THE QUALIFICATIONS OF THEIR MINISTRY. ELEVEN MARKS THAT IT IS CHRISTIAN.

I. THEY were changed men themselves before they went about to change others. Their hearts were rent as well as their garments; and they knew the power and work of God upon them. And this was seen by the great alteration it made, and their stricter course of life, and more godly conversation that immediately followed upon it.

II. They went not forth or preached in their own time or will, but in the will of God; and spoke not their own studied matter, but as they were opened and moved of His spirit, with which they were well acquainted in their own conversion, which cannot be expressed to carnal men, so as to give them any intelligible account; for to such it is, as Christ said, like the blowing of the wind, which no man knows whence it cometh, or whither it goeth. Yet this proof and seal went along with their ministry, that many were turned from their lifeless professions and the evil of their ways to an inward and experimental knowledge of God, and a holy life, as thousands can witness. And as they freely received what they had to say from the Lord, so they freely administered it to others.

III. The bent and stress of their ministry was conversion to God; regeneration and holiness. Not schemes of doctrines and verbal creeds, or new forms of worship; but a leaving off in religion the superfluous, and reducing the ceremonious and formal part, and pressing earnestly the substantial, the necessary, and profitable part to the soul; as all, upon a serious reflection, must and do acknowledge.

IV. They directed people to a principle in themselves, though not of themselves, by which all that they asserted, preached, and exhorted others to, might be wrought in them, and known to them, through experience, to be true: which is a high and distinguishing mark of the truth of their ministry, both that they knew what they said, and were not afraid of coming to the test. For as they were bold from certainty, so they required conformity upon no human authority, but upon conviction, and the conviction of this principle; which they asserted was in them that they preached unto, and unto that they directed them, that they might examine and prove the reality of those things which they had affirmed of it as to its manifestation and work in man. And this is more than the many ministers in the world pretended to. They declare of religion, say many things true, in words of God, Christ, and the spirit; of holiness and heaven; that all men should repent and amend their lives, or they will go to hell, etc.; but which of them all pretend to speak of their own knowledge and experience? Or ever directed to a divine principle, or agent, placed of God in man, to help him; and how to know it, and wait to feel its power to work that good and acceptable will of God in them.

Some of them indeed have spoke of the spirit, and the operations of it to sanctification and performance of worship to God; but where, and how to find it, and wait in it, to perform our duty to God, was yet as a mystery to be declared by this farther degree of reformation. So that this people did not only in words more than equally press repentance, conversion, and holiness, but did it knowingly and experimentally; and directed those to whom they preached to a sufficient principle; and told them where it was, and by what tokens they might know it, and which way they might experience the power and efficacy of it to their souls' happiness. Which is more than theory and speculation upon which most other ministers depend: for here is certainty, a bottom upon which man may boldly appear before God in the great day of account.

V. They reached to the inward state and condition of people, which is an evidence of the virtue of their principle, and of their ministering from it, and not from their own imaginations, glosses, or comments upon Scripture. For nothing reaches the heart but what is from the heart, or pierces the conscience but what comes from a living conscience. Insomuch as it hath often happened where people have under secrecy revealed their state or condition to some choice friends for advice or ease, they have been so particularly directed in the ministry of this people, that they have challenged their friends with discovering their secrets, and telling their preachers their cases to whom a word had not been spoken. Yea, the very thoughts and purposes of the hearts of many have been so plainly detected that they have, like Nathaniel, cried out of this inward appearance of Christ, Thou art the Son of God, Thou art the King of Israel. And those that have embraced this divine principle have found this mark of its truth and divinity (that the woman of Samaria did of Christ when in the flesh, to be the Messiah), viz., it had told them all that ever they had done; shown them their insides, the most inward secrets of their hearts, and laid judgment to the line, and righteousness to the plummet; of which thousands can at this day give in their witness. So that nothing has been affirmed by this people of the power and virtue of this heavenly principle, that such as have turned to it have not found true and more; and that one half had not been told to them of what they have seen of the power, purity, wisdom, and goodness of God therein.

VI. The accomplishments with which this principle fitted even some of the meanest of this people for their work and service, furnishing some of them with an extraordinary understanding in divine things, and an admirable fluency and taking way of expression, which gave occasion to some to wonder, saying of them as of their Master, is not this such a mechanic's Son, how came He by this learning? As from thence others took occasion to suspect and insinuate they were Jesuits in disguise, who had the reputation of learned men for an age past, though there was not the least ground of truth for any such reflection, in that their ministers are known, the places of their abode, their kindred and education.

VII. That they came forth low, and despised and hated as the primitive Christians did, and not by the help of worldly wisdom or power as former reformations in part have done. But in all things it may be said, this people were brought forth in the cross; in a contradiction to the ways, worships, fashions, and customs of this world; yea, against wind and tide, that so no flesh might glory before God.

VIII. They could have no design to themselves in this work, thus to expose themselves to scorn and abuse; to spend and be spent: leaving wife and children, house and land, and all that can be accounted dear to men, with their lives in their hands, being daily in jeopardy, to declare this primitive message, revived in their spirits, by the good spirit and power of God, viz.:

That God is light, and in Him is no darkness at all; and that He has sent His Son a light into the world to enlighten all men in order to salvation; and that they that say they have fellowship with God, and are His children and people, and yet walk in darkness, viz., in disobedience to the light in their consciences, and after the vanity of this world, they lie and do not the truth. But that all such as love the light and bring their deeds to it and walk in the light, as God is light, the blood of Jesus Christ His Son should cleanse them from all sin. Thus John i. 4, 19; iii. 20, 21; 1 John i. 5, 6, 7.

IX. Their known great constancy and patience in suffering

for their testimony in all the branches of it; and that sometimes unto death by beatings, bruisings, long and crowded imprisonments, and noisome dungeons: four of them in New England dying by the hands of the executioner purely for preaching amongst that people: besides banishments and excessive plunders and sequestrations of their goods and estates, almost in all parts, not easily to be expressed, and less to have been endured but by those that have the support of a good and glorious cause; refusing deliverance by any indirect ways or means as often as it was offered unto them.

X. That they did not only not show any disposition to revenge when it was at any time in their power, but forgave their cruel enemies; showing mercy to those that had none for them.

XI. Their plainness with those in authority, like the ancient prophets, not fearing to tell them to their faces of their private and public sins; and their prophecies to them of their afflictions and downfall, when in the top of their glory. Also of some national judgments as of the Plague and Fire of London in express terms; and likewise particular ones to divers persecutors, which accordingly overtook them; and were very remarkable in the places where they dwelt, which in time may be made public for the glory of God.

Thus, reader, thou seest this people in their rise, principles, ministry, and progress, both their general and particular testimony; by which thou mayst be informed how and upon what foot they sprang and became so considerable a people. It remains next that I show also their care, conduct, and discipline as a Christian and reformed society, that they might be found living up to their own principles and profession. And this the rather because they have hardly suffered more in their character from the unjust charge of error than by the false imputation of disorder. Which calumny indeed has not failed to follow all the true steps that were ever made to reformation, and under which reproach none suffered more than the primitive Christians themselves, that were the honour of Christianity, and the great lights and examples of their own and succeeding ages.

CHAPTER IV

OF THE DISCIPLINE AND PRACTICE OF THIS PEOPLE AS A RELIGIOUS SOCIETY. THE CHURCH POWER THEY OWN AND EXERCISE, AND THAT WHICH THEY REJECT AND CONDEMN. WITH THE METHOD OF THEIR PROCEEDINGS AGAINST ERRING AND DISORDERLY PERSONS.

THIS people increasing daily both in town and country, a holy care fell upon some of the elders among them for the benefit and service of the church. And the first business in their view, after the example of the primitive saints, was the exercise of charity; to supply the necessities of the poor, and answer the like occasions. Wherefore collections were early and liberally made for that and divers other services in the church, and entrusted with faithful men, fearing God, and of good report, who were not weary in well-doing; adding often of their own, in large proportions, which they never brought to account or desired should be known, much less restored to them, that none might want nor any service be retarded or disappointed.

They were also very careful that everyone that belonged to them answered their profession in their behaviour among men upon all occasions; that they lived peaceably, and were in all things good examples. They found themselves engaged to record their sufferings and services: and in case of marriage, which they could not perform in the usual methods of the nation, but among themselves they took care that all things were clear between the parties and all others. And it was then rare that anyone entertained an inclination to a person on that account till he or she had communicated it secretly to some very weighty and eminent friends among them that they might have a sense of the matter; looking to the council and unity of their brethren as of great moment to them. But because the charge of the poor, the number of orphans, marriages, sufferings, and other matters multiplied; and that it was good that the churches were in some way and method of proceeding in such affairs among them, to the end they might the better correspond upon occasion where a member of one meeting might have to do with one of another; it pleased the Lord in His wisdom and goodness to open the understanding of the first instrument of this dispensation of life about a good and orderly way of proceeding; who felt a holy concern to visit the churches in person throughout this nation, to begin and establish it among them: and by his epistles the like was done in other nations and provinces abroad; which he also afterwards visited and helped in that service, as shall be observed when I come to speak of him.

Now the care, conduct, and discipline I have been speaking of, and which are now practised among this people, is as followeth.

This godly elder in every country where he travelled exhorted them that some out of every meeting of worship should meet together once in the month to confer about the wants and occasions of the church. And as the case required so those monthly meetings were fewer or more in number in every respective county: four or six meetings of worship usually making one monthly meeting of business. And accordingly the brethren met him from place to place and began the said meetings, viz., for the poor, orphans, orderly walking, integrity to their profession, births, marriages, burials, sufferings, etc. And that these monthly meetings should in each county make up one quarterly meeting where the most zealous and eminent friends of the county should assemble to communicate, advise, and help one another, especially when any business seemed difficult, or a monthly meeting was tender of determining a matter.

Also that these several quarterly meetings should digest the reports of their monthly meetings, and prepare one for each respective county against the yearly meeting, in which all quarterly meetings resolve; which is held in London: where the churches in this nation and other nations and provinces meet by chosen members of their respective counties, both mutually to communicate their church affairs and to advise, and be advised in any depending case to edification. Also to provide a requisite stock for the discharge of general expenses for general services in the church not needful to be here particularised.

At these meetings any of the members of the churches may come, if they please, and speak their minds freely, in the fear of God, to any matter; but the mind of each quarterly meeting therein represented is chiefly understood as to particular cases in the sense delivered by the persons deputed or chosen for that service by the said meeting.

During their yearly meeting, to which their other meetings refer in their order and naturally resolve themselves, care is taken by a select number for that service, chosen by the general assembly, to draw up the minutes of the said meeting upon the several matters that have been under consideration therein, to the end that the respective quarterly and monthly meetings may be informed of all proceedings; together with a general exhortation to holiness, unity, and charity. Of all which proceedings in yearly, monthly, and quarterly meetings, due record is kept by someone appointed for that service, or that hath voluntarily undertaken it. These meetings are opened and usually concluded in their solemn waiting upon God, who is sometimes graciously pleased to answer them with as signal evidences of His love and presence as in any of their meetings of worship.

It is further to be noted that in these solemn assemblies for the churches service there is no one presides among them after the manner of the assemblies of other people; Christ only being their president, as He is pleased to appear in life and wisdom in any one or more of them, to whom, whatever be their capacity or degree, the rest adhere with a firm unity not of authority but conviction, which is the divine authority and way of Christ's power and spirit in His people; making good His blessed promise, that He would be in the midst of His, where and whenever they were met together in His name, even to the end of the world. So be it.

Now it may be expected I should here set down what sort of authority is exercised by this people, upon such members of their society as correspond in their lives with their profession, and that are refractory to this good and wholesome order settled among them; and the rather because they have not wanted their reproach and sufferings from some tongues and pens upon this occasion in a plentiful manner.

The power they exercise is such as Christ has given to His own people, to the end of the world, in the persons of His disciples, viz., to oversee, exhort, reprove, and after long suffering and waiting upon the disobedient and refractory to disown them as any more of their communion, or that they will any longer stand charged in the sight and judgment of God or men with their conversation or behaviour as any of them, until they repent. The subject matter about which this authority in any of the foregoing branches of it is exercised, is first in relation to common and general practice, and secondly, about those things that more strictly refer to their own character and profession, and which distinguish them from all other professors of Christianity; avoiding two extremes upon which many split, viz., persecution and libertinism, that is, a coercive power to whip people into the temple; that such as will not conform, though against faith and conscience, shall be punished in their persons or estates: or leaving all loose and at large as to practice; and so unaccountable to all but God and the magistrate. To which hurtful extreme nothing has more contributed than the abuse of church power, by such as suffer their passion and private interests to prevail with them to carry it to outward force and corporal punishment. A practice they have been taught to dislike by their extreme sufferings as well as their known principle for a universal liberty of conscience.

On the other hand they equally dislike an independency in society; an unaccountableness in practice and conversation to the rules and terms of their own communion, and to those that are the members of it. They distinguish between imposing any practice that immediately regards faith or worship (which is never to be done or suffered or submitted unto) and requiring Christian compliance with those methods that only respect church business in its more civil part and concern; and that regard the discreet and orderly maintenance of the character of the society as a sober and religious community. In short, what is for the promotion of holiness and charity, that men may practise what they profess, live up to their own principles, and not be at liberty to give the lie to their own profession without rebuke, is their use and limit of church power. They compel none to them, but oblige those that are of them to walk suitable, or they are denied by them. That is all the mark they set upon them, and the power they exercise, or judge a Christian society can exercise, upon those that are the members of it.

The way of their proceeding against such as have lapsed or transgressed is this. He is visited by some of them, and the matter of fact laid home to him, be it any evil practice against known and general virtue, or any branch of their particular testimony, which he in common professeth with them. They labour with him in much love and zeal, for the good of his soul, the honour of God, and reputation of their profession, to own his fault and condemn it in as ample a manner as the evil or scandal was given by him; which for the most part is performed by some written testimony under the party's hand. And if it so happen that the party prove refractory, and is not willing to clear the truth they profess from the reproach of his or her evil doing or unfaithfulness, they, after repeated entreaties and due waiting for a token of repentance, give forth a paper to disown such a fact, and the party offending: recording the same as a testimony of their care for the honour of the truth they profess.

And if he or she shall clear their profession and themselves by sincere acknowledgment of their fault and godly sorrow for so doing, they are received and looked upon again as members of their communion. For as God, so His true people upbraid no man after repentance.

This is the account I had to give of the people of God called Quakers, as to their rise, appearance, principles, and practices in this age of the world, both with respect to their faith and worship, discipline and conversation. And I judge it very proper in this place because it is to preface the journal of the first blessed and glorious instrument of this work, and for a testimony to him in his singular qualifications and services, in which he abundantly excelled in this day, and are worthy to be set forth as an example to all succeeding times to the glory of the most high God and for a just memorial to that worthy and excellent man His faithful servant and apostle to this generation of the world.

CHAPTER V

OF THE FIRST INSTRUMENT OR PERSON BY WHOM GOD WAS PLEASED TO GATHER THIS PEOPLE INTO THE WAY THEY PROFESS. HIS NAME G. FOX. HIS MANY EXCELLENT QUALIFICATIONS; SHOWING A DIVINE AND NOT A HUMAN POWER TO HAVE BEEN THEIR ORIGINAL IN HIM. HIS TROUBLES AND SUFFERINGS BOTH FROM WITHOUT AND WITHIN. HIS END AND TRIUMPH.

I AM now come to the third head or branch of my preface, viz., the instrumental author. For it is natural for some to say, well, here is the people and work, but where and who was the man, the instrument? He that in this age was sent to begin this work and people? I shall, as God shall enable me, declare who and what he was; not only by report of others, but from my own long and most inward converse and intimate knowledge of him; for which my soul blesseth God, as it hath often done. And I doubt not but by that time I have discharged myself of this part of my preface, my serious readers will believe I had good cause so to do.

The blessed instrument of, and in this day of God, and of whom I am now about to write, was George Fox, distinguished from another of that name by that other's addition of Younger to his name in all his writings; not that he was so in years, but that he was so in the truth. But he was also a worthy man, witness, and servant of God in his time.

But this George Fox was born in Leicestershire, about the year 1624. He descended of honest and sufficient parents, who endeavoured to bring him up, as they did the rest of their children, in the way and worship of the nation. Especially his mother, who was a woman accomplished above most of her degree in the place where she lived. But from a child he appeared of another frame of mind than the rest of his brethren; being more religious, inward, still, solid, and observing beyond his years, as the answers he would give, and the questions he would put upon occasion manifested to the astonishment of those that heard him, especially in divine things.

His mother taking notice of his singular temper, and the

gravity, wisdom, and piety that very early shined through him, refusing childish and vain sports and company, when very young. She was tender and indulgent over him, so that from her he met with little difficulty. As to his employment, he was brought up in country business, and as he took most delight in sheep so he was very skilful in them; an employment that very well suited his mind in several respects, both for its innocency and solitude; and was a just emblem of his after ministry and service.

I shall not break in upon his own account, which is by much the best that can be given, and therefore desire what I can to avoid saying anything of what is said already as to the particular passages of his coming forth. But, in general, when he was somewhat above twenty he left his friends and visited the most retired and religious people in those parts. And some there were, short of few, if any, in this nation who waited for the consolation of Israel night and day; as Zacharias, Anna, and good old Simeon did of old time. To these he was sent, and these he sought out in the neighbouring counties, and among them he sojourned until his more ample ministry came upon him. At this time he taught, and was an example of, silence, endeavouring to bring them from self-performances: testifying of and turning them to the light of Christ within them, and encouraging them to wait in patience, and to feel the power of it to stir in their hearts that their knowledge and worship might stand in the power of an endless life, which was to be found in the light, as it was obeyed in the manifestation of it in man. For in the word was life, and that life is the light of men. Life in the word, light in men; and life in men too, as the light is obeyed: the children of the light living by the life of the word, by which the word begets them again to God, which is the regeneration and new birth, without which there is no coming into the kingdom of God: and to which, whoever comes, is greater than John; that is, than John's dispensation, which was not that of the kingdom, but the consummation of the legal and forerunning of the gospel times, the time of the kingdom. Accordingly several meetings were gathered in those parts; and thus his time was employed for some years.

In 1652, he being in his usual retirement, his mind exercised towards the Lord, upon a very high mountain in some of the hither parts of Yorkshire, as I take it, he had a visitation of the great work of God in the earth, and of the way that he was to go forth in a public ministry to begin it. He saw people as thick as motes in the sun, that should in time be brought home to the Lord, that there might be but one shepherd and one sheepfold in all the earth. There his eye was directed northward, beholding a great people that should receive him and his message in those parts. Upon this mountain he was moved of the Lord to sound out his great and notable day, as if he had been in a great auditory; and from thence went north, as the Lord had shown him. And in every place where he came, if not before he came to it, he had his particular exercise and service shown to him, so that the Lord was his leader indeed. For it was not in vain that he travelled; God in most places sealing his commission with the convincement of some of all sorts, as well publicans as sober professors of religion. Some of the first and most eminent of those that came forth in a public ministry, and which are now at rest, were Richard Farnsworth, James Nayler, William Dewsberry, Thomas Aldam, Francis Howgil, Edward Burroughs, John Camm, John Audland, Richard Hubberthorn, T. Taylor, T. Holmes, Alexander Parker, William Simson, William Caton, John Stubbs, Robert Withers, Tho. Low, Josiah Coale, John Burnyeat, Robert Lodge, Thomas Salthouse, and many more worthies that cannot be well here named; together with divers yet living of the first and great convincement; who after the knowledge of God's purging judgment in themselves and some time of waiting in silence upon Him, to feel and receive power from on high to speak in His name (which none else rightly can, though they may use the same words), they felt its divine motions, and were frequently drawn forth, especially to visit the public assemblies, to reprove, inform, and exhort them. Sometimes in markets, fairs, streets, and by the highway side; calling people to repentance, and to turn to the Lord with their hearts as well as their mouths; directing them to the light of Christ within them, to see, examine, and consider their ways by, and to eschew the evil and do the good and acceptable will of God. And they suffered great hardships for this their love and goodwill; being often stocked, stoned, beaten, whipped, and imprisoned; though honest men, and of good report where they lived; that had left wives, children, and houses and lands to visit them with a living call to repentance. And though the priests generally set themselves to oppose them, and write against them, and insinuated most false and scandalous stories to defame them; stirring up the magistrates to suppress them, especially in those northern parts; yet God was pleased so to fill them with His living power and give them such an open door of utterance in His service, that there was a mighty convincement over those parts.

And through the tender and singular indulgences of Judge Bradshaw and Judge Fell, and Col. West in the infancy of things, the priests were never able to gain the point they laboured for, which was to have proceeded to blood; and, if possible, Herod-like, by a cruel exercise of the civil power, to have cut them off and rooted them out of the country. But especially Judge Fell, who was not only a check to their rage in the course of legal proceedings, but otherwise, upon occasion; and finally countenanced this people. For his wife receiving the truth with the first, it had that influence upon his spirit, being a just and wise man, and seeing in his own wife and family a full confutation of all the popular clamours against the way of truth, that he covered them what he could, and freely opened his doors, and gave up his house to his wife and her friends; not valuing the reproach of ignorant or of evil-minded people; which I here mention to his or her honour, and which will be I believe an honour and a blessing to such of their name and family as shall be found in that tenderness, humility, love, and zeal for the truth and people of the Lord.

That house was for some years, at first especially, until the truth had opened its way into the southern parts of this island, an eminent receptacle of this people. Others of good note and substance in those northern countries, had also opened their houses, together with their hearts, to the many publishers that in a short time the Lord had raised to declare His salvation to the people; and where meetings of the Lord's messengers were frequently held to communicate their services and exercises, and comfort and edify one another in their blessed ministry.

But lest this may be thought a digression, having touched upon this before, I return to this excellent man. And for his personal qualities, both natural, moral, and divine, as they appeared in his converse with brethren, and in the church of God, take as follows:

I. He was a man that God endued with a clear and wonderful depth. A discerner of other's spirits, and very much a master of his own. And though that side of his understanding which lay next to the world, and especially the expression of it, might sound uncouth and unfashionable to nice ears, his matter was nevertheless very profound; and would not only bear to be often considered, but the more it was so the more weighty and instructing it appeared. And as abruptly and brokenly as sometimes his sentences would seem to fall from him about divine things, it is well known they were often as texts to many fairer declarations. And indeed it showed beyond all contradiction that God sent him; in that no art or parts had any share in the matter of manner of his ministry; and that so many great, excellent, and necessary truths, as he came forth to preach to mankind, had therefore nothing of man's wit or wisdom to recommend them. So that as to man he was an original, being no man's copy. And his ministry and writings show they are from one that was not taught of man, nor had learned what he said by study. Nor were they notional or speculative, but sensible and practical truths, tending to conversion and regeneration, and the setting up of the kingdom of God in the hearts of men: and the way of it was his work. So that I have many times been overcome in myself, and been made to say with my Lord and Master upon the like occasion, I thank Thee, O Father, Lord of heaven and earth, that Thou hast hid these things from the wise and prudent of this world, and revealed them to babes: for many times hath my soul bowed in a humble thankfulness to the Lord, that He did not choose any of the wise and learned of this world to be the first messenger in our age of His blessed truth to men; but that he took one that was not of high degree, or elegant speech, or learned after the way of this world, that His message and work He sent him to do might come with less suspicion, or jealousy of human wisdom and interest, and with more force and clearness upon the consciences of those that sincerely sought the way of truth in the love of it. I say, beholding with the eye of my mind, which the God of heaven had opened in me, the marks of God's finger and hand visibly in this testimony from the clearness of the principle, the power and efficacy of it, in the exemplary, sobriety, plainness, zeal, steadiness, humility, gravity, punctuality, charity, and circumspect care in the government of church affairs, which shined in his and their life and testimony that God employed in this work, it greatly confirmed me that it was of God, and engaged my soul in a deep love, fear, reverence, and thankfulness for His love and mercy therein to mankind: in which mind I remain, and shall I hope through the Lord's strength, to the end of my days.

II. In his testimony of ministry he much laboured to open truth to the people's understandings, and to bottom them upon the principle and principal, Christ Jesus, the light of the world; that by bringing them to something that was from God in themselves they might the better know and judge of Him and themselves.

III. He had an extraordinary gift in opening the Scriptures. He would go to the marrow of things and show the mind, harmony, and fulfilling of them with much plainness, and to great comfort and edification.

IV. The mystery of the first and second Adam, of the fall and restoration of the law and gospel, of shadows and substance, of the servant's and son's state, and the fulfilling of the Scriptures in Christ and by Christ, the true light, in all that are His through the obedience of faith, were much of the substance and drift of his testimonies. In all which he was witnessed to be of God; being sensibly felt to speak that which he had received of Christ, and was his own experience, in that which never errs nor fails.

V. But above all, he excelled in prayer. The inwardness and weight of his spirit, the reverence and solemnity of his address and behaviour, and the fewness and fulness of his words have often struck even strangers with admiration, as they used to reach others with consolation. The most awful, living, reverent frame I ever felt or beheld, I must say, was his in prayer. And truly it was a testimony he knew and lived nearer to the Lord than other men; for they that know Him most will see most reason to approach Him with reverence and fear.

VI. He was of an innocent life, no busybody, nor self-seeker; neither touchy nor critical: what fell from him was very inoffensive, if not very edifying. So meek, contented, modest, easy, steady, tender; it was a pleasure to be in his company. He exercised no authority but over evil, and that everywhere, and in all; but with love, compassion, and long-suffering. A most merciful man, as ready to forgive as unapt to take or give an offence. Thousands can truly say he was of an excellent spirit and savour among them, and because thereof the most excellent spirits loved him with an unfeigned and unfading love.

VII. He was an incessant labourer: for in his younger time, before his many great and deep sufferings and travails had enfeebled his body for itinerant services, he laboured much in the word and doctrine and discipline in England, Scotland, and Ireland; turning many to God, and confirming those that were convinced of the truth, and settling good order as to church affairs among them. And towards the conclusion of his travelling services, between the years seventy-one and seventy-seven, he visited the churches of Christ in the plantations in America, and in the United Provinces, and Germany, as his journal relates; to the convincement and consolation of many. After that time he chiefly resided in and about the city of London: and besides his labour in the ministry, which was frequent and serviceable, he wrote much both to them that are within and those that are without the communion. But the care he took of the affairs of the church in general was very great.

VIII. He was often where the records of the business of the church are kept, and where the letters from the many meetings of God's people over all the world use to come. Which letters he had read to him, and communicated them to the meeting that is weekly held for such services; and he would be sure to stir them up to answer them, especially in suffering cases: showing great sympathy and compassion upon all such occasions; carefully looking into the respective cases, and endeavouring speedy relief, according to the nature of them. So that the churches, or any of the suffering members thereof, were sure not to be forgotten or delayed in their desires if he were there.

IX. As he was unwearied, so he was undaunted in his

services for God and His people; he was no more to be moved to fear than to wrath. His behaviour at Derby, Litchfield, Appleby, before Oliver Cromwell, at Launston, Scarborough, Worcester, and Westminster Hall, with many other places and exercises, did abundantly evidence it to his enemies as well as his friends.

But as in the primitive times some rose up against the blessed apostles of our Lord Jesus Christ, even from among those that they had turned to the hope of the gospel, and they became their greater trouble; so this man of God had his share of suffering from some that were convinced by him, who through prejudice or mistake ran against him, as one that sought dominion over conscience, because he pressed by his presence or epistles a ready and zealous compliance with such good and wholesome things as tended to an orderly conversation about the affairs of the church, and in their walking before men. That which contributed much to this ill work was in some a begrudging of this meek man the love and esteem he had and deserved in the hearts of the people, and weakness in others that were taken with their groundless suggestions of imposition and blind obedience.

They would have had every man independent, that as he had the principle in himself he should only stand and fall to that, and nobody else. Not considering that the principle is one in all; and though the measure of light or grace might differ, yet the nature of it was the same; and being so they struck at the spiritual unity which a people, guided by the same principle, are naturally led into. So that what is an evil to one is so to all, and what is virtuous, honest, and of good repute to one is so to all, from the sense and savour of the one universal principle which is common to all, and which the disaffected also profess to be the root of all true Christian fellowship, and that spirit into which the people of God drink, and come to be spiritually minded, and of one heart and one soul.

Some weakly mistook good order in the government of church affairs for discipline in worship, and that it was so pressed or recommended by him and other brethren. And thereupon they were ready to reflect the same things that dissenters had very reasonably objected upon the national churches that have coercively pressed conformity to their respective creeds and worships. Whereas these things related wholly to conversation and the outward (and as I may say) civil part of the church; that men should walk up to the principles of their belief, and not be wanting in care and charity. But though some have stumbled and fallen through mistakes, and an unreasonable obstinacy, even to a prejudice; yet blessed be God, the generality have returned to their first love, and seen the work of the enemy, that loses no opportunity or advantage by which he may check or hinder the work of God, and disquiet the peace of His church, and chill the love of His people to the truth, and one to another; and there is hope of divers of the few that yet are at a distance.

In all these occasions, though there was no person the discontented struck so sharply at as this good man, he bore all their weakness and prejudice, and returned not reflection for reflection; but forgave them their weak and bitter speeches, praying for them that they might have a sense of their hurt, and see the subtilty of the enemy to rend and divide, and return into their first love that thought no ill.

And truly I must say that though God had visibly clothed him with a divine preference and authority, and indeed his very presence expressed a religious majesty, yet he never abused it, but held his place in the church of God with great meekness, and a most engaging humility and moderation. For upon all occasions, like his blessed Master, he was a servant to all; holding and exercising his eldership in the invisible power that had gathered them with reverence to the head and care over the body: and was received, only in that spirit and power of Christ, as the first and chief elder in this age: who, as he was therefore worthy of double honour, so for the same reason it was given by the faithful of this day; because his authority was inward and not outward, and that he got it and kept it by the love of God, and power of an endless life. I write my knowledge, and not report, and my witness is true; having been with him for weeks and months together on divers occasions; and those of the nearest and most exercising nature; and that by night and by day, by sea and by land; in this and in foreign countries: and I can say, I never saw him out of his place, or not a match for every service or occasion.

For in all things he acquitted himself like a man, yea, a strong man, a new and heavenly-minded man, a divine and a naturalist, and all of God Almighty's making. I have been surprised at his questions and answers in natural things: that whilst he was ignorant of useless and sophistical science, he had in him the grounds of useful and commendable knowledge, and cherished it everywhere. Civil beyond all forms of breeding in his behaviour, very temperate, eating little, and sleeping less, though a bulky person.

Thus he lived and sojourned among us: and as he lived so he died; feeling the same eternal power that had raised and preserved him in his last moments. So full of assurance was he that he triumphed over death; and so even in his spirit to the last as if death were hardly worth notice or a mention; recommending to some of us with him the dispatch and dispersion of an epistle just before given forth by him to the churches of Christ throughout the world, and his own books; but above all, Friends, and of all Friends those in Ireland and America, twice over saying, Mind poor Friends in Ireland and America.

And to some that came in and inquired how he found himself he answered, never heed, the Lord's power is over all weakness and death; the seed reigns, blessed be the Lord: which was about four or five hours before his departure out of this world. He was at the great meetings near Lombard Street on the first day of the week, and it was the third following about ten at night when he left us; being at the house of H. Goldney in the same court. In a good old age he went, after having lived to see his children's children in the truth to many generations. He had the comfort of a short illness, and the blessing of a clear sense to the last. And we may truly say, with a man of God of old, that being dead, he yet speaketh; and though now absent in body he is present in spirit, neither time nor place being able to interrupt the communion of saints, or dissolve the fellowships of the spirits of the just. His works praise him because they are to the praise of Him that wrought by him; for which his memorial is and shall be blessed. I have done as to this part of my preface when I have left this short epitaph to his name: Many sons have done virtuously in this day; but, dear George, thou excellest them all.

CHAPTER VI

CONTAINING FIVE SEVERAL EXHORTATIONS. FIRST, GENERAL, REMINDING THIS PEOPLE OF THEIR PRIMITIVE INTEGRITY AND SIMPLICITY. SECONDLY, IN PARTICULAR, TO THE MINISTRY. THIRDLY, TO THE YOUNG CONVINCED. FOURTHLY, TO THE CHILDREN OF FRIENDS. FIFTHLY, TO THOSE THAT ARE YET STRANGERS TO THIS PEOPLE AND WAY, TO WHOM THIS BOOK (AND THAT IT WAS PREFACE TO IN ITS FORMER EDITION) MAY COME. ALL THE SEVERAL EXHORTATIONS ACCOMMODATED TO THEIR SEVERAL STATES AND CONDITIONS; THAT ALL MAY ANSWER THE END OF GOD'S GLORY AND THEIR OWN SALVATION.

AND now, Friends, you that profess to walk in the way that this blessed man was sent of God to turn us into, suffer, I beseech you, the word of exhortation, as well fathers as children, and elders as young men. The glory of this day, and foundation of the hope that has not made us ashamed since we were a people, you know is that blessed principle of light and life of Christ which we profess, and direct all people to, as the great and divine instrument and agent of man's conversion to God. It was by this that we were first touched, and effectually enlightened as to our inward state; which put us upon the consideration of our latter end, causing us to set the Lord before our eyes, and to number our days that we might apply our hearts to wisdom. In that day we judged not after the sight of the eye, or after the hearing of the ear, but according to the light and sense this blessed principle gave us, so we judged and acted in reference to things and persons, ourselves and others; yea, towards God our Maker. For being quickened by it in our inward man, we could easily discern the difference of things, and feel what was right, and what was wrong, and what was fit, and what not, both in reference to religious and civil concerns. That being the ground of the fellowship of all saints, it was in that our fellowship stood. In this we desired to have a sense of one another, acted towards one another, and all men; in love, faithfulness, and fear.

In feeling of the stirrings and motions of this principle in our hearts, we drew near to the Lord, and waited to be prepared by it, that we might feel drawings and movings before we approach the Lord in prayer, or opened our mouths in ministry. And in our beginning and ending with this stood our comfort, service, and edification. And as we ran faster or fell short we made burthens for ourselves to bear; our services finding in ourselves a rebuke instead of an acceptance; and in lieu of well done, who has required this at your hands? In that day we were an exercised people, our very countenances and deportment declared it.

Care for others was then much upon us, as well as for ourselves; especially of the young convinced. Often had we the burthen of the word of the Lord to our neighbours, relations, and acquaintance; and sometimes strangers also. We were in travail likewise for one another's preservation; not seeking but shunning occasions of any coldness or misunderstanding: treating one another as those that believed and felt God present. Which kept our conversation innocent, serious, and weighty; guarding ourselves against the cares and friendships of the world. We held the truth in the spirit of it, and not in our own spirits, or after our own will and affections.

They were bowed and brought into subjection in so much that it was visible to them that knew us. We did not think ourselves at our own disposal to go where we list, or say or do what we list, or when we list. Our liberty stood in the liberty of the spirit of truth; and no pleasure, no profit, no fear, no favour could draw us from this retired, strict, and watchful frame. We were so far from seeking occasion of company that we avoided them what we could; pursuing our own business with moderation, instead of meddling with other people's unnecessarily.

Our words were few and savoury, our looks composed and weighty, and our whole deportment very observable. True it is that this retired and strict sort of life from the liberty of the conversation of the world exposed us to the censures of many as humourists, conceited, and self-righteous persons, etc. But it was our preservation from many snares to which others were continually exposed by the prevalency of the lust of the eye, the lust of the flesh, and the pride of life that wanted no occasions or temptations to excite them abroad in the converse of the world.

I cannot forget the humility and chaste zeal of that day. O, how constant at meetings, how retired in them, how firm to truth's life, as well as truth's principles! And how entire and united in our communion, as indeed became those that profess one head, even Christ Jesus the Lord.

This being the testimony and example the man of God before mentioned was sent to declare and leave amongst us, and we having embraced the same as the merciful visitation of God to us, the word of exhortation at this time is, that we continue to be found in the way of this testimony, with all zeal and integrity, and so much the more by how much the day draweth near.

And first, as to you, my beloved and much honoured brethren in Christ that are in the exercise of the ministry: O, feel life in your ministry! Let life be your commission, your well-spring and treasury in all such occasions; else you well know there can be no begetting to God, since nothing can quicken or make people alive to God but the life of God. And it must be a ministry in and from life that enlivens any people to God. We have seen the fruit of all other ministers by the few that are turned from the evil of their ways. It is not our parts, or memory, the repetition of former openings in our own will and time that will do God's work. A dry doctrinal ministry, however sound in words, can reach but the ear, and is but a dream at the best: there is another soundness that is soundest of all, viz., Christ the power of God. This is the key of David that opens and none shuts, and shuts, and none can open: as the oil to the lamp and the soul to the body so is that to the best of words. Which made Christ to say, my words, they are spirit, and they are life; that is, they are from life, and therefore they make you alive that receive them. If the disciples that had lived with Jesus were to stay at Jerusalem till they received it, much more must we wait to receive before we minister if we will turn people from darkness to light, and from Satan's power to God.

I fervently bow my knees to the God and Father of our Lord Jesus Christ, that you may always be like-minded, that you may ever wait reverently for the coming and opening of the word of life, and attend upon it in your ministry and service, that you may serve God in His spirit. And be it little, or be it much, it is well; for much is not too much, and the least is enough if from the motion of God's Spirit; and without it, verily, never so little is too much because to no profit.

For it is the spirit of the Lord immediately or through the ministry of His servants that teacheth His people to profit; and to be sure, so far as we take Him along with us in our services, so far we are profitable and no farther. For if it be the Lord that must work all things in us for our salvation, much more is it the Lord that must work in us for the conversion of others. If therefore it was once a cross to us to speak, though the Lord required it at our hands, let us never be so to be silent when He does not.

It is one of the most dreadful sayings in the book of God, that he that adds to the words of the prophecy of this Book God will add to him the plagues written in this Book. To keep back the counsel of God is as terrible; for he that takes away from the words of the Book of this prophecy God shall take away his part out of the Book of Life. And truly, it has great caution in it to those that use the name of the Lord to be well assured the Lord speaks, that they may not be found of the number of those that add to the words of the testimony of prophecy which the Lord giveth them to bear; nor yet to mince or diminish the same, both being so very offensive to God.

Wherefore, brethren, let us be careful neither to outgo our Guide, nor yet loiter behind Him; since he that makes haste may miss his way, and he that stays behind lose his Guide. For even those that have received the word of the Lord had need wait for wisdom that they may see how to divide the word aright. Which plainly implieth that it is possible for one that hath received the word of the Lord to miss in the dividing and application of it, which must come from an impatiency of spirit, and a self-working, which makes an unsound and dangerous mixture; and will hardly beget a right-minded living people to God.

I am earnest in this above all considerations as to public brethren; well knowing how much it concerns the present and future state, and preservation of the Church of Christ Jesus, that has been gathered and built up by a living and powerful ministry, that the ministry be held, preserved, and continued in the manifestations, motions, and supplies of the same life and power from time to time.

And wherever it is observed that any do minister more from gifts and parts than life and power, though they have an enlightened and doctrinal understanding, let them in time be advised and admonished for their preservation, because insensibly such will come to depend upon a self-sufficiency; to forsake Christ the living fountain, and hew out unto themselves cisterns that will hold no living waters: and by degrees such will come to draw others from waiting upon the gift of God in themselves, and to feel it in others, in order to their strength and refreshment, to wait upon them, and to turn from God to man again, and so make shipwreck of the faith, once delivered to the saints, and of a good conscience towards God; which are only kept by that divine gift of life that begat the one and awakened and sanctified the other in the beginning.

Nor is it enough that we have known the divine gift, and in it have reached to the spirits in prison, and been the instruments of the convincing of others of the way of God, if we keep not as low and poor in ourselves, and as depending upon the Lord as ever. Since no memory, no repetitions of former openings, revelations, or enjoyments, will bring a soul to God, or afford bread to the hungry, or water to the thirsty, unless life go with what we say, and that must be waited for.

O that we may have no other fountain, treasure, or dependence! That none may presume at any rate to act of themselves for God, because they have long acted from God; that we may not supply want of waiting with our own wisdom, or think that we may take less care and more liberty in speaking than formerly; and that where we do not feel the Lord by His power, to open us and enlarge us, whatever be the expectation of the people, or has been our customary supply and character, we may not exceed or fill up the time with our own.

I hope we shall ever remember who it was that said, of yourselves you can do nothing: our sufficiency is in Him. And if we are not to speak our own words, or take thought what we should say to men in our defence, when exposed for our testimony, surely we ought to speak none of our own words, or take thought what we shall say in our testimony and ministry, in the name of our Lord to the souls of the people; for then of all times and of all other occasions should it be fulfilled in us, for it is not you that speak, but the spirit of my Father that speaketh in you.

And indeed, the ministry of the spirit must and does keep its analogy and agreement with the birth of the spirit, that as no man can inherit the kingdom of God unless he be born of the spirit, so no ministry can beget a soul to God but that which is from the spirit. For this, as I said before, the disciples waited before they went forth; and in this our elder brethren and messengers of God in our day waited, visited, and reached us. And having begun in the spirit let none ever hope or seek to be made perfect in the flesh. For what is the flesh to the spirit, or the chaff to the wheat? And if we keep in the spirit we shall keep in the unity of it, which is the ground of the fellowship. For by drinking into that one spirit we are made one people to God, and by it we are continued in the unity of the faith and the bond of peace. No envying, no bitterness, no strife can have place with us. We shall watch always for good, and not for evil, one over another, and rejoice exceedingly and not begrudge at one another's increase in the riches of the grace with which God replenisheth His faithful servants.

And, brethren, as to you is committed the dispensation of the oracles of God, which give you frequent opportunities and great place with the people among whom you travail, I beseech you that you would not think it sufficient to declare the word of life in their assemblies; however edifying and comfortable such opportunities may be to you and them. But as was the practice of the man of God, before mentioned, in great measure, when among us, inquire the state of the several churches you visit; who among them are afflicted or sick, who are tempted, and if any are unfaithful or obstinate; and endeavour to issue those things in the wisdom and power of God, which will be a glorious crown upon your ministry. As that prepares your way in the hearts of the people to receive you as men of God, so it gives you credit with them to do them good by your advice in other respects, the afflicted will be comforted by you, the tempted strengthened, the sick refreshed, the unfaithful convicted and restored, and such as are obstinate, softened and fitted for reconciliation, which is clinching the nail, and applying and fastening the general testimony by this particular care of the several branches of it, in reference to them more immediately concerned in it.

For though good and wise men and elders too may reside in such places who are of worth and importance in the general, and in other places; yet it does not always follow that they may have the room they deserve in the hearts of the people they live among; or some particular occasion may make it unfit for him or them to use that authority. But you that travail as God's messengers, if they receive you in the greater shall they refuse you in the less? And if they own the general testimony can they withstand the particular application of it in their own cases? Thus ye will show yourselves workmen indeed, and carry your business before you to the praise of His name that hath called you from darkness to light, that you might turn others from Satan's power unto God and His kingdom, which is within. And O that there were more of such faithful labourers in the vineyard of the Lord! Never more need since the day of God.

Wherefore I cannot but cry and call aloud to you that have been long professors of the truth, and know the truth in the convincing power of it, and have had a sober conversation among men, yet content yourselves only to know truth for yourselves, to go to meetings, and exercise an ordinary charity in the church, and an honest behaviour in the world, and limit yourselves within those bounds; feeling little or no concern upon your spirits, for the glory of the Lord in the prosperity of His truth in the earth, more than to be glad that others succeed in such service. Arise ye in the name and power of the Lord Jesus! Behold how white the fields are unto harvest, in this and other nations, and how few able and faithful labourers there are to work therein! Your country folks, neighbours, and kindred want to know the Lord and His truth, and to walk in it. Does nothing lie at your door upon their account? Search and see, and lose no time, I beseech you, for the Lord is at hand.

I do not judge you, there is one that judgeth all men, and His judgment is true. You have mightily increased in your outward substance. May you equally increase in your inward riches, and do good with both, while you have a day to do good. Your enemies would once have taken what you had from you, for His name sake, in whom you have believed; wherefore He has given you much of the world in the face of your enemies. But O, let it be your servant, and not your master! Your diversion rather than your business! Let the Lord be chiefly in your eye, and ponder your ways, and see if God has nothing more for you to do: and if you find yourselves short in your account with Him, then wait for His preparation, and be ready to receive the word of command, and be not weary of well doing when you have put your hand to the plough, and assuredly you shall reap, if you faint not, the fruit of your heavenly labour in God's everlasting kingdom.

And you young convinced ones, be you entreated and exhorted to a diligent and chaste waiting upon God in the way of His blessed manifestation and appearance of Himself to you. Look not out, but within. Let not another's liberty be your snare: neither act by imitation, but sense and feeling of God's power in yourselves: crush not the tender buddings of it in your souls, nor overrun in your desires and warmness of affections the holy and gentle motions of it. Remember it is a still voice that speaks to us in this day, and that it is not to be heard in the noises and hurries of the mind; but it is distinctly understood in a retired frame. Jesus loved and chose solitudes; often going to mountains, gardens, and seasides to avoid crowds and hurries, to show His disciples it was good to be solitary and sit loose to the world. Two enemies lie near your states, imagination and liberty; but the plain, practical, living, holy truth that has convinced you, will preserve you, if you mind it in yourselves, and bring all thoughts, inclinations, and affections to the test of it, to see if they are wrought in God, or of the enemy, or your own selves: so will a true taste, discerning, and judgment be preserved to you, of what you should do and leave undone. And in your diligence and faithfulness in this way you will come to inherit substance; and Christ the eternal wisdom will fill your treasury. And when you are converted, as well as convinced, then confirm your brethren; and be ready to every good word and work that the Lord shall call you to; that you may be to His praise, who has chosen you to be partakers with the saints in light of a kingdom that cannot be shaken, an inheritance incorruptible in eternal habitations.

And now, as for you, that are the children of God's people, a great concern is upon my spirit for your good: and often are my knees bowed to the God of your Fathers for you that you may come to be partakers of the same divine life and power, that have been the glory of this day; that a generation you may be to God, a holy nation, and a peculiar people, zealous of good works when all our heads are laid in the dust. O you young men and women! Let it not suffice you that you are the children of the people of the Lord; you must also be born again, if you will inherit the kingdom of God. Your fathers are but such after the flesh, and could but beget you into the likeness of the first Adam; but you must be begotten into the likeness of the second Adam, by a spiritual generation, or you will not, you cannot, be of His children or offspring. And therefore look carefully about you, O ye children of the children of God! Consider your standing, and see what you are in relation to this divine kindred, family, and birth! Have you obeyed the light and received and walked in the spirit, which is the incorruptible seed of the word and kingdom of God, of which you must be born again. God is no respecter of persons. The Father cannot save or answer for the child, or the child for the father, but in the sin thou sinnest thou shalt die; and in the righteousness thou dost through Christ Jesus thou shalt live; for it is the willing and obedient that shall eat the good of the land. Be not deceived, God is not mocked, such as all nations and people sow such they shall reap at the hand of the just God. And then your many and great privileges above the children of other people will add weight in the scale against you, if you choose not the way of the Lord. For you have had line upon line, and precept upon precept, and not only good doctrine but good example; and which is more, you have been turned to and acquainted with a principle in yourselves which others have been ignorant of. And you know you may be as good as you please without the fear of frowns and blows, or being turned out of doors, and forsaken of father and mother, for God's sake, and His holy religion, as has been the case of some of your fathers in the day they first entered into this holy path. And if you, after hearing and seeing the wonders that God has wrought in the deliverance and preservation of them through a sea of troubles, and the manifold temporal as well as spiritual blessings that He has filled them with in the sight of their enemies, should neglect and turn your backs upon so great and near a salvation, you would not only be most ungrateful children to God and them, but must expect that God will call the children of those that knew Him not to take the crown out of your hands, and that your lot will be a dreadful judgment at the hand of the Lord: but O that it may never be so with any of you. The Lord forbid, saith my soul.

Wherefore, O ye young men and women, look to the rock of your fathers: there is no other God but Him, no other light but His, no other grace but His, nor spirit but His, to convince you, quicken and comfort you, to lead, guide, and preserve you to God's everlasting kingdom. So will you be possessors as well as professors of the truth, embracing it not only by education, but judgment and conviction; from a sense begotten in your souls, through the operation of the eternal spirit and power of God; by which you may come to be the seed of Abraham, through faith and the circumcision not made with hands; and so heirs of the promise made to the fathers of an incorruptible crown. That, as I said before, a generation you may be to God, holding up the profession of the blessed truth in the life and power of it. For formality in religion is nauseous to God and good men; and the more so where any form and appearance has been new and peculiar, and begun and practised upon a principle with an uncommon zeal and strictness. Therefore, I say, for you to fall flat and formal, and continue the profession without the salt and savour, by which it is come to obtain a good report among men, is not to answer God's love or your parents' care, or the mind of truth in yourselves or in those that are without: who, though they will not obey the truth, have sight and sense enough to see if they do that make a profession of it. For where the divine virtue of it is not felt in the soul, and waited for, and lived in, imperfections will quickly break out, and show themselves, and detect the unfaithfulness of such persons; and that their insides are not seasoned with the nature of that holy principle which they profess.

Wherefore, dear children, let me entreat you to shut your

eyes at the temptations and allurements of this low and perishing world, and not suffer your affections to be captivated by those lusts and vanities that your fathers, for the truth's sake, long since turned their backs upon. But as you believe it to be the truth receive it into your hearts, that you may become the children of God. So that it may never be said of you, as the evangelist writes of the Jews in his time, that Christ, the true light, came to His own, but His own received Him not; but to as many as received Him to them He gave power to become the children of God; which were born, not of blood, nor of the will of the flesh, nor of the will of man, but of God. A most close and comprehensive passage to this occasion. You exactly and peculiarly answer to those professing Jews, in that you bear the name of God's people, by being the children, and wearing of the form of God's people: and He, by His light in you, may be very well said to come to His own, and if you obey it not, but turn your back upon it, and walk after the vanities of your minds, you will be of those that received Him not, which I pray God may never be your case and judgment. But that you may be thoroughly sensible of the many and great obligations you lie under to the Lord for His love, and to your parents for their care: and with all your heart, and all your soul, and all your strength, turn to the Lord, to His gift and spirit in you, and hear His voice and obey it, that you may seal to the testimony of your fathers by the truth and evidence of your own experience; that your children's children may bless you, and the Lord for you, as those that delivered a faithful example, as well as record of the truth of God unto them. So will the grey hairs of your dear parents, yet alive, go down to the grave with joy to see you the posterity of truth as well as theirs, and that not only their nature but spirit shall live in you when they are gone.

I shall conclude this account with a few words to those that are not of our communion, into whose hands this may come; especially those of our own nation.

Friends, as you are the sons and daughters of Adam, and my brethren after the flesh, often and earnest have been my desires and prayers to God on your behalf, that you may come to know your Creator to be your Redeemer and restorer to the holy image, that through sin you have lost, by the power and spirit of His son Jesus Christ, whom He hath given for the light and life of the world. And O that you who are called Christians would receive Him into your hearts! For there it is you want Him, and at that door He stands knocking that you might let Him in, but you do not open to Him. You are full of other guests, so that a manger is His lot among you now, as well as of old. Yet you are full of profession, as were the Jews when He came among them, who knew Him not, but rejected and evilly entreated Him. So that if you come not to the possession and experience of what you profess, all your formality in religion will stand you in no stead in the day of God's judgment.

I beseech you ponder with yourselves your eternal condition, and see what title, what ground and foundation you have for your Christianity. If more than a profession, and an historical belief of the gospel? Have you known the baptism of fire, and the Holy Ghost, and the fan of Christ that winnows away the chaff in your minds, and carnal lusts and affections? That divine leaven of the kingdom, that being received leavens the whole lump of man, sanctifying him throughout in body, soul, and spirit? If this be not the ground of your confidence, you are in a miserable estate.

You will say, perhaps, that though you are sinners, and live in daily commission of sin, and are not sanctified, as I have been speaking, yet you have faith in Christ, who has born the curse for you, and in Him you are complete by faith, His righteousness being imputed to you.

But, my friends, let me entreat you not to deceive yourselves in so important a point as is that of your immortal souls. If you have true faith in Christ your faith will make you clean; it will sanctify you: for the saints' faith was their victory of old: by this they overcame sin within and sinful men without. And if thou art in Christ thou walkest not after the flesh, but after the spirit, whose fruits are manifest. Yea, thou art a new creature: new made, new fashioned; after God's will and mould. Old things are done away, and behold all things are become new: new love, desires, will, affections, and practices. It is not any longer thou that livest; thou disobedient, carnal, worldly one; but it is Christ that liveth in thee; and to live is Christ, and to die is thy eternal gain. Because thou art assured that thy corruptible shall put on incorruption, and thy mortal, immortality, and that thou hast a glorious house eternal in the heavens that will never wax old or pass away. All this follows being in Christ, as heat follows fire, and light the sun.

Therefore have a care how you presume to rely upon such a notion as that you are in Christ, whilst in your old fallen nature. For what communion hath light with darkness, or Christ with Belial? Hear what the beloved disciple tells you: If we say we have fellowship with God, and walk in darkness, we lie, and do not the truth. This is, if we go on in a sinful way, are captivated by our carnal affections, and are not converted to God, we walk in darkness, and cannot possibly in that state have any fellowship with God. Christ clothes them with His righteousness that receive His grace in their hearts, and deny themselves, and take up His cross daily and follow Him. Christ's righteousness makes men inwardly holy; of holy minds, wills, and practices. It is nevertheless Christ's, because we have it; for it is ours, not by nature, but by faith and adoption: it is the gift of God. But still, though not ours, as of or from ourselves, for in that sense it is Christ's, for it is of and from Him; yet it is ours, and must be ours in possession, efficacy, and enjoyment to do us any good; or Christ's righteousness will profit us nothing. It was after this manner that He was made to the primitive Christians, righteousness, sanctification, justification, and redemption; and if ever you will have the comfort, kernel, and marrow of the Christian religion thus you must come to learn and obtain it.

Now, my friends, by what you have read, and will read in what follows, you may perceive that God has visited a poor people among you with this saving knowledge and testimony. Whom He has upheld and increased to this day, notwithstanding the fierce opposition they have met withal. Despise not the meanness of this appearance. It was, and yet is (we know), a day of small things, and of small account with too many; and many hard and ill names are given to it. But it is of God, it came from Him because it leads to Him. This we know, but we cannot make another to know it, unless he will take the same way to know it that we took. The world talks of God, but what do they do? They pray for power, but reject the principle in which it is. If you would know God, and worship and serve God as you should do, you must come to the means He has ordained and given for that purpose. Some seek it in books, some in learned men, but what they look for is in themselves, though not of themselves, but they overlook it. The voice is too still, the seed too small, and the light shineth in darkness; they are abroad, and so cannot divide the spoil. But the woman that lost her silver found it at home after she had lighted her candle and swept her house. Do you so too, and you shall find what Pilate wanted to know, viz., truth. Truth in the inward parts, so valuable in the sight of God.

The light of Christ within, who is the light of the world (and so a light to you that tells you the truth of your condition), leads all that take heed unto it out of darkness unto God's marvellous light. For light grows upon the obedient. It is sown for the righteous, and their way is a shining light that shines forth more and more to the perfect day.

Wherefore, O friends, turn in, turn in, I beseech you. Where is the poison, there is the antidote. There you want Christ, and there you must find Him; and, blessed be God, there you may find Him. Seek and you shall find, I testify for God. But then you must seek aright with your whole heart, as men that seek for their lives, yea, for their eternal lives: diligently, humbly, patiently, as those that can taste no pleasure, comfort, or satisfaction in anything else, unless you find Him whom your souls desire to know and love above all. O it is a travail, a spiritual travail! Let the carnal, profane world think and say as it will. And through this path you must walk to the city of God that has eternal foundations, if ever you will come there.

Well! and what does this blessed light do for you? Why, 1. It sets all your sins in order before you. It detects the spirit of this world in all its baits and allurements, and shows how man came to fall from God, and the fallen estate he is in. 2. It begets a sense and sorrow, in such as believe in it, for this fearful lapse. You will then see Him distinctly whom you have pierced, and all the blows and wounds you have given Him by your disobedience, and how you have made Him to serve with your sins; and you will weep and mourn for it, and your sorrow will be a godly sorrow. 3. After this it will bring you to the holy watch, to take care that you do so no more, and that the enemy surprise you not again. Then thoughts, as well as words and works, will come to judgment, which is the way of holiness in which the redeemed of the Lord do walk. Here you will come to love God above all, and your neighbours as yourselves. Nothing hurts, nothing harms, nothing makes afraid on this holy mountain. Now you come to be Christ's indeed: for you are His in nature and spirit, and not your own. And when you are thus Christ's, then Christ is yours, and not before. And here communion with the Father and with the Son you will know, and the efficacy of the blood of cleansing, even the blood of Jesus Christ, that immaculate Lamb, which speaks better things than the blood of Abel; and which cleanseth from all sin the consciences of those that through the living faith come to be sprinkled with it from dead works to serve the living God.

To conclude, behold the testimony and doctrine of the people called Quakers! Behold their practice and discipline! And behold the blessed man and men (at least many of them) that were sent of God in this excellent work and service! All which is more particularly expressed in the annals of that man of God: which I do heartily recommend to my readers' most serious perusal; and beseech Almighty God that His blessing may go along with both to the convincement of many, as yet strangers to this holy dispensation, and also to the edification of God's Church in general. Who for His manifold and repeated mercies and blessings to His people in this day of His great love is worthy ever to have to glory, honour, thanksgiving, and renown; and be it rendered and ascribed, with fear and reverence, through Him in whom He is well pleased, His beloved Son and Lamb, our light and life, that sits with Him upon the throne, world without end. Amen.

Says one that God has long since mercifully favoured with His fatherly visitation, and who was not disobedient to the heavenly vision and call; to whom the way of truth is more lovely and precious than ever, and that knowing the beauty and benefit of it above all worldly treasures, has chosen it for his chiefest joy; and therefore recommends it to thy love and choice, because He is with great sincerity and affection,

Thy soul's friend,

W. PENN.

PRIMITIVE CHRISTIANITY REVIVED IN THE FAITH AND PRACTICE OF THE PEOPLE CALLED QUAKERS

PRIMITIVE CHRISTIANITY REVIVED

IN THE FAITH AND PRACTICE OF THE PEOPLE CALLED QUAKERS

Written in Testimony to the present Dispensation of God through them to the World; that Prejudices may be removed, the Simple informed, the Well-inclined encouraged, and the Truth and its Innocent Friends rightly represented. By W. P.

THE EPISTLE TO THE READER

Reader,—By this short ensuing treatise thou wilt perceive the subject of it, viz., the light of Christ in man, as the manifestation of God's love for man's happiness. Now, for as much as this is the peculiar testimony and characteristic of the people called Quakers; their great fundamental in religion; that by which they have been distinguished from other professors of Christianity in their time, and to which they refer all people about faith, worship, and practice, both in their ministry and writings; that as the fingers shoot out of the hand and the branches from the body of the tree, so true religion, in all the parts and articles of it, springs from this divine principle in man. And because the prejudices of some are very great against this people and their way; and that others, who love their seriousness, and commend their good life, are yet, through mistakes or want of inquiry, under jealousy of their unsoundness in some points of faith; and that there are not a few in all persuasions which desire earnestly to know and enjoy God in that sensible manner this people speak of, and who seem to long after a state of holiness and acceptance with God; but are under doubts and despondings of their attaining it from the want they find in themselves of inward power to enable them, and are unacquainted with this efficacious agent which God hath given and appointed for their supply.

For these reasons and motives know, Reader, I have taken in hand to write this small tract, Of the Nature and Virtue of the Light of Christ Within Man; what, and where it is, and for what end, and therein of the religion of the people called Quakers; that, at the same time, all people may be informed of their true character, and what true religion is, and the way to it in this age of high pretences, and as deep irreligion. That so the merciful visitation of the God of light and love (more especially to these nations), both immediately and instrumentally, for the promotion of piety (which is religion indeed) may no longer be neglected by the inhabitants thereof, but that they may come to see and say with heart and mouth, this is a dispensation of love and life from God to the world; and this poor people that we have so much despised, and so often trod upon, and treated as the off-scouring of the earth, are the people of God and children of the Most High. Bear with me, Reader, I know what I say, and am not high-minded, but fear. For I write with humility towards God, though with confidence towards thee. Not that thou shouldst believe upon my authority, nothing less; for that is not to act upon knowledge, but trust; but that thou shouldst try and approve what I write. For that is all I ask as well as all I need for thy conviction, and my own justification; the whole, indeed, being but a spiritual experiment upon the soul, and therefore seeks for no implicit credit, because it is self-evident to them that will uprightly try it.

And when thou, Reader, shalt come to be acquainted with this principle, and the plain and happy teachings of it, thou wilt with us admire thou shouldst live so long a stranger to that which was so near thee, and as much wonder that other folks should be so blind as not to see it, as formerly thou thoughtest us singular for obeying it. The day I believe is at hand that will declare this with an uncontrollable authority, because it will be with an unquestionable evidence.

I have done, Reader, with this Preface when I have told thee, First, that I have stated the principle, and opened, as God has enabled me, the nature and virtue of it in religion; wherein the common doctrines and articles of the Christian religion are delivered and improved; and about which I have endeavoured to express myself in plain and proper terms and not in figurative, allegorical, or doubtful phrases. That so I may leave no room for an equivocal or double sense; but that the truth of the subject I treat upon may appear easily and evidently to every common understanding. Next, I have confirmed what I have writ by Scripture, reason, and the effects of it upon so great a people; whose uniform concurrence in the experience and practice thereof through all times and sufferings, since a people, challenge the notice and regard of every serious Reader. Thirdly, I have written briefly, that so it might be everyone's money and reading. And, much in a little is best, when we see daily that the richer people grow, the less money or time they have for God or religion. And perhaps those that would not buy a large book may find in their hearts to give away some of these for their neighbour's good, being little and cheap. Be serious, Reader, be impartial, and then be as inquisitive as thou canst; and that for thine own soul as well as the credit of this most misunderstood and abused people. And the God and Father of lights and spirits so bless thine in the perusal of this short treatise, that thou mayst receive real benefit by it, to His glory and thine own comfort, which is the desire and end of him that wrote it; who is, in the bonds of Christian charity, very much, and very ardently,—Thy real Friend,

WILLIAM PENN.

CHAPTER I

1. THEIR FUNDAMENTAL PRINCIPLE. 2. THE NATURE OF IT. 3. CALLED BY SEVERAL NAMES. 4. THEY REFER ALL TO THIS AS TO FAITH AND PRACTICE, MINISTRY AND WORSHIP.

1. THAT which the people called Quakers lay down, as a main fundamental in religion, is this, that God, through Christ, hath placed a principle in every man to inform him of his duty, and to enable him to do it; and that those that live up to this principle are the people of God, and those that live in disobedience to it are not God's people, whatever name they may bear, or profession they may make of religion. This is their ancient, first, and standing testimony. With this they began, and this they bore, and do bear to the world.

2. By this principle they understand something that is

divine; and though in man, yet not of man, but of God; and that it came from Him, and leads to Him all those that will be led by it.

3. There are divers ways of speaking they have been led to use, by which they declare and express what this principle is, about which I think fit to precaution the reader, viz., they call it the light of Christ within man, or light within,[1] which is their ancient and most general and familiar phrase, also the manifestation [2] or appearance of Christ,[3] the witness of God,[4] the seed of God,[5] the seed of the kingdom,[6] wisdom,[7] the word in the heart,[8] the grace that appears to all men,[9] the spirit given to every man to profit with,[10] the truth in the inward parts,[11] the spiritual leaven that leavens the whole lump of man [12]—which are many of them figurative expressions, but all of them such as the Holy Ghost hath used, and which will be used in this treatise as they are most frequently in the writings and ministry of this people. But that this variety and manner of expression may not occasion any misapprehension or confusion in the understanding of the reader, I would have him know that they always mean by these terms or denominations, not another, but the same principle before mentioned. Which, as I said, though it be in man is not of man but of God, and therefore divine, and one in itself, though diversly expressed by the holy men, according to the various manifestations and operations thereof.

4. It is to this principle of light, life, and grace that this people refer all. For they say it is the great agent in religion; that without which there is no conviction, so no conversion or regeneration; and consequently no entering into the kingdom of God. That is to say, there can be no true sight of sin, nor sorrow for it, and therefore no forsaking or overcoming of it, or remission or justification from it. A necessary and powerful principle indeed, when neither sanctification nor justification can be had without it. In short, there is no

[1] John i. 9.
[2] Rom. i. 19; Tit. iii. 4.
[3] Acts xvii. 28; 2 Pet. iv.
[4] Rom. viii. 6; 1 John v. 10, 12.
[5] 1 Pet. i. 23; 1 John iii. 9.
[6] Mat. xiii. 19, 23.
[7] Prov. i. 20, 21, 22, 23, and viii. 1, 2, 3, 4.
[8] Deut. xxx. 12; Rom. x. 6, 7, 8; Ps. cxix. 10.
[9] Tit. ii. 11, 12.
[10] 1 Cor. xii. 7.
[11] Ps. li. 6; Isa. xxvi. 2; John xiv. 6.
[12] Mat. xiii. 33.

becoming virtuous, holy, and good without this principle; no acceptance with God nor peace of soul but through it. But on the contrary, that the reason of so much irreligion among Christians, so much superstition, instead of devotion, and so much profession without enjoyment, and so little heart reformation is because people in religion overlook this principle, and leave it behind them.

They will be religious without it, and Christians without it, though this be the only means of making them so indeed. So natural is it to man in his degenerate state to prefer sacrifice before obedience, and to make prayers go for practice, and so flatter himself to hope, by ceremonial and bodily service, to excuse himself with God from the stricter discipline of this principle in the soul, which leads man to take up the cross, deny self, and do that which God requires of him. And that is every man's true religion, and every such man is truly religious. That is, he is holy, humble, patient, meek, merciful, just, kind, and charitable; which they say no man can make himself; but that this principle will make them all so, that will embrace the convictions and teachings of it, being the root of all true religion in man, and the good seed from whence all good fruits proceed. To sum up what they say upon the nature and virtue of it as contents of that which follows, they declare that this principle is, first, divine; secondly, universal; thirdly, efficacious; in that it gives man:

First, the knowledge of God and of himself, and therein a sight of his duty and disobedience to it.

Secondly, it begets a true sense and sorrow for sin in those that seriously regard the convictions of it.

Thirdly, it enables them to forsake sin, and sanctifies from it.

Fourthly, it applies God's mercies in Christ for the forgiveness of sins that are past unto justification, upon such sincere repentance and obedience.

Fifthly, it gives to the faithful perseverance unto a perfect man, and the assurance of blessedness, world without end.

To the truth of all which they call in a threefold evidence: First, the Scriptures, which give an ample witness, especially those of the New and better Testament. Secondly, the reasonableness of it in itself. And lastly, a general experience, in great measure, but particularly their own, made credible by the good fruits they have brought forth, and the answer God has given to their ministry, which to impartial observers have commended the principle and gives me occasion to abstract their history in divers particulars for a conclusion to this little treatise.

CHAPTER II

1. THE EVIDENCE OF SCRIPTURE FOR THIS PRINCIPLE, JOHN I. 4, 9. 2. ITS DIVINITY. 3. ALL THINGS CREATED BY IT. 4. WHAT IT IS TO MAN AS TO SALVATION.

1. I SHALL begin with the evidence of the blessed Scriptures of Truth for this divine principle, and that under the name of light, the first and most common word used by them, to express and denominate this principle by, as well as most apt and proper in this dark state of the world.

John i. 1. In the beginning was the Word, and the Word was with God, and the Word was God.

Verse 3. All things were made by Him.

Verse 4. In Him was life, and that life was the light of men.

Verse 9. That was the true light which lighteth every man that cometh into the world.

2. I have begun with him that begun his history with Him that was the beginning of the creation of God; the most beloved disciple, and longest liver of all the apostles, and he that for excellent knowledge and wisdom in heavenly things is justly entitled John the Divine. He tells us first what He was in the beginning, viz., the Word. In the beginning was the Word.

And though that shows what the Word must be, yet he adds and explains that the Word was with God, and the Word was God; lest any should doubt of the divinity of the Word, or have lower thoughts of Him than He deserved. The Word then is divine, and an apt term it is that the Evangelist styles Him by, since it is so great an expression of the wisdom and power of God to men.

3. All things were made by Him. If so, He wants no power. And if we were made by Him, we must be new made by Him too, or we can never enjoy God. His power shows His dignity, and that nothing can be too hard for such a

sufficiency as made all things, and without which nothing was made that was made. As man's Maker must be his husband, so his Creator must be his Redeemer also.

4. In Him was life, and the life was the light of men. This is our point. The Evangelist first begins with the nature and being of the Word. From thence he descends to the works of the Word. And lastly, then he tells us what the Word is with respect to man above the rest of the creation, viz., the Word was life, and the life was the light of men. The relation must be very near and intimate when the very life of the world (that was with God, and was God) is the light of men. As if men were next to the Word and above all the rest of His works; for it is not said so of any other creature.

Man cannot want light then; no, not a divine light: for if this be not divine that is the life of the Divine Word, there can be no such thing at all as divine or supernatural light and life. And the text does not only prove the divinity of the light, but the universality of it also, because man mentioned in it is mankind. Which is yet more distinctly expressed in his 9th verse, that was the true light, which lighteth every man that cometh into the world. Implying that he that lighteth not mankind is not that true light; and therefore John was not that light, but bore witness of Him that was, who lighteth every man; to wit, the Word that took flesh. So that both the divine nature and universality of the light of Christ within are confirmed together.

CHAPTER III

1. HOW THIS SCRIPTURE IS WRESTED. 2. THAT IT IS A NATURAL LIGHT. 3. THAT IT LIGHTETH NOT ALL. 4. THAT IT IS ONLY THE DOCTRINE AND LIFE OF CHRIST WHEN IN THE FLESH. ALL ANSWERED, AND ITS DIVINITY AND UNIVERSALITY PROVED.

1. BUT though there be no passage or proposition to be found in Holy Scripture in which mankind is more interested, or that is more clearly laid down by the Holy Ghost, than this I have produced, yet hardly hath any place been more industriously wrested from its true and plain sense. Especi-

ally since this people have laid any stress upon it in defence of their testimony of the light within. Some will have it to be but a natural light, or a part of man's nature, though it be the very life of the Word by which the world was made; and mentioned within those verses which only concern His eternal power and Godhead. But because I would be understood and treat of things with all plainness, I will open the terms of the objection as well as I can, and then give my answer to it.

2. If by natural be meant a created thing as man is, or anything that is requisite to the composition of man, I deny it. The text is expressly against it; and says, the light with which man is lighted is the life of the Word, which was with God, and was God. But if by natural is only intended that the light comes along with us into the world; or that we have it as sure as we are born or have nature; and is the light of our nature, of our minds and understandings, and is not the result of any revelation from without, as by angels or men; then we mean and intend the same thing. For it is natural to man to have a supernatural light, and for the creature to be lighted by an uncreated light, as is the life of the creating word. And did people but consider the constitution of man it would conduce much to preserve or deliver them from any dilemma upon this account. For man can be no more a light to his mind than he is to his body. He has the capacity of seeing objects when he has the help of light, but cannot be a light to himself by which to see them. Wherefore as the sun in the firmament is the light of the body, and gives us discerning in our temporal affairs, so the life of the Word is the glorious light and sun of the soul; our intellectual luminary that informs our mind and gives us true judgment and distinction about those things that more immediately concern our better, inward, and eternal man.

3. But others will have this text read thus, not that the Word enlightens all mankind, but that all who are enlightened are enlightened by Him, thereby not only narrowing and abusing the text, but rendering God partial and so severe to His creatures as to leave the greatest part of the world in darkness, without the means or opportunity of salvation; though we are assured from the Scriptures that all have light,[1] that

[1] John i. 4, 9.

Christ is the light of the world,[1] and that He died for all;[2] yea, the ungodly,[3] and that God desires not the death of any, but rather that all should repent and come to the knowledge of the truth and be saved;[4] and that the grace of God has appeared to all men,[5] etc.

4. There is a third sort that will needs have it understood, not of any illumination by a divine light or spirit in man, but by the doctrine Christ preached and the life and example He lived and led in the world; and which yet neither reached the thousandth part of mankind, nor can consist with what the apostle John intends in the beginning of his history, which wholly relates to what Christ was before He took flesh, or at least what He is to the soul by His immediate inshinings and influences. It is most true Christ was in a sense the light of the world in that very appearance, and shined forth by His heavenly doctrine, many admirable miracles, and His self-denying life and death. But still that hinders not, but that He was and is that spiritual light which shineth more or less in the hearts of the sons and daughters of men. For as He was a light in His life and conversation, He was only a light in a more excellent sense than He spoke of to His disciples when He said, ye are the lights of the world. But Christ the Word enlightened them, and enlightens us, and enlightens all men that come into the world; which He could not be said to do if we only regard His personal and outward appearance. For in that sense it is long since He was that light, but in this He is continually so. In that respect He is remote, but in this sense He is present and immediate, else we should render the text, that was the true light which did lighten instead of which lighteth every man that cometh into the world. And that the Evangelist might be so understood as we speak he refers to this as an evidence of His being the Messiah, and not John; for whom many people had much reverence, for verse 8 he said of John, he was not that light, but was sent to bear witness of that light. Now comes his proof and our testimony, That was the true light which lighteth every man that cometh into the world; which was not John, or any else, but the Word that was with God, and was God. The Evangelist did not describe Him by His

[1] Ch. viii. 12. [2] Rom. v. 6. [3] 2 Cor. v. 15.
[4] 1 Tim. ii. 4. [5] Tit. ii. 11, 12.

fasting forty days, preaching so many sermons, working so many miracles, and living so holy a life; and after all so patiently suffering death (which yet Christ did) thereby to prove Him the light of the world; but says the Evangelist, that was the true light, the Word in flesh, the Messiah, and not John or any else, which lighteth every man that cometh into the world. So that Christ is manifested and distinguished by giving light. And indeed so are all His followers from other people, by receiving and obeying it. There are many other scriptures of both testaments that refer to the light within; either expressly or implicity; which, for brevity's sake, I shall waive reciting; but the reader will find some directions at the foot of the page[1] which will guide him to them.

CHAPTER IV

1. THE VIRTUE OF THE LIGHT WITHIN; IT GIVES DISCERNING. 2. IT MANIFESTS GOD. 3. IT GIVES LIFE TO THE SOUL. 4. IT IS THE APOSTOLICAL MESSAGE. 5. OBJECTION ANSWERED ABOUT TWO LIGHTS. 6. ABOUT NATURAL AND SPIRITUAL LIGHT: NOT TWO DARKNESSES WITHIN, THEREFORE NOT TWO LIGHTS WITHIN. 7. THE APOSTLE JOHN ANSWERS THE OBJECTION FULLY: THE LIGHT THE SAME, 1 JOHN II. 8, 9.

1. THE third thing is the virtue and efficacy of this light for the end for which God hath given it, viz., to lead and guide the soul of man to blessedness. In order to which the first thing it does in and for man is to give him a true sight or discerning of himself: what he is, and what he does; that he may see and know his own condition, and what judgment to make of himself with respect to religion and a future state. Of which let us hear what the Word Himself saith that cannot err, as John relates it, Chap. iii. 20, 21. For everyone that doth evil hateth the light, neither cometh to the light, lest his deeds should be reproved. But he that doth truth cometh to the light that his deeds may be made manifest

[1] Job xviii. 5, xxi. 17, xxv. 3, xxxviii. 5; Ps. xviii. 28, xxvii. 1, xxxiv. 5, xxxvi. 9, cxviii. 27, cxix. 105; Prov. xiii. 9, xx. 20, 27, xxiv. 20; Isa. ii. 5, viii. 20, xlii. 6, xlix. 6; 1 Pet. ii. 9; 1 John ii. 8.

that they are wrought in God. A most pregnant instance of the virtue and authority of the light. First, it is that which men ought to examine themselves by. Secondly, it gives a true discerning betwixt good and bad, what is of God from what is not of God. And, lastly, it is a judge, and condemneth or acquitteth, reproveth or comforteth the soul of man as he rejects or obeys it. That must needs be divine and efficacious which is able to discover to man what is of God from what is not of God; and which gives him a distinct knowledge in himself of what is wrought in God from what is not wrought in God. By which it appears that this place does not only regard the discovery of man and his works, but in some measure it manifesteth God and His works also, which is yet something higher; for as much as it gives the obedient man a discovery of what is wrought or performed by God's power and after His will from what is the mere workings of the creature of himself. If it could not manifest God it could not tell man what was God's mind nor give him such a grounded sense and discerning of the rise, nature, and tendency of the workings of his mind or inward man, as is both expressed and abundantly implied in this passage of our Saviour. And if it reveals God to be sure it manifests Christ that flows and comes from God. Who then would oppose or slight this blessed light?

2. But that this light doth manifest God is yet evident from Rom. i. 19. Because that which may be known of (God) is manifest in men, for God hath showed it unto them. A universal proposition; and we have the apostle's word for it, who was one of a thousand, and inspired on purpose to tell us the truth. Let it then have its due weight with us. If that which may be known of God is manifest in men, the people called Quakers cannot certainly be out of the way in preaching up the light within, without which nothing can be manifested to the mind of man; as saith the same apostle to the Ephesians, Eph. v. 13. Whatsoever doth make manifest is light. Well then may they call this light within a manifestation or appearance of God that showeth in and to man all that may be known of God. A passage much like unto this is that of the prophet Micah, chap. vi. 8. God hath showed thee, O man, what is good; and what doth the Lord require of thee but to do justly, and to love mercy, and to

walk humbly with thy God? God hath showed thee, O man! It is very emphatical. But how hath He showed him? Why by His light in the conscience which the wicked rebel against, Job xxiv. 13. Who for that cause know not the ways nor abide in the paths thereof: for its ways are ways of pleasantness, and all its paths are peace to them that obey it.

3. But the light giveth the light of life, which is eternal life to them that receive and obey it. Thus says the blessed Saviour of the world, John viii. 12, I am the light of the world, he that followeth Me shall not abide in darkness, but shall have the light of life. Now He is the light of the world because He lighteth every man that cometh into the world, and they that obey that light obey Him, and therefore have the light of life. That is, the light becomes eternal life to the soul; that as it is the life of the Word, which is the light in man, so it becomes the life in man through his obedience to it as his heavenly light.

4. Farthermore, this light was the very ground of the apostolical message, as the beloved disciple assures us. 1 John i. 5, 6, 7. This then is the message which we have heard of Him, and declare unto you, that God is light, and in Him is no darkness at all. If we say we have fellowship with Him, and walk in darkness, we lie, and do not the truth. But if we walk in the light, as He is in the light, we have fellowship one with another, and the blood of Jesus Christ cleanseth us from all sin. Which is so comprehensive of the virtue and excellency of the light in reference to man that there is little need that more should be said upon it; for as much as, first, it reveals God, and that God Himself is light. Secondly, it discovers darkness from light, and that there is no fellowship between them. Thirdly, that man ought to walk in the light. Fourthly, that it is the way to obtain forgiveness of sin and sanctification from it. Fifthly, that it is the means to have peace and fellowship with God and His people; His true church redeemed from the pollutions of the world.

5. Some perhaps may object, as indeed it hath been more than once objected upon us, that this is another light, not that light wherewith every man is enlightened. But the same apostle in his evangelical history tells us that in the Word was life, and the life was the light of men, and that that very light that was the life of the world was the true light

which lighteth every man that cometh into the world, John i. 4, 9. Where is there so plain a text to be found against the sufficiency as well as universality of the light within; or a plainer for any article of faith in the whole book of God? Had the beloved disciple intended two lights in his evangelical history and his epistles, to be sure he would have noted to us his distinction. But we read of none, and by the properties ascribed in each writing we have reason to conclude he meant the same.

6. But if any shall yet object, that this is to be understood a spiritual light, and that ours is to be a natural one, I shall desire them to do two things: First, to prove that a natural light, as they phrase it, doth manifest God other than as I have before explained and allowed. Since whatever is part of man in his constitution, but especially in his degeneracy from God, is so far from yielding him the knowledge of God that it cannot rightly reprove or discover that which offends Him without the light we speak of. And it is granted that what we call divine, and some mistakedly call natural light, can do both. Secondly, if this light be natural, notwithstanding it doth manifest our duty and reprove our disobedience to God, they would do well to assign us some certain medium or way whereby we may truly discern and distinguish between the manifestations and reproofs of the natural light within from those of the divine light within, since they allow the manifestation of God and reproof of evil as well to the one as to the other. Let them give us but one Scripture that distinguishes between a natural and a spiritual light within. They may with as much reason talk of a natural and spiritual darkness within. It is true there is a natural proper darkness, to wit, the night of the outward world; and there is a spiritual darkness, viz., the clouded and benighted understandings of men through disobedience to the light and spirit of God. But let them assign us a third if they can. People used indeed to say improperly of blind men they are dark, we may call a natural or idiot so if we will; but where is there another darkness of the understanding in the things of God? If they can, I say, find that in and about the things of God, they do something.

Christ distinguished not between darkness and darkness,

or light and light in any such sense; nor did any of His disciples. Yet both have frequently spoken of darkness and light. What difference, pray, doth the Scripture put between spiritual darkness and darkness mentioned in these places. Luke i. 7, 9. Mat. iv. 16. John i. 5 and iii. 19 and viii. 12, 31, 46. 1 Thess. v. 4. 1 John i. 6. Acts xxvi. 18. Rom. xiii. 12. 2 Cor. vi. 14, 22. Eph. v. 8. Col. i. 13. Upon the strictest comparison of them I find none. It is all one spiritual darkness. Neither is there so much as one Scripture that affords us a distinction between light within and light within; or that there are really two lights from God in man that regard religion. Peruse Mat. iv. 16. Luke ii. 32 and xv. 8. John i. 4, 5, 7, 8, 9, and iii. 19, 20, 21, and viii. 12. Acts xxvi. 18. Rom. xiii. 12. 2 Cor. iv. 6 and vi. 14. Eph. v. 8, 13. Col. i. 12. 1 Thess. v. 5. 1 Tim. vi. 16. 1 Pet. ii. 9. 1 John i. 5, 7, and ii. 8. Rev. xxi. 23, 24, and xxii. 5. And we believe the greatest opposer to our assertion will not be able to sever light from light, or find out two lights within in the passages here mentioned or any other to direct man in his duty to God and his neighbour. And if he cannot, pray let him forbear his mean thoughts and words of the light of Christ within man as man's guide in duty to God and man. For as he must yield to us that the light manifesteth evil and reproveth for it, so doth Christ Himself teach us of the light, John iii. 20. For everyone that doth evil hateth the light, neither cometh unto the light lest his deeds should be reproved. And the apostle Paul plainly saith, Eph. v. 13. But all things that are reproved are made manifest by the light; therefore there are not two distinct lights within, but one and the same manifesting, reproving, and teaching light within. And this the apostle John in his first epistle makes plain beyond all exception to all considerate people. First, in that he calls God light, chap. i. 5. Secondly, in that he puts no medium or third thing between that light and darkness, verse 6. If we say we have fellowship with Him and walk in darkness we lie, etc. Intimating that men must walk either in light or darkness and not in a third or other state or region. I am sure that which manifests and reproves darkness cannot be darkness. This all men must confess.

7. And as if the apostle John would have anticipated their objection, viz., it is true your light within reproves for evil,

but it is not therefore the divine light which leads into higher things, and which comes by the gospel; he thus expresseth himself, 1 John ii. 8, 9. The darkness is past and the true light now shineth. He that saith he is in the light and hateth his brother is in darkness even until now; which is not another light than that mentioned before, chap. 1. For as light is put there in opposition to darkness so light here is put in opposition to darkness. And as the darkness is the same so must the light be the same. Wherefore we may plainly see that it is not another light than that which reproves a man for hating his brother which brings a man into fellowship with God and to the blood of cleansing as the next verse speaks: therefore that light which reproveth a man for hating his brother is of a divine and efficacious nature. In short, that light which is opposite to and reproves spiritual darkness in a man and woman is a spiritual light; but such a light is that which we confess, testify to, and maintain: therefore it is a spiritual light. It is also worth our notice that the apostle useth the same manner of expression here, chap. ii. 8, the true light shineth, that he doth in his evangelical history, chap. i. 9, that was the true light; intimating the same divine Word, or true light now shineth; and that is the same true light in his account that reproveth such as hate their brethren. Consequently that light that so reproveth them is the true light. And strange it is that Christ and His disciples, but especially His beloved one, should so often make that very light, which stoops to the lowest step of immorality and to the reproof of the grossest evil, to be no other than the same divine light in a farther degree of manifestation which brings such as follow it to the light of life, to the blood of cleansing, and to have fellowship with God and one with another. Nay, not only so, but the apostle makes a man's being a child of God to depend upon his answering of this light in a palpable and common case, viz., not hating of his brother: and that yet any should shut their eyes so fast against beholding the virtue of it as to conclude it a natural and insufficient light is both unscriptural and unreasonable. Shall we slight it because we come so easily by it, and it is so familiar and domestic to us? Or make its being so common an argument to undervalue so inestimable a mercy? What is more common than light and air and water? And should we therefore condemn them or prize them? Prize them, certainly, as what we cannot live nor live comfortably without. The more general the mercy is the greater and therefore the greater obligation upon man to live humbly and thankfully for it. And to those alone that do so are its divine secrets revealed.

CHAPTER V

1. THE LIGHT THE SAME WITH THE SPIRIT—IT IS OF GOD; PROVED BY ITS PROPERTIES. 2. THE PROPERTIES OF THE SPIRIT COMPARED WITH THOSE OF THE LIGHT. 3. THE LIGHT AND GRACE FLOW FROM THE SAME PRINCIPLE PROVED BY THEIR AGREEING PROPERTIES. 4. AN OBJECTION ANSWERED. 5. DIFFERENCE IN MANIFESTATION, OR OPERATION, ESPECIALLY IN GOSPEL TIMES, BUT NOT IN PRINCIPLE, ILLUSTRATED.

1. *Objection.* But some may say, we could willingly allow to the spirit and grace of God, which seemed to be the peculiar blessing of the new and second covenant and the fruit of the coming of Christ, all that which you ascribe to the light within; but except it appeared to us that this light were the same in nature with the spirit and grace of God, we cannot easily bring ourselves to believe what you say in favour of the light within.

Answer. This objection at first look seems to carry weight with it. But upon a just and serious review it will appear to have more words than matter, show than substance. Yet because it gives occasion to solve scruples that may be flung in the way of the simple, I shall attend it throughout. I say then if it appear that the properties ascribed to the light within are the same with those that are given to the Holy Spirit and grace of God; and that those several terms or epithets are only to express the divers manifestations or operations of one and the same principle, then it will not, it cannot, be denied, but this light within is divine and efficacious as we have asserted it. Now that it is of the same nature with the spirit and grace of God and tends to the same end, which is to bring people to God, let the properties of the light be compared with those of the spirit and grace of God. I say they are the same in that, first, the light proceeds from the one Word and one life of that one Word, which was with God and was God, John i. 4 and i. 9. Secondly, it is universal, it lighteth every man. Thirdly, it giveth the knowledge of God and fellowship with Him. Rom. i. 19. John iii. 21. 1 John i. 5, 6. Fourthly, it manifesteth and reproveth evil, John iii. 20. Eph. v. 13. Fifthly, it is made the rule and guide of Christian walking, Psalm xliii. 3. John viii. 12. Eph. v. 13, 15. Sixthly, it is the path for God's people to go in, Psalm cxix., 105. Prov. iv. 18. Isaiah ii. 5. 1 John i. 7. Rev. xxiv. 23. And the nations of them that are saved shall walk in the light of the (Lamb). Lastly, it is the armour of the children of God against Satan, Psalm xxvii. 1. The Lord is my light, whom shall I fear? Rom. xiii. 12. Let us put on the armour of light.

2. Now let all this be compared with the properties of the Holy Spirit, and their agreement will be very manifest. First, it proceedeth from God, because it is the spirit of God, Rom. vi. 11. Secondly, it is universal. It strove with the old world, Gen. vi. 3. Then to be sure with the new one: everyone hath a measure of it given to profit withal, 1 Cor. xii. 7. Thirdly, it revealeth God, Job xxxii. 8. 1 Cor. ii. 10, 11. Fourthly, it reproveth sin, John xvi. 8. Fifthly, it is a rule and guide for the children of God to walk by, Rom. viii. 14. Sixthly, it is also the path they are to walk in, Rom. viii. 1. Gal. v. 15. Walk in the spirit. Lastly, this is not all; it is likewise the spiritual weapon of a true Christian, Eph. vi. 17. Take the sword of the spirit, which is the Word of God. After this I hope none will deny that this light and this spirit must be of one and the same nature, that work one and the same effect, and tend evidently to one and the same holy end.

3. And what is said of the light and spirit may also very well be said of the light and grace of God; in that, first, the grace floweth from Christ, the Word that took flesh as well as the light; for as in Him was life and that life the light of men, so He was full of grace and truth, and of His fulness have all we received, and grace for grace, John i. 4, 9, 14, 16. Secondly, it is universal; both from this text and what the

apostle to Titus teacheth; for the grace of God that bringeth salvation hath appeared to all men, Tit. ii. 11, 12. Thirdly, it manifesteth evil, for if it teaches to deny ungodliness and worldly lusts, it must needs detect them, and so says the text. Fourthly, it revealeth godliness, and consequently it must manifest God. Fifthly, it is an instructor and guide; for, says the apostle, it teaches to deny ungodliness and worldly lusts, and to live soberly, righteously, and godly in this present world, and herein a rule of life, Tit. ii. 11, 12. Sixthly, it is to all that receive it all that they can need or desire. 2 Cor. xii. 9. My grace is sufficient for thee. A high testimony from heaven to the power of this teaching and saving grace, under the strongest temptations.

4. *Objection.* But there is little mention made of the spirit and none of the grace before Christ's coming, and therefore the spirit as spoken of in the writings of the New Testament, and especially the grace, must be another and a nobler thing than the light within.

Answer. By no means another thing, but another name, from another manifestation or operation of the same principle. It is called light from the distinction and discerning it gives. Let there be light, and there was light, said God in the beginning of the old world; so there is first light in the beginning of the new creation of God in man. It is called spirit because it giveth life, sense, motion, and vigour. And it is as often mentioned in the writings of the Old as New Testament; which every reader may see if he will but please to look into his Scripture concordance. Thus God's spirit strove with the old world, Gen. vi. 3., and with Israel in the wilderness, Neh. ix. 30. And David asked in the agony of his soul, whither shall I go from thy spirit? Ps. cxxxix. 7, and the prophets often felt it. It is styled grace not from its being another principle, but because it was a fuller dispensation of the virtue and power of the same divine principle: and that being purely God's favour and mercy, and not man's merit, is aptly and deservedly called the grace, favour, or good-will of God to undeserving man. The wind does not always blow fresh, nor heaven send down its rain freely, nor the sun shine forth clearly; shall we therefore say it is not of the same kind of wind, rain, or light when it blows, rains, or shines but a little, as when it blows, rains, or shines much?

It is certainly the same in nature and kind; and so is this blessed principle under all its several dispensations, manifestations, and operations for the benefit of man's soul ever since the world began.

5. But this is most freely, humbly, and thankfully acknowledged by us that the dispensation of the gospel was the clearest, fullest, and noblest of all others; both with regard to the coming of Christ in the flesh and being our one holy offering to God for sin through the Eternal Spirit; and the breaking forth of His light, the effusion of His spirit, and appearance of His grace in and to man in a more excellent manner after His ascension. For though it was not another light or spirit than that which He had given to man in former ages, yet it was another and greater measure; and that is the privilege of the gospel above former dispensations. What before shined but dimly shines since with great glory. Then it appeared but darkly, but now with open face. Types, figures, and shadows veiled its appearances and made them look low and faint; but in the gospel time the veil is rent and the hidden glory manifest. It was under the law but as a dew or small rain, but under the gospel it may be said to be poured out upon men, according to that gracious and notable promise of God by the prophet Joel, in the latter days I will pour out of my spirit upon all flesh. Thus we say when it rains plentifully, look how it pours. So God augments His light, grace, and spirit to these latter days. They shall not have it sparingly and by small drops, but fully and freely, and overflowing too. And thus Peter, that deep and excellent apostle, applies that promise in Joel on the day of Pentecost as the beginning of the accomplishment of it. This is grace and favour and goodness indeed. And therefore well may this brighter illumination and greater effusion of the spirit be called grace; for as the coming of the Son excelled that of the servant, so did the manifestation of the light and spirit of God since the coming of Christ excel that of the foregoing dispensations; yet ever sufficient to salvation to all those that walked in it. This is our sense of the light, spirit, and grace of God. And by what is said it is evident they are one and the same principle, and that He that has light need not want the spirit or grace of God if he will but receive it in the love of it. For the very principle that

is light to show him is also spirit to quicken him, and grace to teach, help, and comfort him. It is sufficient in all circumstances of life to them that diligently mind and obey it.

CHAPTER VI

1. AN OBJECTION ANSWERED: ALL ARE NOT GOOD THOUGH ALL ARE LIGHTED. 2. ANOTHER OBJECTION ANSWERED, THAT GOSPEL TRUTHS WERE KNOWN BEFORE CHRIST'S COMING. 3. ANOTHER: THE GENTILES HAD THE SAME LIGHT THOUGH NOT WITH THOSE ADVANTAGES: PROVED FROM SCRIPTURE.

1. *Objection.* But some may yet say, if it be as you declare, how comes it that all who are enlightened are not so good as they should be or as you say this would make them?

Answer. Because people do not receive and obey it: all men have reason, but all men are not reasonable. Is it the fault of the grain in the granary that it yields no increase or of the talent in the napkin that it is not improved? It is plain a talent was given; and as plain that it was improvable; both because the like talents were actually improved by others, and that the just judge expected his talent with advantage; which else, to be sure, he would never have done. Now when our objectors will tell us whose fault it was the talent was not improved we shall be ready to tell them why the unprofitable servant was not so good as he should have been. The blind must not blame the sun, nor sinners tax the grace of insufficiency. It is sin that darkens the eye and hardens the heart, and that hinders good things from the sons of men. If we do His will we shall know of His divine doctrine, so Christ tells us. Men not living to what they know cannot blame God that they know no more. The unfruitfulness is in us, not in the talent. It were well indeed that this were laid to heart. But, alas! men are too apt to follow their sensual appetites, rather than their reasonable mind, which renders them brutal instead of rational. For the reasonable part in man is his spiritual part, and that guided by the divine λογος or Word, which Tertullian interprets reason in the most excellent sense, makes man truly reasonable;

and then it is that man comes to offer up himself to God a reasonable sacrifice. Then a man indeed; a complete man; such a man as God made when He made man in His own image and gave him paradise for his habitation.

2. *Objection.* But some yet object if mankind had always this principle, how comes it that gospel truths were not so fully known before the coming of Christ to those that were obedient to it.

Answer. Because a child is not a grown man, nor the beginning the end; and yet He that is the beginning is also the end. The principle is the same, though not the manifestation. As the world has many steps and periods of time towards its end, so hath man to his perfection. They that are faithful to what they know of the dispensation of their own day shall hear the happy welcome of well done, good and faithful servant. And yet many of God's people in those days had a prospect of the glory of the latter times, the improvement of religion, the happiness of the Church of God.

This we see in the Prophecies of Jacob and Moses concerning the restoration of Israel by Christ. So David in many of his excellent Psalms expressing most sensible and extraordinary enjoyments as well as Prophecies; particularly his ii., xv., xviii., xxii., xxiii., xxv., xxvii., xxxii., xxxvi., xxxvii., xlii., xliii., xlv., li., lxxxiv., etc. The prophets are full of it, and for that reason have their name; particularly Isaiah, chap. ii., ix., xi., xxv., xxviii., xxxii., xxxv., xlii., xlix., l., li., lii., liii., liv., lix., lx., lxi., lxiii., lxv., lxvi. Jeremiah also, chap. xxiii., xxx., xxxi., xxxiii. Ezekiel, chap. xx., xxxiv., xxxvi., xxxvii. Daniel, chap. viii., ix., x., xi., xii. Hosea, chap. i., iii. Joel, chap. ii., iii. Amos, chap. ix. Micah, chap. iv., v. Zachariah, chap. vi., viii., ix., xi., xiii., xiv. Malachi, chap. iii., iv. This was not another principle though another manifestation of the same principle, nor was it common, but particular and extraordinary in the reason of it.

It was the same spirit that came upon Moses which came upon John the Baptist, and it was also the same spirit that came upon Gideon and Samson that fell upon Peter and Paul; but it was not the same dispensation of that spirit. It hath been the way of God to visit and appear to men according to their states and conditions, and as they have been prepared to receive Him, be it more outwardly or inwardly, sensibly or spiritually. There is no capacity too low or too high for this divine principle, for as it made and knows all, so it reaches unto all people. It extends to the meanest, and the highest cannot subsist without it. Which made David break forth in his expostulations with God, whither shall I go from Thy spirit, or whither shall I flee from Thy presence? Psal. cxxxix. 7, 8, 9, 10, implying it was everywhere, though not everywhere nor at every time alike. If I go to heaven, to hell, or beyond the seas even there shall Thy hand lead me, and Thy right hand shall hold me. That is, there will this divine word, this light of men, this spirit of God find me, lead me, help me, and comfort me. For it is with me wherever I am and wherever I go in one respect or other; Prov. vi. 22, When thou goest it shall lead thee; when thou sleepest it shall keep thee; and when thou awakest, it shall talk with thee: and I can no more get rid of it if I would than of myself or my own nature; so present is it with me and so close it sticks unto me. Isa. xliii. 2, When thou passest through the waters I will be with thee; and through the rivers, they shall not overflow thee; when thou walkest through the fire thou shalt not be burnt, neither shall the flame kindle upon thee. David knew it, and therefore had a great value for it. In Thy light shall we see light, or we shall be enlightened by Thy light. Thou wilt light my candle; the Lord my God will lighten my darkness. Again, the Lord is my light, whom shall I fear. It was His armour against all danger. It took fear away from him, and he was undaunted because he was safe in the way of it. Of the same blessed word he says elsewhere, it is a lamp unto my feet, and a lanthorn to my paths. In short, a light to him in his way to blessedness.

3. *Objection.* But if the Jews had this light it does not follow that the Gentiles had it also; but by your doctrine all have it.

Answer. Yes, and it is the glory of this doctrine which we profess that God's love is therein held forth to all. And besides the texts cited in general and that are as full and positive as can be expressed, the apostle is very particular in the second chapter of his epistle to the Romans, that the Gentiles having not the law, did by nature the things contained in the law, and were a law unto themselves. That is, they had not an outward law circumstanced as the Jews had; but they had the work of the law written in their hearts, and therefore might well be a law to themselves that had the law in themselves. And so had the Jews too, but then they had greater outward helps to quicken their obedience to it, such as God afforded not unto any other nation: and therefore the obedience of the Gentiles, or uncircumcision, is said to be by nature, or naturally, because it was without those additional, external, and extraordinary ministries and helps which the Jews had to provoke them to duty. Which is so far from lessening the obedient Gentiles, that it exalts them in the apostle's judgment; because though they had less advantages than the Jews, yet the work of the law written in their hearts was made so much the more evident by the good life they lived in the world. He adds, their consciences bearing witness (or as it may be rendered, witnessing with them) and their thoughts meanwhile accusing or else excusing one another in the day when God shall judge the secrets of all hearts by Jesus Christ, according to my gospel. Which presents us with four things to our point, and worth our serious reflection. First, that the Gentiles had the law written in their hearts. Secondly, that their conscience was an allowed witness or evidence about duty. Thirdly, that the judgment made thereby shall be confirmed by the apostle's gospel at the great day, and therefore valid and irreversible. Fourthly, that this could not be if the light of this conscience were not a divine and sufficient light. For conscience truly speaking is no other than the sense a man hath, or judgment he maketh of his duty to God according to the understanding God gives him of His will. And that no ill but a true and scriptural use may be made of this word conscience, I limit it to duty, and that to a virtuous and holy life, as the apostle evidently doth, about which we cannot miss or dispute. Read verses 7, 8, and 9. It was to that therefore the apostles of our Lord Jesus Christ desired to be made manifest, for they dared to stand the judgment of conscience in reference to the doctrine they preached and pressed upon men. The beloved disciple also makes it a judge of man's present and future state, under the term heart, for if our heart condemn us, God is greater than our heart and knoweth all things. Beloved, if our heart condemn us not then have we confidence towards God. Plain and strong words: and what were they about, but whether we love God in deed and in truth? And how must that appear? Why, in keeping His commandments, which is living up to what we know. And if any desire to satisfy themselves farther of the divinity of the Gentiles, let them read Plato, Seneca, Plutarch, Epictetus, Marcus Aurelius Antoninus, and the Gentile writers. They will also find many of their sayings collected in the first part of a book called *The Christian Quaker*, and compared with the testimonies of scripture not for their authority but agreeableness. In them they may discern many excellent truths and taste great love and devotion to virtue: a fruit that grows upon no tree but that of life, in no age or nation. Some of the most eminent writers of the first ages, such as Justin Martyr, Origen, Clemens, Alexandrinus, etc., bore them great respect, and thought it no lessening to the reputation of Christianity that it was defended in many Gentile authors, as well as that they used and urged them to engage their followers to the faith, as Paul did the Athenians with their own poets.

CHAPTER VII

1. AN OBJECTION ANSWERED ABOUT THE VARIOUS DISPENSATIONS OF GOD: THE PRINCIPLE THE SAME. 2. GOD'S WORK OF A PIECE AND TRUTH THE SAME UNDER DIVERS SHAPES. 3. THE REASON OF THE PREVALENCY OF IDOLATRY. 4. THE QUAKER'S TESTIMONY THE BEST ANTIDOTE AGAINST IT, VIZ., WALKING BY A DIVINE PRINCIPLE IN MAN. 5. IT WAS GOD'S END IN ALL HIS MANIFESTATIONS THAT MAN MIGHT BE GOD'S IMAGE AND DELIGHT.

1. *Objection.* But it may be said if it were one principle why so many modes and shapes of religion since the world began? For the Patriarchal, Mosaical, and Christian have their great differences, to say nothing of what has befallen the Christian since the publication of it to the world.

Answer. I know not how properly they may be called divers religions that assert the true God for the object of worship; the Lord Jesus Christ for the only Saviour; and the light or spirit of Christ for the great agent and means of man's conversion and eternal felicity, any more than infancy, youth, and manhood make three men instead of three growths or periods of time of one and the same man. But passing that, the many modes or ways of God's appearing to men arise, as hath been said, from the divers states of men, in all which it seems to have been his main design to prevent idolatry and vice by directing their minds to the true object of worship, and pressing virtue and holiness. So that though mediately He spoke to the patriarchs mostly by angels in the fashion of men and by them to their families over and above the illumination in themselves; so to the prophets for the most part by the revelation of the Holy Ghost in them, and by them to the Jews; and since the gospel dispensation by His Son, both externally, by His coming in the flesh, and internally, by His spiritual appearance in the soul, as He is the great light of he world. Yet all its flowings mediately through others have still been from the same principle, co-operating with the manifestation of it immediately in man's own particular.

2. This is of great weight for our information and encouragement that God's work in reference to man is all of a piece, and in itself lies in a narrow compass, and that His eye has ever been upon the same thing in all His dispensations, viz., to make men truly good by planting His holy awe and fear in their hearts. Though He has condescended, for the hardness and darkness of men's hearts, to approach and spell out His holy mind to them by low and carnal ways, as they may appear to our more enlightened understandings, suffering truth to put on divers sorts of garments the better to reach to the low state of men, to engage them from false gods and ill lives; seeing them sunk so much below their nobler part and what He made them, that like brute beasts they knew not their own strength and excellency.

3. And if we do but well consider the reason of the prevalency of idolatry upon the earlier and darker times of the world, of which the Scripture is very particular, we shall find that it ariseth from this; that it is more sensual and therefore calculated to please the senses of men; being more outward or visible or more in their own power to perform than one more spiritual in its object. For as their gods were the

workmanship of men's hands they could not prefer them, that being the argument which did most of all gall their worshippers, and what of all things for that reason they were most willing to forget. But their incidency to idolatry, and the advantages it had upon the true religion with them, plainly came from this, that it was more outward and sensual. They could see the object of their devotion, and had it in their power to address it when they would. It was more fashionable too, as well as better accommodated to their dark and too brutal state. And therefore it was that God by many afflictions and greater deliverances brought forth a people to endear Himself to them, that they might remember the hand that saved them, and worship Him and Him only; in order to root up idolatry and plant the knowledge and fear of Him in their minds for an example to other nations. Whoever reads Deuteronomy, which is a summary of the other four books of Moses, will find the frequent and earnest care and concern of that good man for Israel about this very point; and how often that people slipped and lapsed notwithstanding God's love, care, and patience over them into the idolatrous customs of the nations about them. Divers other scriptures inform us also, especially those of the prophets, Isaiah xliv. and xlv., Psalms xxxvii. and cxv., and Jer. x., where the Holy Ghost confutes and rebukes the people and mocks their idols with a sort of holy disdain.

4. Now that which is farthest from idolatry and the best antidote against it is the principle we have laid down, and the more people's minds are turned and brought to it, and that they resolve their faith, worship, and obedience into the holy illuminations and power of it, the nearer they grow to the end of their creation, and consequently to their Creator. They are more spiritually qualified, and become better fitted to worship God as He is, who, as we are told by our Lord Jesus Christ, is a spirit, and will be worshipped in spirit and in truth, and that they are such sort of worshippers which God seeketh to worship Him in this gospel day. The hour cometh, saith He, and now is. That is, some now do so, but more shall. A plain assertion in present, and a promise and prophecy of the increase of such worshippers in future. Which shows a change intended from a ceremonial worship and state of the Church of God to a spiritual one. Thus the

text, but the time cometh, and now is, when true worshippers shall worship the Father in spirit and in truth. Which is as much as to say, when the worship of God shall be more inward than outward, and so more suitable to the nature of God and the nobler part of man, his inside, or his inward and better man. For so those blessed words import, in spirit and in truth. In spirit, that is, through the power of the spirit. In truth, that is in realities not in shadows, ceremonies, or formalities, but in sincerity with and in life, being divinely prepared and animated; which brings man not only to offer up right worship, but also into intimate communion and fellowship with God, who is a spirit.

5. And if it be duly weighed it will appear that God in all His manifestations of Himself hath still come nearer and nearer to the insides of men that He might reach to their understandings and open their hearts and give them a plainer and nearer acquaintance with Himself in spirit. And then it is that man must seek and find the knowledge of God for his eternal happiness. Indeed, all things that are made show forth the power and wisdom of God and His goodness too to mankind; and therefore many men urge the creation to silence atheistical objections. But though all those things show a God, yet man does it above all the rest. He is the precious stone of the ring, and the most glorious jewel of the globe; to whose reasonable use, service, and satisfaction the whole seems to be made and dedicated. But God's delight (by whom man was made, we are told by the Holy Ghost) is in the habitable parts of the earth with the sons of men, Prov. viii. 31, and with those that are contrite in spirit, Isaiah lxvi. 1. And why is man His delight, but because man only of all His works was of His likeness. This is the intimate relation of man to God. Somewhat nearer than ordinary; for of all other beings man only had the honour of being His image; and by his resemblance to God, as I may say, came his kindred with God and knowledge of Him. So that the nearest and best way for man to know God and be acquainted with Him is to seek Him in Himself, in His image; and as he finds that he comes to find and know God. Now man may be said to be God's image in a double respect. First, as He is of an immortal nature; and next, as that nature is endued with those excellencies in small, and proportionable to a

creature's capacity, that are by nature infinitely and incomparably in his Creator. For instance, wisdom, justice, mercy, holiness, patience, and the like. As man becomes holy, just, merciful, patient, etc. By the copy he will know the Original, and by the workmanship in himself he will be acquainted with the Holy Workman. This, reader, is the regeneration and new creature we press (Gal. vi. 15, 16), and according to this rule we say men ought to be religious and walk in this world. Man, as I said just now, is a composition of both worlds; his body is of this, his soul of the other world. The body is as the temple of the soul, the soul the temple of the Word, and the Word the great temple and manifestation of God. By the body the soul looks into and beholds this world, and by the Word it beholds God and the world that is without end. Much might be said of this order of things and their respective excellencies, but I must be brief.

CHAPTER VIII

1. THE DOCTRINES OF SATISFACTION AND JUSTIFICATION OWNED AND WORDED ACCORDING TO SCRIPTURE. 2. WHAT CONSTRUCTIONS WE CAN'T BELIEVE OF THEM, AND WHICH IS AN ABUSE OF THEM. 3. CHRIST OWNED A SACRIFICE AND A MEDIATOR. 4. JUSTIFICATION TWOFOLD FROM THE GUILT OF SIN, AND FROM THE POWER AND POLLUTION OF IT. 5. EXHORTATION TO THE READER UPON THE WHOLE.

1. *Objection.* Though there be many good things said how Christ appears and works in a soul to awaken, convince, and convert it, yet you seem not particular enough about the death and sufferings of Christ. And it is generally rumoured and charged upon you by your adversaries that you have little reverence to the doctrine of Christ's satisfaction to God for our sins, and that you do not believe that the active and passive obedience of Christ when He was in the world is the alone ground of a sinner's justification before God.

Answer. The doctrines of satisfaction and justification truly understood are placed in so strict a union that the one is a necessary consequence of the other, and what we say of them is what agrees with the suffrage of Scripture, and for the most part in the terms of it; always believing that in points where there arises any difficulty, be it from the obscurity of expression, mistranslation, or the dust raised by the heats of partial writers or nice critics, it is ever best to keep close to the text, and maintain charity in the rest. I shall first speak negatively, what we do not own, which perhaps hath given occasion to those who have been more hasty than wise to judge us defective in our belief of the efficacy of the death and sufferings of Christ to justification, as:

2. First, we cannot believe that Christ is the cause but the effect of God's love, according to the testimony of the beloved disciple, John iii., God so loved the world that He gave His only begotten Son into the world, that whosoever believeth in Him should not perish but have everlasting life.

Secondly, we cannot say God could not have taken another way to have saved sinners than by the death and sufferings of His Son to satisfy His justice, or that Christ's death and sufferings were a strict and rigid satisfaction for that eternal death and misery due to man for sin and transgression: for such a notion were to make God's mercy little concerned in man's salvation; and indeed we are at too great a distance from His infinite wisdom and power to judge of the liberty or necessity of His actings.

Thirdly, we cannot say Jesus Christ was the greatest sinner in the world (because He bore our sins on His cross, or because He was made sin for us, who knew no sin), an expression of great levity and unsoundness, yet often said by great preachers and professors of religion.

Fourthly, we cannot believe that Christ's death and sufferings so satisfies God or justifies men, as that they are thereby accepted of God. They are indeed thereby put into a state capable of being accepted of God, and through the obedience of faith and sanctification of the spirit are in a state of acceptance. For we can never think a man justified before God while self-condemned; or that any man can be in Christ who is not a new creature; or that God looks upon men otherwise than they are. We think it a state of presumption and not of salvation to call Jesus Lord, and not by the work of the Holy Ghost; Master, and He not yet master of their affections; Saviour, and they not saved by

Him from their sins; Redeemer, and yet they not redeemed by Him from their passion, pride, covetousness, wantonness, vanity, vain honours, friendships, and glory of this world: which were to deceive themselves; for God will not be mocked, such as men sow, such they must reap. And though Christ did die for us, yet we must, by the assistance of His grace, work out our salvation with fear and trembling. As He died for sin so we must die to sin, or we cannot be said to be saved by the death and sufferings of Christ, or thoroughly justified and accepted with God. Thus far negatively. Now positively what we own as to justification.

3. We do believe that Jesus Christ was our holy sacrifice, atonement, and propitiation; that He bore our iniquities, and that by His stripes we were healed of the wounds Adam gave us in his fall; and that God is just in forgiving true penitents upon the credit of that holy offering Christ made of Himself to God for us; and that what He did and suffered satisfied and pleased God, and was for the sake of fallen man that had displeased God. And that through the offering up of Himself once for all, through the eternal spirit, he hath for ever perfected those (in all times) that were sanctified, who walked not after the flesh but after the spirit, Rom. viii. 1. Mark that.

4. In short, justification consists of two parts, or hath a twofold consideration, viz., justification from the guilt of sin, and justification from the power and pollution of sin, and in this sense justification gives a man a full and clear acceptance before God. For want of this latter part it is that so many souls religiously inclined are often under doubts, scruples, and despondencies, notwithstanding all that their teachers tell them of the extent and efficacy of the first part of justification. And it is too general an unhappiness among the professors of Christianity that they are apt to cloak their own active and passive disobedience with the active and passive obedience of Christ. The first part of justification we do reverently and humbly acknowledge is only for the sake of the death and sufferings of Christ, nothing we can do, though by the operation of the Holy Spirit, being able to cancel old debts or wipe out old scores. It is the power and efficacy of that propitiatory offering upon faith and repentance that justifies us from the sins that are past; and it

is the power of Christ's spirit in our hearts that purifies and makes us acceptable before God. For until the heart of man is purged from sin, God will never accept of it. He reproves, rebukes, and condemns those that entertain sin there, and therefore such cannot be said to be in a justified state; condemnation and justification being contraries. So that they that hold themselves in a justified state by the active and passive obedience of Christ while they are not actively and passively obedient to the spirit of Christ Jesus are under a strong and dangerous delusion; and for crying out against this sin-pleasing imagination, not to say doctrine, we are staged and reproached as deniers and despisers of the death and sufferings of our Lord Jesus Christ. But be it known to such, they add to Christ's sufferings and crucify to themselves afresh the Son of God, and trample the blood of the covenant under their feet, that walk unholily under a profession of justification; for God will not acquit the guilty nor justify the disobedient and unfaithful. Such deceive themselves, and at the great and final judgment their sentence will not be, come ye blessed, because it cannot be said to them, well done, good and faithful, for they cannot be so esteemed that live and die in a reprovable and condemnable state; but, go ye cursed, etc.

5. Wherefore, O my reader! rest not thyself wholly satisfied with what Christ has done for thee in His blessed person without thee, but press to know His power and kingdom within thee, that the strong man that has too long kept thy house may be bound, and his goods spoiled, his works destroyed, and sin ended, according to 1 John iii. 7. For which end, says that beloved disciple, Christ was manifested, that all things may become new: new heavens and new earth in which righteousness dwells. Thus thou wilt come to glorify God in thy body and in thy spirit, which are His; and live to Him and not to thyself. Thy love, joy, worship, and obedience; thy life, conversation, and practice; thy study, meditation, and devotion will be spiritual. For the Father and the Son will make their abode with thee, and Christ will manifest Himself to thee; for the secrets of the Lord are with them that fear Him; and a holy unction or anointing have all those which leads them unto all truth, and they need not the teachings of men. They are better

taught being instructed by the divine oracle. No bare hearsay or traditional Christians, but fresh and living witnesses. Those that have seen with their own eyes and heard with their own ears, and have handled with their own hands the word of life, in the divers operations of it, to their souls' salvation. In this they meet, in this they preach, and in this they pray and praise. Behold the new covenant fulfilled, the Church and worship of Christ, the great anointed of God, and the great anointing of God in His holy high priesthood and offices in His Church!

CHAPTER IX

1. A CONFESSION TO CHRIST AND HIS WORK BOTH IN DOING AND SUFFERING. 2. THAT OUGHT NOT TO MAKE VOID OUR BELIEF AND TESTIMONY OF HIS INWARD AND SPIRITUAL APPEARANCE IN THE SOUL. 3. WHAT OUR TESTIMONY IS IN THE LATTER RESPECT: THAT IT IS IMPOSSIBLE TO BE SAVED BY CHRIST WITHOUT US, WHILE WE REJECT HIS WORK AND POWER WITHIN US. 4. THE DISPENSATION OF GRACE IN ITS NATURE AND EXTENT. 5. A FARTHER ACKNOWLEDGMENT TO THE DEATH AND SUFFERINGS OF CHRIST. 6. THE CONCLUSION, SHOWING OUR ADVERSARY'S UNREASONABLENESS.

1. AND lest any should say we are equivocal in our expressions and allegorise away Christ's appearance in the flesh; meaning only thereby our own flesh; and that as often as we mention Him we mean only a mystery or a mystical sense of Him, be it as to His coming, birth, miracles, sufferings, death, resurrection, ascension, mediation and judgment; I would yet add, to preserve the well-disposed from being staggered by such suggestions, and to inform and reclaim such as are under the power and prejudice of them, that we do, we bless God, religiously believe and confess to the glory of the Father, and the honour of His dear and beloved Son, that Jesus Christ took our nature upon Him, and was like unto us in all things, sin excepted; that He was born of the Virgin Mary, suffered under Pontius Pilate, the Roman governor, was crucified, dead, and buried in the sepulchre of Joseph of

Arimathea; rose again the third day, and ascended into heaven, and sits on the right hand of God in the power and majesty of His Father; who will one day judge the world by Him, even that blessed man, Christ Jesus, according to their works.

2. But because we so believe, must we not believe what Christ said? He that is with you shall be in you, John xiv. I in them, and they in Me, etc., xvii. When it pleased God to reveal His Son in me, etc., Gal. The mystery hid from ages is Christ in the Gentiles, the hope of glory, Col. i. Unless Christ be in you, ye are reprobates, 2 Cor. xiii. Or must we be industriously represented deniers of Christ's coming in the flesh, and the holy ends of it, in all the parts and branches of His doing and suffering, only because we believe and press the necessity of believing, receiving, and obeying His inward and spiritual appearance and manifestation of Himself through His light, grace, and spirit in the hearts and consciences of men and women to reprove, convict, convert, and change them? This we esteem hard and unrighteous measure; nor would our warm and sharp adversaries be so dealt with by others. But to do as they would be done to is too often no part of their practice, whatever it be of their profession.

3. Yet we are very ready to declare to the whole world that we cannot think men and women can be saved by their belief of the one without the sense and experience of the other; and that is what we oppose, and not His blessed manifestation in the flesh. We say that He then overcame our common enemy, foiled him in the open field, and in our nature triumphed over him that had overcome and triumphed over it in our forefather Adam and his posterity. And that as truly as Christ overcame him in our nature in His own person, so by His divine grace, being received and obeyed by us, He overcomes him in us. That is, He detects the enemy by His light in the conscience, and enables the creature to resist him and all his fiery darts; and finally, so to fight the good fight of faith as to overcome him and lay hold on eternal life.

4. And this is the dispensation of grace which we declare has appeared to all more or less; teaching those that will receive it to deny ungodliness and worldly lusts, and to live

soberly, righteously, and godly in this present world; looking for (which none else can justly do) the blessed hope and glorious appearing of the great God and our Saviour Jesus Christ, etc., Tit. ii. 11, 12, 13. And as from the teachings, experience, and motion of this grace we minister to others, so the very drift of our ministry is to turn people's minds to this grace in themselves that all of them may up and be doing, even the good and acceptable will of God, and work out their salvation with fear and trembling, and make their high and heavenly calling and election sure, which none else can do, whatever be their profession, church, and character. For such as men sow they must reap; and his servants we are whom we obey. Regeneration we must know or we cannot be children of God and heirs of eternal glory. And to be born again another spirit and principle must prevail, leaven, season, and govern us than either the spirit of the world or our own depraved spirits; and this can be no other spirit than that which dwelt in Christ; for unless that dwells in us we can be none of His, Rom. viii. 9. And this spirit begins in conviction and ends in conversion and perseverance; and the one follows the other. Conversion being the consequence of convictions obeyed, and perseverance a natural fruit of conversion and being born of God; for such sin not, because the seed of God abides in them, John iii. 7, 8. But such through faithfulness continue to the end and obtain the promise, even everlasting life.

5. But let my reader take this along with him, that we do acknowledge that Christ, through His holy doing and suffering (for being a Son He learned obedience), has obtained mercy of God His Father for mankind, and that His obedience has an influence to our salvation in all the parts and branches of it, since thereby He became a conqueror, and led captivity captive, and obtained gifts for men with divers great and precious promises, that thereby we might be partakers of the divine nature, having (first) escaped the corruption that is in the world through lust. I say, we do believe and confess that the active and passive obedience of Christ Jesus affects our salvation throughout as well from the power and pollution of sin as from the guilt, He being a conqueror as well as a sacrifice, and both through suffering. Yet they that reject His divine gift so obtained (and which He has given to them,

by which to see their sin and the sinfulness of it, and to repent and turn away from it, and do so no more; and to wait upon God for daily strength to resist the fiery darts of the enemy, and to be comforted through the obedience of faith in and to this divine grace of the Son of God) such do not please God, believe truly in God, nor are they in a state of true Christianity and salvation. Woman, said Christ, to the Samaritan at the well, hadst thou known the gift of God, and who it is that speaketh to thee, etc. People know not Christ and God, whom to know is life eternal, John xvii., because they are ignorant of the gift of God, viz., a measure of the spirit of God that is given to every one to profit with, 1 Cor. xii. 7, which reveals Christ and God to the soul, chap. ii. Flesh and blood cannot do it, Oxford and Cambridge cannot do it, tongues and philosophy cannot do it. For they that by wisdom knew not God had these things for their wisdom. They were strong, deep, and accurate in them; but, alas! they were clouded, puffed up, and set farther off from the inward and saving knowledge of God, because they sought for it in them, and thought to find God there. But the key of David is another thing, which shuts and no man opens, and opens and no man shuts; and this key have all they that receive the gift of God into their hearts, and it opens to them the knowledge of God and themselves, and gives them a quite other sight, taste, and judgment of things than their educational or traditional knowledge afforded them. This is the beginning of the new creation of God, and thus it is we come to be new creatures.

And we are bold to declare there is no other way like this by which people can come into Christ; or be true Christians, or receive the advantage that comes by the death and sufferings of the Lord Jesus Christ. Wherefore we say, and upon good authority, even that of our own experience as well as that of the Scriptures of truth, Christ will prove no saving sacrifice for them that refuse to obey Him for their example. They that reject the gift deny the giver instead of themselves for the giver's sake. O that people were wise that they would consider their latter end, and the things that make for the peace thereof! Why should they perish in a vain hope of life while death reigns? Of living with God who live not to Him nor walk with Him? Awake thou that sleepest in thy sin, or at best in thy self-righteousness! Awake, I say, and Christ shall give thee life! For He is the Lord from heaven, the quickening spirit, that quickens us by His spirit if we do not resist it and quench it by our disobedience, but receive, love, and obey it in all the holy leadings and teachings of it. Rom. viii. 14, 15. To which holy spirit I commend my reader, that he may the better see where he is, and also come to the true belief and advantage of the doings and sufferings of our dear and blessed Lord and Saviour Jesus Christ, who saves from the power and pollution as well as guilt of sin all those that hear His knocks, and open the door of their hearts to Him that He may come in and work a real and thorough reformation in and for them; and so the benefit, virtue, and efficacy of His doings and sufferings without us will come to be livingly and effectually applied and felt, and fellowship with Christ in His death and sufferings known, according to the doctrine of the apostle; which those that live in that which made Him suffer know not, though they profess to be saved by His death and sufferings. Much more might be said as to this matter, but I must be brief.

6. To conclude this chapter, we wonder not that we should be mistaken, misconstrued, and misrepresented in what we believe and do to salvation, since our betters have been so treated in the primitive times. Nor indeed is it only about doctrines of religion; for our practice in worship and discipline have had the same success. But this is what I earnestly desire, that however bold people are pleased to make with us, they would not deceive themselves in the great things of their own salvation. That while they would seem to own all to Christ, they are not found disowned of Christ in the last day. Read the 7th of Matthew. It is he that hears Christ, the great word of God, and does what He enjoins, what He commands, and by His blessed example recommends, that is a wise builder that has founded his house well, and built with good materials, and whose house will stand the last shock and judgment. For which cause we are often plain, close, and earnest with people to consider, that Christ came not to save them in, but from, their sins; and that they that think to discharge and release themselves of His yoke and burden, His cross and example, and secure themselves and compliment Christ with His having done all for them (while

He has wrought little or nothing in them, nor they parted with anything for the love of Him), will finally awake in a dreadful surprise at the sound of the last trumpet, and at this sad and irrevocable sentence, depart from me, ye workers of iniquity, I know you not. Which terrible end may all timely avoid by hearkening to wisdom's voice and turning at her reproof that she may lead them in the ways of righteousness and in the midst of the paths of judgment that their souls may come to inherit substance; even durable riches and righteousness in the kingdom of the Father, world without end.

CHAPTER X

1. OF THE TRUE WORSHIP OF GOD IN WHAT IT STANDS. 2. OF THE TRUE MINISTRY, THAT IT IS BY INSPIRATION. 3. THE SCRIPTURE PLAIN IN THAT CASE. 4. CHRIST'S MINISTERS TRUE WITNESSES, THEY SPEAK WHAT THEY KNOW, NOT BY REPORT. 5. CHRIST'S MINISTERS PREACH FREELY, IT IS ONE OF THEIR MARKS.

1. As the Lord wrought effectually by His divine grace in the hearts of this people, so He thereby brought them to a divine worship and ministry; Christ's words they came to experience, viz., that God was a spirit, and that He would therefore be worshipped in the spirit and in the truth, and that such worshippers the Father would seek to worship Him. For bowing to the convictions of the spirit in themselves in their daily course of living, by which they were taught to eschew that which was made manifest to them to be evil, and to do that which was good, they in their assembling together sat down and waited for the preparation of this holy spirit, both to let them see their states and conditions before the Lord, and to worship Him acceptably; and as they were sensible of wants, or shortness, or infirmities, so in the secret of their own hearts prayer would spring to God, through Jesus Christ, to help, assist, and supply. But they did not dare to awake their beloved before His time; or approach the throne of the King of Glory till He held out His sceptre; or take thought what they should say, or after their own or other men's studied words and forms, for

this were to offer strange fire; to pray, but not by the spirit; to ask, but not in the name, that is, in the power of our Lord Jesus Christ, who prayed as well as spoke like one having authority, that is, power, a divine energy and force to reach and pierce the heavens, which He gives to all that obey His light, grace, and spirit in their solemn waitings upon him. So that it is this people's principle that fire must come from heaven, life and power from God, to enable the soul to pour out itself acceptably before Him. And when a coal from His holy altar touches our lips, then can we pray and praise Him as we ought to do. And as this is our principle, and that according to Scripture so it is, blessed be God, our experience and practice. And therefore it is we are separated from the worships of men under their several forms because they do not found it in the operation, motion, and assistance of the spirit of Christ, but the appointment, invention, and framing of man, both as to matter, words, and time. We do not dissent in our own wills, and we dare not comply against His that has called us and brought us to His own spiritual worship; in obedience to whom we are what we are, in our separation from the divers ways of worship in the world.

2. And as our worship stands in the operation of the spirit and truth in our inward parts, as before expressed, so does our ministry. For as the holy testimonies of the servants of God of old were from the operation of His blessed spirit, so must those of His servants be in every age, and that which has not the spirit of Christ for its spring and source is of man and not of Christ. Christian ministers are to minister what they receive: this is Scripture; now that which we receive is not our own, less another man's, but the Lord's. So that we are not only not to steal from our neighbours, but we are not to study nor speak our own words. If we are not to study what we are to say before magistrates for ourselves, less are we to study what we are to say for and from God to the people. We are to minister as the oracles of God; if so, then must we receive from Christ, God's great oracle, what we are to minister. And if we are to minister what we receive then not what we study, collect, and beat out of our own brains, for that is not the mind of Christ, but our imaginations, and this will not profit the people.

3. This was recommended to the Corinthians by the

apostle Paul, 1 Cor. xiv., that they should speak as they were moved, or as anything was revealed to them by the spirit, for the edification of the Church; for, says he, ye may all prophesy; that is, ye may all preach to edification as anything is revealed to you for the good of others, and as the spirit giveth utterance. And if the spirit must give Christ's ministers their utterance, then those that are His are careful not to utter anything in His name to the people without His spirit; and by good consequence they that go before the true Guide and utter words without the knowledge of the mind of the spirit, are none of Christ's ministers. Such certainly run, and God has not sent them, and they cannot profit the people. And indeed how should they, when it is impossible that mere man, with all his parts, arts, and acquirements, can turn people from darkness to light, and from the power of Satan to God, which is the very end and work of the gospel ministry? It must be inspired men, men gifted by God, taught and influenced by His heavenly spirit, that can be qualified for so great, so inward, and so spiritual a work.

4. Ministers of Christ are His witnesses, and the credit of a witness is that he has heard, seen, or handled. And thus the beloved disciple states the truth and authority of their mission and ministry, 1 John i. 1, 3. That which we have heard, which we have seen with our eyes, which we have looked upon, and our hands have handled, that declare we unto you that your fellowship may be with us, and truly our fellowship is with the Father and with His Son Jesus Christ. I say, if Christ's ministers are His witnesses they must know what they speak; that is, they must have experienced and passed through those states and conditions they preach of, and practically know those truths they declare of to the people, or they come not in by the door but over the wall, and are thieves and robbers. He that has the key of David comes in at the door, Christ Jesus, and has His admission and approbation from Him, anointed by Him, the alone high priest of the gospel dispensation. He it is that breathes and lays His hands upon His own ministers; He anoints them, and recruits their cruise, and renews their horn with oil, that they may have it fresh, and fresh for every occasion and service He calls them to and engages them in.

5. Nor is this all, but as they receive freely, freely they

give. They do not teach for hire, divine for money, nor preach for gifts or rewards. It was Christ's holy command to His ministers to give freely, and it is our practice. And truly we cannot but admire that this should be made a fault, and that preaching for hire should not be seen to be one; yea, a mark of false prophets when it has been so frequently and severely cried out upon by the true prophets of God in former times. I would not be uncharitable, but the guilty are desired to call to mind who it was that offered money to be made a minister, and what it was for, if not to get money and make a trade or livelihood by it; and what answer he met with from the apostle Peter, Acts viii. 18, 19, 20. The Lord touch the hearts of those that are giving money to be made ministers in order to live by their preaching that they may see what ground it is they build upon, and repent and turn to the Lord that they may find mercy and become living witnesses of His power and goodness in their own souls; so may they be enabled to tell others what God has done for them, which is the root and ground of the true ministry; and this ministry it is that God does bless. I could say much on this subject, but let what has been said suffice at this time, only I cannot but observe that where any religion has a strong temptation of gain to induce men to be ministers there is great danger of their running faster to that calling than becomes a true gospel minister.

1. *Objection.* But does not this sort of ministry and worship tend to make people careless, and to raise spiritual pride in others, may it not give an occasion to great mischief and irreligion?

Answer. By no means, for when people are of age they of right expect their inheritances; and the end of all words is to bring people to the great Word, and then the promise of God is accomplished, they shall be all taught of Me from the least to the greatest, and in righteousness (pray mark that) they shall be established, and great shall be their peace. To this of the evangelical prophet the beloved disciple agrees, and gives a full answer to the objection: these things have I written unto you concerning them that seduce you. But the anointing, which ye have received of Him, abideth in you, and ye need not that any man teach you, but as the same anointing teacheth you of all things, and is truth, and is no lie: and even as it hath taught you ye shall abide in Him. In which three things are observable: First, that he wrote his epistle upon an extraordinary occasion, viz., to prevent their delusion. Secondly, that he asserts a nearer and superior minister than himself, viz., the anointing or grace they had received; and that not only in that particular exigency, but in all cases that might attend them. Thirdly, that if they did but take heed to the teachings of it they would have no need of man's directions, or fear of his seducings. At least of no ministry that comes not from the power of the anointing: though I rather take the apostle in the highest sense of the words. Thus also the apostle Paul to the Thessalonians. But as touching brotherly love, ye need not that I write unto you: for ye yourselves are taught of God to love one another, 1 Thess. iv. 9. But helps are useful and a great blessing if from God, such was John the Baptist; but remember he pointed all to Christ, 1 John i. 26. Lo, the Lamb of God! I baptise you with water, but He shall baptise you with the Holy Ghost and with fire, Matt. iii. 11. And so the true ministry does. And while people are sensual and under such an eclipse by the interposition of sin and satan, God is pleased to send forth His enlightening servants to awaken and turn them from the darkness to the light in themselves, that through obedience to it they may come to be children of the light, John xii. 36, and have their fellowship one with another in it, and an inheritance at last with the saints in light for ever.

And as it is the way God has taken to call and gather people, so a living and holy ministry is of great advantage to watch over and build up the young, and comfort and establish the feeble and simple ones. But still I say the more inward, the less outward. The more people come to be taught immediately of God by the light of His word and spirit in their hearts, the less need of outward means, read Isa. xvi. 19, 20. Which is held by all to be a gospel promise, and the sun and moon there are generally understood to mean the external means in the Church. Compare them with John i. 13; Rom. i. 19; 1 Cor. ii. 11, 15; 1 Thess. iv. 9; 1 John ii. 20, 27; Rev. xxi. 22, 23, 24. All which places prove what we assert of the sufficiency and glorious privilege of inward and spiritual teachings. And most certainly as men grow in grace and know the anointing of the word in themselves, the dispensation will be less in words (though in words) and more in life; and preaching will in great measure be turned into praising and the worship of God, more into walking with than talking of God. For that is worship indeed that bows to His will at all times and in all places, the truest, the highest worship man is capable of in this world. And it is that conformity that gives communion, and there is no fellowship with God, no light of His countenance to be enjoyed, no peace and assurance to be had farther than their obedience to His will, and a faithfulness to His word, according to the manifestation of the light thereof in the heart.

I say this is the truest and highest state of worship; for set days and places, with all the solemnity of them, were most in request in the weakest dispensation. Altars, ark, and temples, Sabbaths and festivals, etc., are not to be found in the writings of the New Testament. There every day is alike and every place is alike; but if there were a dedication let it be to the Lord. Thus the apostle, but he plainly shows a state beyond it, for to live (with him) was Christ, and to die was gain; for the life he lived was by the faith of the Son of God, and therefore it was not he that lived, but Christ that lived in him; that is, that ruled, conducted, and bore sway in him, which is the true Christian life, the supersensual life, the life of conversion and regeneration, to which all the dispensations of God and ministry of His servants have ever tended as the consummation of God's work for man's happiness. Here every man is a temple, and every family a church, and ever place a meeting-place, and every visit a meeting. And yet a little while and it shall be so yet more and more; and a people the Lord is now preparing to enter into this Sabbath or degree of rest.

Not that we would be thought to undervalue public and solemn meetings: we have them all over the nation where the Lord has called us. Yea, though but two or three of us be in a corner of a country we meet as the apostle exhorted the saints of his time, and reproved such as neglected to assemble themselves. But yet show we unto thee, O reader, a more excellent way of worship. For many may come to those meetings and go away carnal, dead, and dry; but the worshippers in spirit and in truth, whose hearts bow, whose minds adore the eternal God, that is a spirit, in and by His spirit, such as conform to His will, and walk with him in a spiritual life, they are the true, constant, living, and acceptable worshippers; whether it be in meetings or out of meetings; and as with such all outward assemblies are greatly comfortable, so also do we meet for a public testimony of religion and worship, and for the edification and encouragement of those that are yet young in the truth, and to call and gather others to the knowledge of it who are yet going astray; and blessed be God, it is not in vain, since many are thereby added to the Church that we hope and believe shall be saved.

CHAPTER XI

1. AGAINST TITHES. 2. AGAINST ALL SWEARING. 3. AGAINST WAR AMONG CHRISTIANS. 4. AGAINST THE SALUTATIONS OF THE TIMES. 5. AND FOR PLAINNESS OF SPEECH. 6. AGAINST MIXED MARRIAGES. 7. AND FOR PLAINNESS IN APPAREL, ETC. NO SPORTS AND PASTIMES AFTER THE MANNER OF THIS WORLD. 8. OF OBSERVING DAYS. 9. OF CARE OF POOR, PEACE, AND CONVERSATION.

1. AND as God has been pleased to call us from a human ministry, so we cannot for conscience sake support and maintain it, and upon that score, and not out of humour or covetousness, we refuse to pay tithes or such-like pretended dues, concerning which many books have been written in our defence. We cannot support what we cannot approve, but have a testimony against; for thereby we should be found inconsistent with ourselves.

2. We dare not swear, because Christ forbids it, Mat. v. 34, 37, and James, His true follower. It is needless as well as evil for the reason of swearing being untruth, that men's yea was not yea. Swearing was used to awe men to truth speaking, and to give others satisfaction that what was sworn was true. But the true Christian's yea being yea the end of an oath is answered, and therefore the use of it is needless, superfluous, and cometh of evil. The apostle James taught the same doctrine, and the primitive Christians practised it, as may be seen in the book of martyrs; as also the earliest and best of the reformers.

3. We also believe that war ought to cease among the followers of the Lamb Christ Jesus, who taught His disciples to forgive and love their enemies, and not to war against them and kill them; and that therefore the weapons of His true followers are not carnal but spiritual; yea mighty, through God, to cut down sin and wickedness, and dethrone him that is the author thereof. And as this is the most Christian, so the most rational way; love and persuasion having more force than weapons of war. Nor would the worst of men easily be brought to hurt those that they really think love them. It is that love and patience must in the end have the victory.

4. We dare not give worldly honour or use the frequent and modish salutations of the times, seeing plainly that vanity, pride, and ostentation belong to them. Christ also forbade them in His day, and made the love of them a mark of declension from the simplicity of purer times; and His disciples and their followers were observed to have obeyed their Master's precept. It is not to distinguish ourselves a party, or out of pride, ill-breeding, or humour, but in obedience to the sight and sense we have received from the spirit of Christ, of the evil rise and tendency thereof.

5. For the same reason we have returned to the first plainness of speech, viz., thou and thee to a single person, which though men give no other to God they will hardly endure it from us. It has been a great test upon pride, and shown the blind and weak insides of many. This also is out of pure conscience, whatever people may think or say of us for it. We may be despised, and have been so often, yea, very evilly entreated, but we are now better known, and people better informed. In short, it is also both scripture and grammar, and we have propriety of speech for it as well as peace in it.

6. We cannot allow of mixed marriages, that is, to join with such as are not of our society; but oppose and disown them, if at any time any of our profession so grossly err from the rule of their communion; yet restore them upon sincere repentance, but not disjoin them. The book I wrote of the rise and progress of the people called Quakers is more full and express herein.

7. Plainness in apparel and furniture is another testimony

peculiar to us in the degree we have bore it to the world. As also few words, and being at a word. Likewise temperance in food, and abstinence from the recreations and pastimes of the world. All which we have been taught by the spirit of our Lord Jesus Christ to be according to godliness; and therefore we have long exhorted all that their moderation may be known unto all men for that the Lord was at hand to enter into judgment with us for every intemperance or excess; and herein we hope we have been no ill examples or scandals unto any that have a due consideration of things.

8. We cannot in conscience to God observe Holy Days (so called), the public fasts and feasts, because of their human institution and ordination, and that they have not a divine warrant, but are appointed in the will of man.

9. Lastly, we have been led by this good spirit of our Lord Jesus Christ, of which I have treated in this discourse, according to primitive practice to have a due care over one another for the preservation of the whole society in a conversation more suitable to their holy profession.

First, in respect to a strict walking both towards those that are without and those that are within; that their conversation in the world, and walking in and towards the Church, may be blameless. That as they may be strict in the one so they may be faithful in the other.

Secondly, that collections be made to supply the wants of the poor, and that care be taken of widows and orphans and such as are helpless, as well in counsel as about substance.

Thirdly, that all such as are intended to marry, if they have parents or are under the direction of guardians or trustees, are obliged, first, to declare to them their intention and have their consent before they propose it to one another, and the meeting they relate to, who are also careful to examine their clearness, and being satisfied with it they are by them allowed to solemnise their marriage in a public select meeting for that purpose appointed, and not otherwise; whereby all clandestine and indirect marriages are prevented among us.

Fourthly, and to the end that this good order may be observed, for the comfort and edification of the society in the ways of truth and soberness, select meetings (of care and business) are fixed in all parts where we inhabit, which are held monthly, and which resolve into quarterly meetings, and those into one yearly meeting for our better communication one with another in those things that maintain piety and charity; that God who by His grace has called us to be a people to His praise may have it from us, through His beloved Son, and our ever-blessed and only Redeemer, Jesus Christ, for He is worthy, worthy, now and ever. Amen.

Thus, reader, thou hast the character of the people called Quakers in their doctrine, worship, ministry, practice, and discipline. Compare it with Scripture and primitive example, and we hope thou wilt find that this short discourse hath in good measure answered the title of it, viz.:

Primitive Christianity Revived in the Principles and Practice of the People called Quakers.

A LETTER FROM WILLIAM PENN

PROPRIETARY AND GOVERNOR OF PENNSYLVANIA IN AMERICA, TO THE COMMITTEE OF THE FREE SOCIETY OF TRADERS OF THAT PROVINCE RESIDING IN LONDON. CONTAINING A GENERAL DESCRIPTION OF THE SAID PROVINCE, ITS SOIL, AIR, WATER, SEASONS, AND PRODUCE, BOTH NATURAL AND ARTIFICIAL, AND THE GOOD INCREASE THEREOF. WITH AN ACCOUNT OF THE NATIVES OR ABORIGINES.

MY KIND FRIENDS,—The kindness of yours by the ship *Thomas* and *Anne* doth much oblige me; for by it I perceive the interest you take in my health and reputation, and the prosperous beginning of this province which you are so kind as to think may much depend upon them. In return of which I have sent you a long letter, and yet containing as brief an account of myself and the affairs of this province as I have been able to make.

In the first place, I take notice of the news you sent me whereby I find some persons have had so little wit, and so much malice, as to report my death, and to mend the matter, dead a Jesuit too. One might have reasonably hoped that this distance, like death, would have been a protection against spite and envy; and indeed absence being a kind of death ought alike to secure the name of the absent as the dead; because they are equally unable as such to defend themselves. But they that intend mischief do not use to follow good rules to effect it. However, to the great sorrow and shame of the inventors, I am still alive, and no Jesuit, and, I thank God, very well. And without injustice to the authors of this I may venture to infer that they that wilfully and falsely report would have been glad it had been so. But I perceive many frivolous and idle stories have been invented since my departure from England, which perhaps at this time are no more alive than I am dead.

But if I have been unkindly used by some I left behind me

I found love and respect enough where I came; a universal kind welcome, every sort in their way. For here are some of several nations, as well as divers judgments. Nor were the natives wanting in this, for their kings, queens, and great men both visited and presented me; to whom I made suitable returns, etc.

For the Province, the General Condition of it take as followeth.

I. The country itself in its soil, air, water, seasons, and produce, both natural and artificial, is not to be despised. The land containeth divers sorts of earth, as sand yellow and black, poor and rich: also gravel both loamy and dusty; and in some places a fast fat earth, like to our best vales in England, especially by inland brooks and rivers, God in His wisdom having ordered it so, that the advantages of the country are divided, the back lands being generally three to one richer than those that lie by navigable waters. We have much of another soil, and that is a black hasel mould upon a stony or rocky bottom.

II. The air is sweet and clear, the heavens serene, like the south parts of France, rarely overcast; and as the woods come by numbers of people to be more cleared that itself will refine.

III. The waters are generally good, for the rivers and brooks have mostly gravel and stony bottoms, and in number hardly credible. We have also mineral waters that operate in the same manner with Barnet and North Hall, not two miles from Philadelphia.

IV. For the seasons of the year, having by God's goodness now lived over the coldest and hottest that the oldest liver in the province can remember, I can say something to an English understanding.

First, of the fall, for then I came in: I found it from October 24 to the beginning of December as we have it usually in England in September, or rather like an English mild spring. From December to the beginning of the month called March we had sharp frosty weather; not foul, thick, black weather as our north-east winds bring with them in England, but a sky as clear as in summer, and the air dry, cold, piercing, and hungry; yet I remember not that I wore more clothes than in England. The reason of this cold is given from the great lakes that are fed by the fountains of Canada. The winter before was as mild, scarce any ice at all; while this, for a few days, froze up our great River Delaware. From that month to the month called June we enjoyed a sweet spring, no gusts but gentle showers and a fine sky. Yet this I observe, that the winds here as there are more inconstant spring and fall, upon that turn of nature, than in summer or winter. From thence to this present month, which endeth the summer (commonly speaking), we have had extraordinary heats, yet mitigated sometimes by cool breezes. The wind that ruleth the summer season is the south-west; but spring, fall, and winter it is rare to want the wholesome north-western seven days together. And whatever mists, fogs, or vapours foul the heavens by easterly or southerly winds, in two hours time are blown away; the one is followed by the other. A remedy that seems to have a peculiar Providence in it to the inhabitants; the multitude of trees yet standing being liable to retain mists and vapours, and yet not one quarter so thick as I expected.

V. The natural produce of the country of vegetables is trees, fruits, plants, flowers. The trees of most note are the black walnut, cedar, cyprus, chestnut, poplar, gumwood, hickory, sassafrax, ash, beech, and oak of divers sorts, as red, white, and black; Spanish chestnut and swamp, the most durable of all. Of all which there is plenty for the use of man.

The fruits that I find in the woods are the white and black mulberry, chestnut, walnut, plums, strawberries, cranberries, hurtleberries, and grapes of divers sorts. The great red grape (now ripe) called by ignorance the fox grape (because of the relish it hath with unskilful palates), is in itself an extraordinary grape, and by art doubtless may be cultivated to an excellent wine, if not so sweet, yet little inferior to the Frontiniack, as it is not much unlike in taste, ruddiness set aside, which in such things, as well as mankind, differs the case much. There is a white kind of muskatel, and a little black grape like the cluster grape of England, not yet so ripe as the other; but they tell me, when ripe, sweeter, and that they only want skilful vinerons to make good use of them. I intend to venture on it with my Frenchman this season, who shows some knowledge in those things. Here are also peaches, and very good and in great quantities, not an Indian plantation without them; but whether naturally here at first I know not. However, one may have them by bushels for little; they make a pleasant drink, and I think not inferior to any peach you have in England, except the true Newington. It is disputable with me whether it be best to fall to fining the fruits of the country, especially the grape, by the care and skill of art, or send for foreign stems and sets already good and approved. It seems most reasonable to believe that not only a thing groweth best where it naturally grows, but will hardly be equalled by another species of the same kind that doth not naturally grow there. But to solve the doubt I intend, if God give me life, to try both, and hope the consequence will be as good wine as any European countries of the same latitude do yield.

VI. The artificial produce of the country is wheat, barley,[1] oats, rye, peas, beans, squashes, pumpkins, water-melons, musk-melons, and all herbs and roots that our gardens in England usually bring forth.

VII. Of living creatures, fish, fowl, and the beasts of the woods, here are divers sorts, some for food and profit, and some for profit only. For food as well as profit, the elk, as big as a small ox, deer bigger than ours, beaver, racoon, rabbits, squirrels, and some eat young bear, and commend it. Of fowl of the land there is the turkey (forty and fifty pound weight), which is very great; pheasants, heath birds, pigeons, and partridges in abundance. Of the water, the swan, goose, white and gray; brands, ducks, teal, also the snipe and curloe, and that in great numbers; but the duck and teal excel, nor so good have I ever eat in other countries. Of fish, there is the sturgeon, herring, rock, shad, catshead, sheeps-head, eel, smelt, perch, roach; and in inland rivers, trout, some say salmon above the falls. Of shell fish, we have oysters, crabs, cockles, conchs, and muscles; some oysters six inches long; and one sort of cockles as big as the stewing oysters, they make a rich broth. The creatures for profit only, by skin or fur, and that are natural to these parts, are

[1] Note, that Edward Jones, son-in-law to Thomas Wynn, living on the Schulkil, had, with ordinary cultivation, for one grain of English barley, seventy stalks and ears of barley; and it is common in this country from one bushel sown to reap forty, often fifty, and sometimes sixty; and three pecks of wheat sows an acre here.

the wild cat, panther, otter, wolf, fox, fisher, minx, musk-rat: and of the water, the whale for oil, of which we have good store, and two companies of whalers, whose boats are built, will soon begin their work, which hath the appearance of a considerable improvement. To say nothing of our reasonable hopes of good cod in the bay.

VIII. We have no want of horses, and some are very good and shapely enough. Two ships have been freighted to Barbadoes with horses and pipe-staves since my coming in. Here is also plenty of cow cattle and some sheep; the people plough mostly with oxen.

IX. There are divers plants, that not only the Indians tell us, but we have had occasion to prove by swellings, burnings, cuts, etc., that they are of great virtue, suddenly curing the patient. And for smell, I have observed several, especially one, the wild myrtle; the other I know not what to call, but are most fragrant.

X. The woods are adorned with lovely flowers, for colour, greatness, figure, and variety. I have seen the gardens of London best stored with that sort of beauty, but think they may be improved by our woods. I have sent a few to a person of quality this year for a trial.

Thus much of the Country, next of the Natives or Aborigines.

XI. The natives I shall consider in their persons, language, manners, religion, and government, with my sense of their original. For their persons they are generally tall, straight, well-built, and of singular proportion; they tread strong and clever, and mostly walk with a lofty chin. Of complexion, black, but by design, as the gypsies in England. They grease themselves with bear's fat clarified, and using no defence against sun or weather their skins must needs be swarthy. Their eye is little and black, not unlike a straight-looked Jew. The thick lip and flat nose so frequent with the East Indians and blacks are not common to them; for I have seen as comely European-like faces among them of both as on your side the sea; and truly an Italian complexion hath not much more of the white, and the noses of several of them have as much of the Roman.

XII. Their language is lofty yet narrow, but like the

Hebrew; in signification full, like short-hand in writing; one word serveth in the place of three, and the rest are supplied by the understanding of the hearer; imperfect in their tenses, wanting in their moods, participles, adverbs, conjunctions, interjections. I have made it my business to understand it, that I might not want an interpreter on any occasion. And I must say that I know not a language spoken in Europe that hath words of more sweetness or greatness in accent and emphasis than theirs. For instance, *Octocockon, Rancocas, Oricton, Shak, Marian, Poquesien,* all which are names of places, and have grandeur in them. Of words of sweetness *anna,* is mother; *issimus,* a brother; *netcap,* friend; *usque oret,* very good; *pane,* bread; *metse,* eat; *matta,* no; *hatta,* to have; *Payo,* to come; *Sepassen, Passijon,* the names of places; *Tamane, Secane, Menanse, Secatereus,* are the names of persons. If one ask them for anything they have not they will answer, *mattá ne hattá,* which to translate is, not I have instead of I have not.

XIII. Of their customs and manners there is much to be said, I will begin with children. So soon as they are born they wash them in water, and while very young and in cold weather to choose they plunge them in the rivers to harden and embolden them. Having wrapped them in a clout they lay them on a straight thin board a little more than the length and breadth of the child, and swadle it fast upon the board to make it straight; wherefore all Indians have flat heads; and thus they carry them at their backs. The children will go very young, at nine months commonly; they wear only a small clout round their waist till they are big; if boys, they go fishing till ripe for the woods, which is about fifteen; then they hunt, and after having given some proofs of their manhood by a good return of skins they may marry, else it is a shame to think of a wife. The girls stay with their mothers and help to hoe the ground, plant corn, and carry burthens, and they do well to use them to that young, they must do when they are old; for the wives are the true servants of the husbands; otherwise the men are very affectionate to them.

XIV. When the young women are fit for marriage they wear something upon their heads for an advertisement, but so as their faces are hardly to be seen but when they please.

The age they marry at, if women, is about thirteen and fourteen; if men, seventeen and eighteen; they are rarely older.

XV. Their houses are mats or barks of trees set on poles in the fashion of an English barn, but out of the power of the winds, for they are hardly higher than a man; they lie on reeds or grass. In travel they lodge in the woods about a great fire, with the mantle of duffills they wear by day wrapt about them, and a few boughs stuck round them.

XVI. Their diet is maize or Indian corn, divers ways prepared; sometimes roasted in the ashes, sometimes beaten and boiled with water, which they call *homine;* they also make cakes, not unpleasant to eat. They have likewise several sorts of beans and peas that are good nourishment, and the woods and rivers are their larder.

XVII. If a European comes to see them, or calls for lodging at their house or *wigwam,* they give him the best place, and first cut. If they come to visit us they salute us with an *itah,* which is as much as to say, good be to you, and set them down, which is mostly on the ground, close to their heels, their legs upright; it may be they speak not a word, but observe all passages. If you give them anything to eat or drink, well, for they will not ask; and be it little or much, if it be with kindness, they are well pleased, else they go away sullen, but say nothing.

XVIII. They are great concealers of their own resentments, brought to it, I believe, by the revenge that hath been practised among them; in either of these they are not exceeded by the Italians. A tragical instance fell out since I came into the country. A king's daughter thinking herself slighted by her husband, in suffering another woman to lie down between them, rose up, went out, plucked a root out of the ground, and eat it, upon which she immediately died; and for which, last week, he made an offering to her kindred for atonement and liberty of marriage; as two others did to the kindred of their wives that died a natural death. For till widowers have done so they must not marry again. Some of the young women are said to take undue liberty before marriage, for a portion; but when married, chaste; when with child, they know their husbands no more till delivered; and during their month they touch no meat they eat but with a stick, less they should defile it; nor do their husbands frequent them till that time be expired.

XIX. But in liberality they excel, nothing is too good for their friend; give them a fine gun, coat, or other thing, it may pass twenty hands before it sticks; light of heart, strong affections, but soon spent; the most merry creatures that live, feast, and dance perpetually; they never have much, nor want much. Wealth circulateth like the blood, all parts partake; and though none shall want what another hath, yet exact observers of property. Some kings have sold, others presented me with several parcels of land; the pay or presents I made them were not hoarded by the particular owners, but the neighbouring kings and their clans being present when the goods were brought out, the parties chiefly concerned consulted what and to whom they should give them. To every king then, by the hands of a person for that work appointed, is a proportion sent, so sorted and folded, and with that gravity that is admirable. Then that king sub-divideth it in like manner among his dependants, they hardly leaving themselves an equal share with one of their subjects. And be it on such occasions as festivals, or at their common meals, the kings distribute, and to themselves last. They care for little, because they want but little, and the reason is, a little contents them. In this they are sufficiently revenged on us; if they are ignorant of our pleasures they are also free from our pains. They are not disquieted with bills of lading and exchange, nor perplexed with Chancery suits and Exchequer reckonings. We sweat and toil to live; their pleasure feeds them; I mean, their hunting, fishing, and fowling, and this table is spread everywhere. They eat twice a day, morning and evening; their seats and table are the ground. Since the Europeans came into these parts they are grown great lovers of strong liquors, rum especially, and for it exchange the richest of their skins and furs. If they are heated with liquors they are restless till they have enough to sleep; that is their cry, some more and I will go to sleep; but when drunk, one of the most wretchedest spectacles in the world.

XX. In sickness, impatient to be cured, and for it give anything, especially for their children, to whom they are extremely natural; they drink at those times a teran or decoction of roots in spring water; and if they eat any flesh it must be of the female of any creature. If they die they bury them with their apparel, be they man or woman, and the nearest of kin fling in something precious with them as a token of their love: their mourning is blacking of their faces, which they continue for a year. They are choice of the graves of their dead; for lest they should be lost by time and fall to common use, they pick off the grass that grows upon them, and heap up the fallen earth with great care and exactness.

XXI. These poor people are under a dark night in things relating to religion, to be sure, the tradition of it; yet they believe a God and immortality without the help of metaphysics; for they say, there is a great king that made them, who dwells in a glorious country to the southward of them, and that the souls of the good shall go thither where they shall live again. Their worship consists of two parts, sacrifice and cantico: their sacrifice is their first fruits; the first and fattest buck they kill goeth to the fire where he is all burnt, with a mournful ditty of him that performeth the ceremony, but with such marvellous fervency and labour of body that he will even sweat to a foam. The other part is their cantico, performed by round dances, sometimes words, sometimes songs, then shouts, two being in the middle that begin, and by singing and drumming on a board direct the chorus. Their postures in the dance are very antic, and differing, but all keep measure. This is done with equal earnestness and labour, but great appearance of joy. In the fall, when the corn cometh in, they begin to feast one another; there have been two great festivals already, to which all come that will. I was at one myself; their entertainment was a great seat by a spring, under some shady trees, and twenty bucks with hot cakes of new corn, both wheat and beans, which they make up in a square form in the leaves of the stem, and bake them in the ashes; and after that they fell to dance. But they that go must carry a small present in their money, it may be sixpence, which is made of the bone of a fish; the black is with them as gold, the white, silver; they call it all wampum.

XXII. Their government is by kings, which they call Sachema, and those by succession, but always of the mother's side. For instance, the children of him that is now king will not succeed, but his brother by the mother or the children of his sister, whose sons (and after them the children of her daughter) will reign; for no woman inherits; the reason they render for this way of descent is that their issue may not be spurious.

XXIII. Every king hath his council, and that consists of all the old and wise men of his nation, which perhaps is two hundred people. Nothing of moment is undertaken, be it war, peace, selling of land, or traffic, without advising with them; and which is more, with the young men too. It is admirable to consider how powerful the kings are, and yet how they move by the breath of their people. I have had occasion to be in council with them upon treaties for land, and to adjust the terms of trade; their order is thus: the king sits in the middle of a half moon, and hath his council, the old and wise, on each hand; behind them, or at a little distance, sit the younger fry in the same figure. Having consulted and resolved their business the king ordered one of them to speak to me; he stood up, came to me, and in the name of his king saluted me, then took me by the hand and told me he was ordered by his king to speak to me, and that now it was not he but the king that spoke, because what he should say was the king's mind. He first prayed me to excuse them that they had not complied with me the last time; he feared there might be some fault in the interpreter, being neither Indian nor English; besides it was the Indian custom to deliberate and take up much time in council before they resolve; and that if the young people and owners of the land had been as ready as he, I had not met with so much delay. Having thus introduced his matter he fell to the bounds of the land they had agreed to dispose of, and the price (which now is little and dear, that which would have bought twenty miles, not buying now two). During the time that this person spoke not a man of them was observed to whisper or smile; the old grave, the young reverend in their deportment; they do speak little, but fervently and with elegancy: I have never seen more natural sagacity, considering them without the help (I was going to say the spoil) of tradition; and he will deserve the name of wise that outwits them in any treaty about a thing they understand. When the purchase was agreed, great promises passed between us of kindness and good neighbourhood, and that the Indians and English must live in love as long as the sun gave light. Which done another made a speech to the Indians in the name of all the sachamakers or kings, first to tell them what was done; next, to charge and command them to love the Christians, and particularly live in peace with me and the people under my government; that many governors had been in the river, but that no governor had come himself to live and stay here before; and having now such a one that had treated them well, they should never do him or his any wrong. At every sentence of which they shouted and said, Amen, in their way.

XXIV. The justice they have is pecuniary. In case of any wrong or evil fact, be it murder itself, they atone by feasts and presents of their wampum, which is proportioned to the quality of the offence or person injured, or of the sex they are of: for in case they kill a woman they pay double, and the reason they render is that she breedeth children, which men cannot do. It is rare that they fall out, if sober; and if drunk, they forgive it, saying, it was the drink and not the man that abused them.

XXV. We have agreed that in all differences between us six of each side shall end the matter: do not abuse them, but let them have justice, and you win them: the worst is that they are the worse for the Christians who have propagated their vices and yielded them tradition for ill, and not for good things. But as low an ebb as these people are at, and as glorious as their own condition looks, the Christians have not outlived their sight with all their pretensions to a higher manifestation: what good then might not a good people graft, where there is so distinct a knowledge left between good and evil? I beseech God to incline the hearts of all that come into these parts to outlive the knowledge of the natives by a fixed obedience to their greater knowledge of the will of God; for it were miserable indeed for us to fall under the just censure of the poor Indian conscience, while we make profession of things so far transcending.

XXVI. For their original, I am ready to believe them of the Jewish race, I mean, of the stock of the ten tribes, and that for the following reasons: first, they were to go to a land not planted or known, which to be sure Asia and Africa were, if not Europe; and he intended that extraordinary judgment upon them might make the passage not uneasy to them, as it is not impossible in itself, from the easternmost parts of Asia to the westernmost of America. In the next place I find them of like countenance, and their children of so lively resemblance, that a man would think himself in Dukes Place or Berry Street in London when he seeth them. But this is not all; they agree in rites, they reckon by moons; they offer their first fruits, they have a kind of feast of tabernacles; they are said to lay their altar upon twelve stones; their mourning a year, customs of women, with many things that do not now occur.

So much for the natives, next the old planters will be considered in this relation, before I come to our colony, and the concerns of it.

XXVII. The first planters in these parts were the Dutch, and soon after them the Swedes and Finns. The Dutch applied themselves to traffic, the Swedes and Finns to husbandry. There were some disputes between them some years, the Dutch looking upon them as intruders upon their purchase and possession, which was finally ended in the surrender made by John Rizeing, the Swedish governor, to Peter Styresant, governor for the states of Holland, Anno 1655.

XXVIII. The Dutch inhabit mostly those parts of the province that lie upon or near to the bay, and the Swedes the freshes of the river Delaware. There is no need of giving any description of them, who are better known there than here; but they are a plain, strong, industrious people, yet have made no great progress in culture or propagation of fruit trees, as if they desired rather to have enough than plenty of traffic. But I presume the Indians made them the more careless by furnishing them with the means of profit, to wit, skins and furs for rum and such strong liquors. They kindly received me as well as the English, who were few, before the people concerned with me came among them: I must needs commend their respect to authority and kind behaviour to the English; they do not degenerate from the old friendship between both kingdoms. As they are people proper and strong of body, so they have fine children and almost every house full; rare to find one of them without three or four boys and as many girls; some six, seven, and eight sons. And I must do them that right, I see few young men more sober and laborious.

XXIX. The Dutch have a meeting place for religious worship at Newcastle, and the Swedes three, one at Christina, one at Tenecum, and one at Wicoco, within half a mile of this town.

XXX. There rests that I speak of the condition we are in, and what settlement we have made, in which I will be as short as I can; for I fear, and not without reason, that I have tried your patience with this long story. The country lieth bounded on the east by the river and bay of Delaware and Eastern Sea; it hath the advantage of many creeks, or rivers rather, that run into the main river or bay; some navigable for great ships, some for small craft: those of most eminency are Christina, Brandywine, Skilpot, and Skulkill; any one of which have room to lay up the royal navy of England, there being from four to eight fathom water.

XXXI. The lesser creeks or rivers yet convenient for sloops and ketches of good burthen are Lewis, Mespilion, Cedar, Dover, Cranbrook, Feversham, and Georges below, and Chichester, Chester, Toacawny, Pemmapecka, Portquessin, Neshimenck, and Pennberry in the freshes; many lesser that admit boats and shallops. Our people are mostly settled upon the upper rivers, which are pleasant and sweet, and generally bounded with good land. The planted part of the province and territories is cast into six counties, Philadelphia, Buckingham, Chester, Newcastle, Kent, and Sussex, containing about four thousand souls. Two general assemblies have been held, and with such concord and dispatch that they sate but three weeks, and at least seventy laws were past without one dissent in any material thing. But of this more hereafter, being yet raw and new in our gear. However, I cannot forget their singular respect to me in this infancy of things, who by their own private expenses so early considered mine for the public, as to present me with an impost upon certain goods imported and exported: which after my acknowledgments of their affection, I did as freely remit to the province and the traders to it. And for the well government of the said counties courts of justice are established in every county, with proper officers, as justices, sheriffs, clerks, constables, etc., which courts are held every two months: but to prevent lawsuits there are three peacemakers chosen by every county court in the nature of common arbitrators, to hear and end differences betwixt man and man; and spring and fall there is an orphan's court in each county to inspect and regulate the affairs of orphans and widows.

XXXII. Philadelphia, the expectation of those that are concerned in this province, is at last laid out, to the great content of those here that are anyways interested therein. The situation is a neck of land, and lieth between two navigable rivers, Delaware and Skulkill, whereby it hath two fronts upon the water, each a mile, and two from river to river. Delaware is a glorious river, but the Skulkill being a hundred miles boatable above the falls and its course northeast toward the fountain of Susquahannah (that tends to the heart of the province, and both sides our own) it is like to be a great part of the settlement of this age. I say little of the town itself, because a platform will be shown you by my agent, in which those who are purchasers of me will find their names and interests. But this I will say for the good providence of God, that of all the many places I have seen in the world I remember not one better seated; so that it seems to me to have been appointed for a town, whether we regard the rivers or the conveniency of the coves, docks, springs, the loftiness and soundness of the land and the air, held by the people of these parts to be very good. It is advanced within less than a year to about four score houses and cottages, such as they are, where merchants and handicrafts are following their vocations as fast as they can, while the countrymen are close at their farms. Some of them got a little winter corn in the ground last season, and the generality have had a handsome summer crop, and are preparing for their winter corn. They reaped their barley this year in the month called May; the wheat in the month following; so that there is time in these parts for another crop of divers things before the winter season. We are daily in hopes of shipping to add to our number; for blessed be God, here is both room and accommodation for them; the stories of our necessity being either the fear of our friends or the scarecrows of our enemies;

for the greatest hardship we have suffered hath been salt meat, which by fowl in winter, and fish in summer, together with some poultry, lamb, mutton, veal, and plenty of venison the best part of the year hath been made very passable. I bless God, I am fully satisfied with the country and entertainment I can get in it; for I find that particular content which hath always attended me, where God in His providence hath made it my place and service to reside. You cannot imagine my station can be at present free of more than ordinary business, and as such I may say it is a troublesome work; but the method things are putting in will facilitate the charge, and give an easier motion to the administration of affairs. However, as it is some men's duty to plough, some to sow, some to water, and some to reap; so it is the wisdom as well as duty of a man to yield to the mind of Providence, and cheerfully, as well as carefully, embrace and follow the guidance of it.

XXXIII. For your particular concern I might entirely refer you to the letters of the president of the society; but this I will venture to say, your provincial settlements both within and without the town for situation and soil are without exception. Your city lot is a whole street, and one side of a street, from river to river, containing near one hundred acres, not easily valued, which is, besides your four hundred acres in the city liberties, part of your twenty thousand acres in the country. Your tannery hath such plenty of bark; the saw mill for timber and the place of the glass house are so conveniently posted for water carriage, the city lot for a dock, and the whalery for a sound and fruitful bank, and the town Lewis by it to help your people, that by God's blessing the affairs of the society will naturally grow in their reputation and profit. I am sure I have not turned my back upon any offer that tended to its prosperity; and though I am ill at projects I have sometimes put in for a share with her officers to countenance and advance her interest. You are already informed what is fit for you farther to do; whatsoever tends to the promotion of wine, and to the manufacture of linen in these parts, I cannot but wish you to promote it; and the French people are most likely in both respects to answer that design: to that end I would advise you to send for some thousands of plants out of France, with some able vinerons, and people of the other vocation. But because I believe you have been entertained with this and some other profitable subjects by your president, I shall add no more, but to assure you that I am heartily inclined to advance your just interest, and that you will always find me,

Your kind cordial friend,

W. PENN.

PHILADELPHIA, *the 16th of the 6th month, called August*, 1683.

THE TEMPLE PRESS LETCHWORTH ENGLAND